AF334645

STATESMAN
OF THE PIANO

STATESMAN OF THE PIANO

*Jazz, Race, and History
in the
Life of Lou Hooper*

Edited by

SEAN MILLS, ERIC FILLION, AND DÉSIRÉE ROCHAT

Carleton Library Series 266

McGILL-QUEEN'S UNIVERSITY PRESS
Montreal & Kingston · London · Chicago

ISBN 978-0-2280-1880-3 (cloth)
ISBN 978-0-2280-1915-2 (ePDF)
ISBN 978-0-2280-1916-9 (ePUB)

Legal deposit third quarter 2023
Bibliothèque nationale du Québec

Printed in Canada on acid-free paper that is 100% ancient forest free (100% post-consumer recycled), processed chlorine free

This book has been published with the help of a grant from the Canadian Federation for the Humanities and Social Sciences, through the Awards to Scholarly Publications Program, using funds provided by the Social Sciences and Humanities Research Council of Canada.

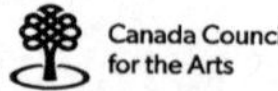

We acknowledge the support of the Canada Council for the Arts.
Nous remercions le Conseil des arts du Canada de son soutien.

Library and Archives Canada Cataloguing in Publication

Title: Statesman of the piano : jazz, race, and history in the life of Lou
    Hooper / edited by Sean Mills, Eric Fillion, and Désirée Rochat
Names: Hooper, Louis, 1894-1977, author. | Mills, Sean, 1978- editor. |
    Fillion, Eric, editor. | Rochat, Désirée, editor. | Hooper, Louis, 1894-1977.
    That happy road.
Series: Carleton library series ; 266.
Description: Series statement: Carleton library series 266 | Includes Lou
    Hooper's autobiography, titled That happy road. | Includes biblio-
    graphical references and index.
Identifiers: Canadiana (print) 20230192998 | Canadiana (ebook)
    20230193625 | ISBN 9780228018803 (cloth) | ISBN 9780228019169 (ePUB) |
    ISBN 9780228019152 (ePDF)
Subjects: LCSH: Hooper, Louis, 1894-1977. | LCSH: Pianists—Canada—
    Biography. | LCSH: Jazz musicians—Canada—Biography. | LCSH:
    Musicians, Black—Canada—Biography.
Classification: LCC ML417.H786 S79 2023 | DDC 786.2165092—dc23

Contents

Figures

Concert Programs

Preface

This book has its origins in May 2016, when one of our editors (Sean Mills)
travelled to Ypsilanti, Michigan, to see if he could find any information about
Louis Stanley Hooper. A year or so earlier, he had been doing research on the
history of jazz and had stumbled upon the Canadian-born pianist's archival
fonds in Ottawa. Hooper's collection at Library and Archives Canada (LAC)
opened up a whole new world to him, revealing the multi-faceted dimensions
of a musician who had grown up in Ypsilanti and had lived and played
throughout North America, notably in Detroit, New York, Toronto, and Montreal. The fonds in Ottawa contained correspondence, photographs, concert
programs, the original thesis that the pianist had written for his bachelor of
music degree at the Detroit Conservatory of Music in 1920, and many other
documents related to his musical life that spanned much of the twentieth
century. Most important, it contained a draft of an autobiography that the
jazzman had written, but which remained unpublished at the time of his
death in 1977. After spending a few months going over the material, Sean set
out to search for traces of Hooper's life in other archives in Montreal, New
York, and Buxton (the place of Hooper's birth). It was then that he decided
to visit the Ypsilanti Museum and Archives. Once there, Sean and a friend
with whom he was travelling asked the archivist if he had any information
on Hooper. After coming up empty, the embarrassed archivist asked: was
Hooper Black? When they answered yes, they were informed that the archive

primarily contained records of the white population of Ypsilanti, and that this explained why it did not have anything on Hooper.

Sean sat with this story for a long time, not quite sure what to do with it, realizing how powerfully it spoke to the role of race in shaping archival legacies. He also realized how valuable it was that Hooper had collected his own material throughout his life and had written his autobiography. It was also extremely fortunate that his family recognized the value of these documents and decided to donate them to LAC after his death. Inspired by the Black Lives Matter movement, and during the uprisings that followed the killing of George Floyd, the answer of what to do with these documents became clear: it was time to publish Hooper's autobiography and let the world finally hear his story, in his own words. And so in the summer of 2020, Sean reached out to the jazz and cultural historian Eric Fillion and Désirée Rochat, a community educator and preserver of Black diasporic archives, and together they began working on the project that would become *Statesman of the Piano: Jazz, Race, and History in the Life of Lou Hooper.*

This book emerged out of our discussions about history, jazz, race, transnationalism, and the power of archives. In consultation with members of Hooper's family and with their enthusiastic support, we prepared a critical edition of *That Happy Road* (the title that Hooper gave to his autobiography), along with a select number of other documents and photographs. From the beginning, our goal was not only to publish these materials, but to make them live in our present by sparking new conversations about Hooper's legacy and the meanings of his archival collection. We therefore reached out to five different contributors, asking each of them to speak about the documents and photographs from their own perspective and to reflect upon what they can teach us about the importance of stories and archives that have remained largely overlooked. Cultural critic Sunita Nigam reads *That Happy Road* as an ecobiography, following Hooper as he travelled throughout the United States and Canada, while musician and historian Jason Wilson reflects on Hooper's service in the Canadian military overseas during the Second World War. Historian Arshad Suliman Desai and archivist Kristen Young write about the meaning of the Hooper fonds to Black Canadian history and archives. Finally, musician, artist-researcher, and cultural worker Julie Richard considers Hooper as a composer across different musical genres and situates him within a lineage of Black voices who have been, until recently, largely ignored. Taken together, these various contributions offer different ways of thinking about Hooper in the present. We hope that they will be a starting point in a larger conversation about music, identity, race, and archives, a conversation that is at once anchored in the past, but set with an eye (and an ear) towards the future.

Acknowledgments

Our first and most important thanks go to the Hooper family. In particular, we would like to thank Adam Barken, Hooper's grandson, who has done everything possible to assist us in this project, from providing access to his own collection of photographs, recordings, and manuscripts to coordinating the rights for this material. Most important of all, his enthusiasm and desire to share his grandfather's story has been heartening and inspiring.

Since the beginning of our research on Hooper, many individuals have discussed different iterations or facets of the project with us. In particular, we would like to thank Mark Miller, Robin Elliott, Funké Aladejebi, LK Bertram, Dimitry Anastakis, Heidi Bohaker, Scott Rutherford, Brian Gettler, Dan Horner, Simon Orpana, Karen Dubinsky, Steve Penfold, Suzanne Mills, Rodney Saint-Éloi, Rick Halpern, Luis Van Isschot, Bronwyn Jaques, Dave St Onge, Andy Williams, and John Gilmore. Philippe J. Fournier deserves special thanks for accompanying Sean on his original research trip to Ypsilanti and visiting various music venues in Detroit with him. Archivists, especially those at Library and Archives Canada, Buxton National Historic Site and Museum, Concordia University Special Collections, Alex Dworkin Canadian Jewish Archives, Clara Thomas Archives and Special Collections, and the Institute of Jazz Studies at Rutgers-Newark, have offered exceptional assistance in tracking down documents pertaining to Hooper's life and work. A special word of gratitude for James Kidd, who shared valuable research material with us, and who – along with his colleagues in the Montreal Vintage Music Society – did so much to bring Hooper to prominence in the first place.

The original research was funded by a SSHRC Insight Development Grant, and in its final stages we drew on funds from the Canada Research Chair Program, as well as funds from the University of Toronto in support of the Canada Research Chair. Post-doctoral fellowships and funding from SSHRC, FRQSC, and the University of Toronto, and a Buchanan post-doctoral fellowship at Queen's University, supported Eric during the making of this book. The members of the Montreal History Group have offered constant encouragement. Moreover, the group's FRQSC grant funded some of the early research as well as a post-doctoral fellowship for Désirée, who also benefited from a Faculty of Arts and Science post-doctoral fellowship in the Department of History at the University of Toronto, for which she is grateful. The history departments at the University of Toronto, as well as Queen's and Concordia Universities have provided stimulating environments for us to carry out this project.

We owe a particular debt to Mayar Shahin, who worked with us in transcribing Hooper's autobiography while researching and writing some of the early annotations. Matthieu Caron also helped with the transcription of some of the documents, and we are grateful for his assistance in preparing the manuscript for submission. A number of research assistants offered additional support, including Kieran McKormick, Elspeth Gibson, and Christopher McGoey. Also, thanks to Tim Pearson for his work on the index.

At McGill-Queen's University Press, we would like to thank Jonathan Crago for his expert guidance and James Leahy for copy-editing. Our thanks extend to the Carleton Library Series for accepting this book in their series. We also want to acknowledge the five authors who left their valuable imprint on the pages of this book: Julie Richard, Sunita Nigam, Jason Wilson, Arshad Suliman Desai, and Kristen Young.

Désirée would like to thank her multiple collaborators (including her amazing co-editors Sean and Eric) on the inspiring, collaborative journey of preserving and activating the archives of Black lives.

Eric is filled with gratitude for the time spent working on *Statesman of the Piano* with Sean and Désirée, the best co-editors one could wish for. He gives thanks to Valérie Dumaine, his life, travelling, and music-listening partner (with a preference for Hooper instrumentals) for more than fifteen years.

Sean would like to thank Eric and Désirée, both outstanding colleagues and good friends. He is very fortunate that they accepted the invitation to work on this project, which now bears the marks of their invaluable expertise, knowledge, and insight. This book would not be the same without their perspectives and exacting work. He would also like to thank Esme Allen-Creighton for her love and constant support, as well as Cecile Grace, who was born just as the manuscript went out to review. May she know a better world.

Abbreviations

AFM	American Federation of Musicians
ATS	Auxiliary Territorial Service
BBC	British Broadcasting Corporation
BSM	Band Sergeant Major
CAHU	Canadian Artillery Holding Unit
CARU	Canadian Army Reinforcement Unit
CAS	Canadian Army Show
CBC	Canadian Broadcasting Corporation
CLWS	Canadian Legion War Services
CMHQ	Canadian Military Headquarters
CNE	Canadian National Exhibition
IAJRC	International Association of Jazz Record Collectors
JATP	Jazz at the Philharmonic
LAC	Library and Archives Canada
MWSO	Montreal Women's Symphony Orchestra
NAACP	National Association for the Advancement of Colored People
NAAFI	Navy, Army and Air Force Institutes
NCO	Non-Commissioned Officer
RCA	Royal Canadian Artillery
RCAF	Royal Canadian Air Force
RCASC	Royal Canadian Army Service Corps

RSM	Regimental Sergeant Major
TLS	Tank Landing Ship
UNIA	Universal Negro Improvement Association (also known as United Negro Improvement Association)
USNARA	US National Archives and Records Administration
WO	Warrant Officer
YMCA	Young Men's Christian Association
YWCA	Young Women's Christian Association

STATESMAN
OF THE PIANO

INTRODUCTION

Lou Hooper's "Rediscovery"

SEAN MILLS, ERIC FILLION,
AND DÉSIRÉE ROCHAT

In the 1960s Montreal was the largest and most powerful city in Canada, and its political and cultural life was in an exhilarating state of turmoil. Montreal acted as the central battleground for Quebec nationalists working to lay greater claim to public space, and it was the country's most important site of transnational Black Power and Caribbean activism. Social movements proliferated and protesters filled the streets. Heated arguments about identity, race, class, language, the sexual revolution, and the global climate of rebellion filled the air, much of it to the beat of sounds and songs about hope, resistance, and change. It was amid this turbulent atmosphere that Louis Stanley Hooper (or "Lou," as most people called him), a Black pianist in his seventies living in Montreal, came to widespread public attention for the first time. His music spoke of a different era, but it found a receptive audience among those who sought to understand the city's place in the broader history of jazz in North America. In the coming years, he would give interviews and speak at record collectors' conventions and conferences. Journalists marvelled at his storied chronicles of participating in the blues and jazz worlds of 1910s and 1920s Detroit and New York. However fascinating, Hooper's anecdotes and reminiscences always sat somewhat uneasily alongside the broader atmosphere of revolt that surrounded him.

The story of Hooper's "rediscovery" began with the Montreal Vintage Music Society, a group of jazzophiles that started meeting informally in 1964 to discuss their record collections and to identify musicians who played on rare and classic recordings. James Kidd, one of the club's instigators and its president after it was officially established in 1966, was particularly interested in the Ajax label, on which Hooper had recorded extensively. It came as a shock and surprise when Kidd learned that Hooper was apparently not only "still alive, but living in Montreal and still professionally active!"[1] Hooper had played alongside the greatest figures of the Jazz Age in Detroit and Harlem, before moving to Toronto and then Montreal, where he became one of the backbones of the city's music scene. He performed with Myron Sutton's Canadian Ambassadors, possibly the country's first organized Black jazz band, promoted music education through his Hooper Southern Singers of Canada, taught Oscar Peterson, played on concert stages in England and entertained troops throughout Europe during the war, collaborated with notable collectives such as the Negro Theatre Guild, and then played in various clubs and resorts in the 1950s. Hooper would come to form a close relationship with Kidd, helping him with his goal of learning more about early jazz and blues recordings. "As we sit with a tape recorder listening to sides made forty years ago," Kidd wrote in the mid-1960s, Hooper's "eyes light up, his mind zeroes in on the session, and the stories start."[2]

The synergy between Hooper and Kidd was remarkable, bringing the once-prolific pianist publicity and prompting him to both re-examine his early work and reflect on his career. In this new chapter of his life that began in the 1960s, Hooper returned to the stage and became the subject of numerous news stories and features. He gave interviews and recounted tales about the great artists with whom he had worked over the years. The list of names was impressive: Ethel Waters, Ma Rainey, Bessie Smith, Paul Robeson, and many more. Hooper was "blessed with an amazing memory," noted Kidd, astonished by his new friend's ability to recall the "exact placement of horns, musicians, and instruments from [decades-old] sessions."[3] Together, they helped prepare the "discographical notes" for a series of reissue albums that the New Jersey–based Historical Records released in the late 1960s, one of which featured a new recording by Hooper.[4] Titled "Cakewalk," it was his first piano solo. It was followed in early 1973 by a full solo album entitled simply *Lou Hooper, piano*, produced by Radio Canada International. At the time of the recording, Hooper was nearly eighty years old, and the album had a nostalgic air, with one reviewer writing that it was intended for "academically-minded ragtimers."[5] In the flurry of discussions about his life, Hooper wrote an autobiography entitled *That Happy Road*, a document that offers testimony of a life in jazz lived on both sides of the Canada–US border. It is also an intimate window into both the social history of the North American jazz scene and the relationship between race and music in the twentieth century. Until now, the autobiography has remained unpublished, sitting in a folder at LAC, long overlooked by researchers.

In the late 1960s and 1970s, Hooper, building on his work with Kidd, became a figure of fascination for record-collecting jazzophiles, notably those who gravitated around the Montreal Vintage Music Society, which he himself joined. In 1967, Hooper and Kidd travelled to Toronto for the convention of the International Association of Jazz Record Collectors (IAJRC). The participants listened to old 78 rpm discs, traded notes, and watched rare films.[6] In 1970, a group of jazz collectors met at St Lawrence University, in Canton, New York. The two friends travelled there from Montreal: Kidd talked about the Berliner and Compo record companies while Hooper told anecdotes and performed for the crowd. One of the highlights of the convention was Hooper's participation in a jam session that also featured bassist Irving Stone, saxophonist Raymond Shiner, and cornetist Robert Fertig.[7] When the IAJRC met at Montreal's Berkeley Hotel in 1973, Hooper once again acted as a major draw for the 500 in attendance.[8] He played at conventions as late as 1977, when he appeared at the Canadian Collectors' Congress in Barrie, Ontario. One jazzophile recalled hearing Hooper playing on the airwaves of the Canadian Broadcasting Corporation (CBC) while driving to the event. At the congress itself, there was "nary a dry eye in the house" when Hooper played "I Can't Give You Anything but Love Baby." That day, a member of the Toronto-based collectors' society the Muddies presented Hooper with a plaque made specially for the occasion.[9]

During this period, Hooper also developed a following in the broader public. This was largely due to the combined effects of his exposure in the national media and the concerts that he performed. In May 1973, for example, his *Music through the Years* retrospective advertised itself as "A Concert of Original Compositions by Lou Hooper from 1918 to 1970." Presented in the Westmount High School Auditorium on Saint-Catherine Street West in Montreal, it featured Hooper accompanied by a fifteen-piece orchestra and forty singers from the St Lambert Choral Society.[10] The concert included his oratorio *Ruth*, "a 90-minute work for chorale and orchestra based on the Old

Testament story of Ruth," which he had composed as a student at the Detroit Conservatory of Music in 1920. It also included ragtime tunes as well as lyrical works, notably "In the Candlelight," a song that Hooper wrote while in London during the wartime blackout. The program drew, of course, from his "experience as a blues pianist in the days of Ma Rainey and Bessie Smith" when he worked as "a recording artist in the heyday of 'race records' 78s." *Music through the Years* was "a 'balanced diet' of styles," and it demonstrated the extent of Hooper's movement across borders, both national and musical.[11]

Classically trained at the Detroit Conservatory of Music, Hooper was something of an anomaly in the jazz world. True, there were many jazz musicians who had classical training. Fletcher Henderson began his career as a prodigy of classical piano before then turning to jazz, and one could easily point to many others, some of whom were following in Hooper's footsteps.[12] When Oscar Peterson began playing at the Alberta Lounge in Montreal in the second half of the 1940s, he started the evening with a set of classical music, before playing jazz with his trio in the second set.[13] Still, Hooper's formal training at the conservatory gave him skills that set him apart from many other musicians in his circles, giving him versatility and mobility. In Harlem during the 1920s he juggled a schedule that included not only working in pit orchestras and playing piano during blues and jazz studio sessions, but also teaching classical music during the day. In 1924, Hooper performed at the Copley Plaza Hotel in Boston and Rutgers University with singer Paul Robeson. On both occasions, he performed "In the Bottoms" by Black classical composer Robert Nathaniel Dett.[14] When he arrived in Montreal, he did a lot of arranging since he had a stronger musical foundation, "superior knowledge and ability," according to his son, than many of the other musicians with whom he worked. Reminiscing about his childhood, Lou Hooper Jr explained that when his father practised – and he practised for five or six hours a day – he nearly always practised classical music. And when his father visited his school and was asked to play, he "never played anything in the jazz idiom."[15]

From the very beginning of his career, then, Hooper was interested in and worked across different musical genres. The "organ music that attracted [him] as a boy," and which inspired his interest in performance and composition, included Richard Wagner, Giuseppe Verdi, and Felix Mendelssohn.[16] At the Detroit Conservatory of Music he both learned the foundations of classical music while also writing his 1920 thesis for his bachelor of music on the originality of the African American folk song tradition, a tradition that originated in the musical culture of the enslaved. In his thesis he challenged the interpretation of Richard Wallaschek, who argued in his book *Primitive Music* (1893), that African American music was simply derivative of European traditions, and not original in its own right.[17] Despite his varied background and training, as a Black musician, Hooper's career options were limited. According to Hooper Jr, his father's true ambition was to become a concert pianist, but that pathway was not open to him because of the racism that pervaded the world of classical music.[18] So he turned to jazz to secure a livelihood, showing one of the many ways that his life was shaped by race and the unequal opportunities afforded to Black artists.

Even if jazz was not his first musical love (and he would later write that his training "caused some lack of real abandon" in the "interpretation of the genuine black music"), Hooper clearly derived a lot of meaning and pleasure from playing it.[19] As he told Frank Rasky of the Canadian magazine *Star Weekly* in 1973, jazz is "when you're doodling on the piano extemporaneously, looking for a lick or a phrase that'll express your happy, don't-give-a-damn feeling."[20] Around this time, he was working through a provisional draft of *That Happy Road*, a detailed and vibrant chronicle of his brilliant career. *The Gazette* reporter Dane Lanken read parts of the manuscript, and he felt that once finished it would be an important component of the pianist's "sizeable contributions to Canadian and North American music."[21] The work certainly is a contribution to music history, but it is also much more. It is filled with cunning observations on an array of topics, from growing up as a Black child in Ypsilanti to living in Detroit, New York, and Montreal. It discusses gender and sexuality in Harlem in the 1920s, the difficult economic circumstances of the Depression of the 1930s, and talks extensively about the experience of a Black musician overseas during the Second World War and the difficulties of settling back into civilian life when the conflict came to a close.

Hooper completed a first draft of *That Happy Road* in the winter of 1972. This version of his autobiography ended in 1953, when he met a "young fellow" who would eventually help bring him back to the limelight. "This episode forms a vital link in my story," Hooper wrote, adding that it "will be elaborated upon in later chapters."[22] He had planned to continue writing, but at the time of his death in 1977 he had neither completed nor published the work.

The record collectors who first brought Hooper back to prominence searched for the essence of an art form and were concerned with reconstructing his recording career in New York in the 1920s. They paid minute attention to discographical details, but were far less concerned with Hooper's history in Montreal. Although their project brought a great deal of new information to light, it did not align with the sense of urgency and rebellion that fuelled the city's exploding cultural scene. Hooper was celebrated as an embodiment of a different age, as a living artifact that could illuminate the present, but his rediscovery did not register with the experimentalist artists of the 1960s and 1970s. It is true that Hooper achieved a certain acclaim in Montreal as well as in the national media in the final years of his life. Yet one cannot help but be struck by the extent to which his "rediscovery" was a non-event for the city's most daring artists. If Hooper was well known among some of the city's older Black musicians, he also remained out of step with the younger (and whiter) members of the avant-garde. For them, the history of jazz embodied by Hooper was off-key, so to speak. They were impatient with the pace of change in their society, and embraced revolutionary politics and national liberation. For inspiration, they were more likely to listen to the radical free jazz of figures like Ornette Coleman, Albert Ayler, and Archie Shepp in the US than to their own city's musical past.[23]

Montreal was undergoing profound transformations in those years. The Quiet Revolution opened up a new space of creativity, and an increasing number of French-speaking artists and intellectuals found themselves drawn to the international literature on decolonization. Inspired by the works of Frantz Fanon, Albert Memmi, Aimé Césaire, and others, they saw themselves as participants in a global anti-imperialist and anti-capitalist movement. Modern forms of jazz acted as the soundtrack to much of this cultural ferment. On the airwaves of Radio-Canada in the early 1960s, the poetry of writers from the decolonizing world was read out to a backdrop of music performed by Serge Garant's quartet, and in the mid-1960s jazz mixed with poetry during the famed evenings of the *Lundi littéraire*, mythic events held at the restaurant Le perchoir d'Haïti. There, Haitian and francophone Quebec poets met, exchanged ideas about art and anti-colonialism, and learned from one another amid a warm and politically charged atmosphere.[24] Francophone

Quebec artists and musicians also listened and learned from the uncompromising and largely improvised forms of jazz that many associated with Black political activism in the US. The list of writers who theorized about the subversiveness of bebop and free jazz included Yves Préfontaine in *Liberté*, Patrick Straram in *Parti pris*, and Raymond Gervais in *Tilt*.[25] They were joined by musicians, notably Quatuor de Jazz Libre du Québec, who championed collective improvisation as a social practice and a driving force of change. In the context of this revolutionary sentiment, few gave much thought to the city's own rich jazz history.[26]

Young English-speaking musicians in Montreal were also shaped by these developments. They may not have embraced the left nationalist discourse that was prevalent among many of their French-speaking counterparts, but they still shared their interest in the more modern forms of jazz coming from south of the border. As such, few took note of the activities surrounding Hooper's "rediscovery." Whether they championed a modern aesthetic agenda or advocated a radical break with the past, those who sought to remake jazz culture in 1960s and 1970s Montreal rarely saw themselves as part of a local jazz tradition. As this tradition had been largely forged by Black musicians, they missed out on an opportunity to grapple with the complexities of race and music in their own city's past. To be fair, the scene that prevailed from the 1930s to the early 1950s had been transformed beyond recognition when local authorities launched a series of efforts to clean up vice and corruption by cracking down on nightlife, something which took on new dimensions when Jean Drapeau became mayor in 1954.[27] Because of this, there was a generational divide among musicians, as artists of Hooper's generation had their careers profoundly disrupted, and by the 1960s most were no longer active in the city's jazz scene. Not only this, but as few had ever had a chance to record their music, there was therefore little with which the new generation could engage.[28] As for those who were still active, they had moved on to bigger and better stages outside Quebec. In this context, Hooper appeared to belong to an old and largely forgotten world.

If we know more today about Montreal's early jazz history, it is because of the hugely important research carried out by jazz historians John Gilmore and Mark Miller, starting in the 1980s. Their respective works, notably *Swinging in Paradise* and *Such Melodious Racket*, and the invaluable archival repository that Gilmore helped establish at Concordia University, provided much-needed insight on the genealogies of the Montreal jazz scene, thus making it possible to write Hooper and dozens of other pioneering Black artists back into the history of the city's cultural life. Both made great use of Hooper's personal papers and photographs held at LAC. Gilmore and Miller evidently learned much from reading the manuscript of *That Happy Road*, mining it as a source of information and quoting from it to add depth and colour to their respective histories.[29] Neither, however, reflected on the importance of the manuscript itself.

Had *That Happy Road* been published in the early 1970s, Hooper might have been able to communicate something about his life and struggles to younger musicians, most of whom lacked an understanding of the resilience and resolve with which he and others – in New York during the Harlem Renaissance and in Depression-era Montreal – created a new culture of affirmation and belonging in the face of a great deal of adversity. It is impossible today to revisit Hooper's autobiography and not see its non-publication in the 1970s as a missed opportunity to make connections and foster dialogue – a squandered occasion to think more deeply about the meanings and breadth of jazz culture in Montreal and elsewhere. What is *That Happy Road* if not an invitation to engage in a conversation about music's relationship to time, place, and community?

The act of writing an autobiography, like the effort of organizing personal archives, speaks to a desire to preserve and pass on stories for others to engage with. It conveys the need to narrate, which must be understood as "a process of responding to the world and connecting with it."[30] In jazz culture, self-narratives also constitute a way of assigning meaning to the politics of music making – of embracing experiences of affirmation and resistance.[31] Writing about one's life is a profoundly relational exercise, and it is as much about the past and the present as it is about the future, which Hooper understood. From his childhood in Ypsilanti in the opening years of the twentieth century to the sense of community he found in booming Harlem in the 1920s, or the bonds he created with fellow soldiers during both world wars, as well as the racial discrimination he faced at different moments in his life, the intimate stories that Hooper shares in *That Happy Road* bear witness to a lived and embodied history. These stories invite us to examine the wide-reaching connections that he nurtured throughout his life, and the autobiography adds a rare first-person perspective of a Canadian-born Black musician who navigated borders, communities, music styles, and cultural life throughout much of the twentieth century.

Preserved at LAC, the Lou Hooper fonds is the outcome of Hooper's process of actively memorializing his life. In the same way that he meticulously revisited the past in *That Happy Road*, Hooper carefully collected and organized his personal papers, photographs, and other materials with the help of his family who arranged for all of it to be preserved and made accessible to researchers, artists, and community members. Through this archive, he consciously inscribed his life, work, and voice in history, on his own terms, at a moment when the presence and experiences of Black musicians – and Black Canadians more generally – remained largely invisible to the mainstream.[32] As Dorothy Williams explains in her study of Black publications in Montreal, this invisibility was – and still is – due to the limited presence of records about the Black diaspora in libraries and institutional archival repositories.[33] This explains in part why, for instance, the young experimentalists who played jazz in 1960s and 1970s Montreal sought to connect their music to political and historical movements in the US rather than engage with the city's older and largely invisibilized and forgotten generation of Black musicians. This process of invisibilization and forgetting also operated far beyond the realm of music. As artists and activists in 1960s Montreal took inspiration from anti-colonial movements across the Global South and from the American Black Power and civil rights movements, they largely ignored the history of Black Montreal itself. Relegated to the margins of political and cultural life, the Black population of Montreal existed as an "absented presence."[34] Whether consciously or not, Hooper worked against this tendency and sought to preserve documents and chronicle his personal journey, bringing to light the histories of which he had been a part. Through his archive, he also consciously attempted to connect with those who would go on to use it.

One of the unique aspects of Hooper's approach to archiving and storytelling is the extent to which he carefully and creatively cultivated his source material, in writing as well as in music. To cultivate one's archive is to assign meaning and value to its content by organizing and using it. It is, according to Eric Ketelaar, "a political act, an act of memory politics" that sees the making of archival heritage as a "dynamic open-ended process" involving a multitude of actors – from those behind the creation of an archive to those who use it and those who are responsible for both its preservation and access.[35] Hooper cultivated his archive years before his family donated it to LAC. For instance, he did so by bringing his musical archive to life in various contexts such as in his *Music through the Years* concert, during which he revisited the oratorio *Ruth*, situating it vis-à-vis his ragtime repertoire, a testament to the depth and breadth of his musical literacy and legacy. When he collaborated with Kidd to record and publish interviews, and for the reissue albums that the Historical Records label produced in the late 1960s, he also drew upon his musical knowledge and past experiences. Similarly, at a concert that he performed at the Confederation Centre of the Arts in Charlottetown, Prince Edward Island, he played a mix of Felix Mendelssohn with James P. Johnson, Ethel Waters, and Bix Beiderbecke. It is important to note that during these concerts in the 1960s and 1970s, when he chose to present highlights of his life in music, he placed works from the classical tradition alongside jazz and blues, again exemplary of his constant practice of working in various musical styles.[36] Writing *That Happy Road* provided Hooper with other opportunities to bring his archive to life, notably in the ways he integrated passages from his war diaries into the narrative, weaving together various textual records and memories sparked by looking at old photographs or listening to old 78 rpm records.

The significance of *That Happy Road* therefore rests not only in its content, but also in the conscious act of memory preservation and cultivation that underlies it. On the one hand, the autobiography helps structure the other elements of Hooper's archive, suggesting ways of reading through its folders and files, or of studying its photographs and listening to its rare acetate discs and shellac records. On the other hand, it reveals Hooper's "fingerprints" on the materials, which points to his conscious effort to construct and activate an archival heritage for jazz, both in Canada and internationally.[37] In the last decade of his life, Hooper laid the foundation for others – musicians, collectors, researchers, and community members – to engage with his archive and contribute to its meaning.

In *That Happy Road* and through the other documents that he left behind, Hooper comes to us as a figure bridging cultures and places, connecting cities and forms of music, illuminating the differing meanings and cultural politics of jazz at various moments in time. When authors turn their attention to the Jazz Age, they generally focus on the singular genius of artists such as Louis Armstrong, Billie Holiday, Duke Ellington, or Bessie Smith, but jazz was also made by the innumerable studio musicians, live accompanists, and music instructors whose contributions and experiences are no less fundamental to the history of the music. His status as a sideman was one of the reasons for which he has not occupied a larger role in jazz historiography, but the fact that he lived and worked for most of his career outside of the US has also contributed to his lack of visibility, as scholars of jazz have rarely extended their gaze into Canada. At the same time, scholars of Canadian culture have seldom thought about jazz.[38]

Despite his relative absence from historical narratives in both Canada and the US, Hooper's cross-border story helps us understand how the movement and circulation of musicians between different sites reshaped the meaning of jazz outside of its main centres of production.[39] We hope that the publication of *That Happy Road* will appeal to audiences with interests in race, migration, war, and culture. While Hooper's autobiography speaks to literatures on all of these topics, we in particular see it contributing to a growing body of works that explore Black migration across the Canada–US border. In this new literature, scholars such as Afua Cooper, dann Broyld, Debra Thompson, and Wendell Adjetey have worked to develop an understanding of the long history of cross-border Black migration, attending to the ways in which migrants have travelled in both directions, fleeing racism and violence, building political movements, connecting with extended family and community, and seeking new opportunities.[40]

The Lou Hooper fonds, in which different iterations of *That Happy Road* can be found, is only one slice of what we see as the broader "Hooper Archive." This "Archive" encompasses the various materials about his life and work that are preserved primarily in his fonds at LAC, but also at other institutions in places as diverse as Montreal and Buxton, as well as those kept privately by his family. Like Hooper's life, that "Archive" is characteristically transnational and is connected to multiple communities, musical and otherwise. In other words, it reveals what Maria Tamboukou describes as the "entanglement of space/time rhythms [that] extends into the world."[41] Hooper not only lived a life in jazz, but he also relied on music to travel and forge relationships with the people and the communities that helped him grow into the person he became. The traces of his life that one can find in the above cities are crucial to understanding the broader story of how he was able to operate across so many boundaries – political and generational, aesthetic and professional. And while these repositories "can never add up to the whole of a life lived and experienced organically," to borrow from Sue Breakell and Victoria Worsley, "viewed together this cacophony of tales functions as an unstructured biography" that one can read alongside Hooper's actual autobiography, thus creating further opportunities to reflect on the politics of preserving, remembering, and narrating transnational, artistic, and racialized lives.[42]

For Hooper, the cultural explosion that first went off in Ypsilanti and the crucial insights that he honed playing music in Detroit and New York, and later in Toronto and Montreal, were still reverberating in Charlottetown, where he settled in 1975 for what would end up being the final years of his life. He had many friends there from his time serving during the Second World War, and he felt right at home and immediately set out to organize concerts.[43] On 14 December 1975, he performed at the Confederation Centre of the Arts, and the following year he put together a musical performance of the poem "The Congo" by Vachel Lindsay, featuring music that he had written in 1947 at the request of Montreal's Negro Theatre Guild. This epic "musical fantasy," described as "one of the most important local theatrical events" of the season, saw Hooper share the stage with an eleven-piece band and the Island Dance Ensemble.[44] These well-attended events confirmed his status as a cherished member of the local community, inspiring many letters of praise and generating a great deal of interest from the island's arts world. Hooper, who had started teaching at the University of Prince Edward Island, continued right up until the last year of his life to entertain crowds with his piano playing at church events, when not performing for packed audiences of students at Holland College or speaking to reporters eager to hear his stories of his life in music.[45] For reasons that we will never fully know, he had yet to revisit *That Happy Road* and add chapters dealing with the years after 1953, as he had intended to do.

Hooper died on 17 September 1977, just as the CBC was preparing a documentary on his life and career. The tributes began to pour in, attesting to the multi-faceted influence that he had had throughout his life. Frank J. Storey, a staff officer to the board of the Confederation Centre of the Arts, had moving words to share: "The earth is just a little more empty because Lou Hooper

Figure 1
Lou Hooper rehearsing *The Congo* at the Confederation Centre of the Arts in
Charlottetown, Prince Edward Island (ca 1975–76). Courtesy of Adam Barken.

lives here no more." "We are a little more sad," he added, "because a great and
gentle man walks with us no more. The sound of music will be a little less
sweet because a master musician will play no more. And so it is that a man
came into our community and in such a very short time touched many lives,
made us hear and helped us understand just a little more than we did before.
Of him it can be said, he left the world just a little better because he lived."[46]
Some of the homages paid were musical, such as when Alan Reesor of St
Peter's Cathedral led an orchestra and soloists through a performance of
Hooper's oratorio *Ruth*.[47] In 1978, Oscar Peterson came to Charlottetown to
perform at the Confederation Centre of the Arts. He took the occasion to
play "Night Child," pausing to explain that he had written the work in honour
of Hooper, his former teacher and mentor.[48] There were many other tributes
and memorials, all of which spoke of Hooper's influence on lives throughout
North America.

Figure 2
Lou Hooper during a broadcast performance (n.d.). Courtesy of Adam Barken.

That Happy Road does not have an ending and that suits us well, as it is our hope that the conversation will continue beyond this book. "Stories do many things," explains Tamboukou; "they produce realities as much as they are produced by them and within their own discursive constraints and limitations, they keep creating conditions of possibilities for other stories to be told, and written."[49] Hooper's self-narrative, his activation of the textual, iconographic, and audio materials that he amassed over the years, a significant portion of which is now preserved at LAC, compel us to connect with his world and his music. They urge us to continue rediscovering Hooper, as well as the events and contexts that made him. His stories are an invitation to add our layers of meaning next to or atop his. In the early 1970s, Hooper's wife Alice Margaret and a friend of the family added their fingerprints to *That*

Happy Road by commenting on the manuscript and suggesting revisions. The editorial and research team for *Statesman of the Piano* contributed theirs, by annotating and lightly editing the autobiography, and by choosing excerpts of other archival records to accompany it. The contributors then added their perspectives by responding to the material. It is our hope that the readers will also find a way to engage with these documents in their own way and add their own fingerprints, therefore helping ensure that the history recounted in these documents will inform new ways of thinking about the past and imagining the future.

NOTES

1 Kidd, "Louis Hooper," 2.
2 LAC, Hooper Fonds, Vol. 1, No. 11, Jim Kidd, "[N.B.] Louis Hooper," typed document, n.d.
3 Kidd, "Louis Hooper," 2.
4 Among other records, The Three Jolly Miners, *The Three Jolly Miners*; Various, *Collectors' Items*; and Various, RARE AND HOT!
5 Wyndham, "Record Review: *Lou Hooper, piano*," 7.
6 Norris, "Jazz," 12.
7 LAC, Hooper Fonds, Vol. 1, Nos. 4–5. "Jazz of Yesterday Is Theme at SLU Meet," *The Post-Standard*, 2 November 1970.
8 LAC, Hooper Fonds, Vol. 1, No. 11, Frank Rasky, "Homage to Hooper – Jazzman for Nearly 80 Years," *Canadian Panorama, Star Weekly*, 21 July 1973.
9 LAC, Hooper Fonds, Vol. 1, No. 12, Montreal Vintage Music Society, pamphlet, Hankus, "The Canadian Collector's Convention/Congress at Barrie, Ontario April 30th, 1977, Success!"
10 The cover image of the program for the concert and a transcription of its content are included in this book under Documents.
11 Lanken, "A Life-Time of Music on Stage," 18.
12 Ross, *The Rest Is Noise*, 139–40. See also Magee, *The Uncrowned King of Swing*.
13 Winfried Siemerling also points out that in 1946 Peterson performed both classical and jazz piano at a major concert held at His Majesty's Theatre. See National Museum of American History, Archives Center, Smithsonian Jazz Oral History Program Collection, Oscar Peterson, interview, 19–20 March

1997; and Siemerling, "Jazz, Diaspora, and the History and Writing of Black Anglophone Montreal," 499.

14 Born in Canada in 1882, Robert Nathaniel Dett received his music education in the United States and in France, followed by a distinguished career as a composer-educator and choir conductor. He died in Michigan in 1943 while on tour with United Service Organizations, a group that provided entertainment to members of the United States Armed Forces and their families. Schomburg Center for Research in Black Culture, The Paul Robeson Collection, MG170 3/2, Ballantine Gymnasium Rutgers College Concert program, 17 December 1924, and MG170 3/2, Copley-Plaza concert program, 2 November 1924.

15 Concordia University Special Collections, Gilmore Fonds, Interview with Lou Hooper Jr, 1 September 1982.

16 Hooper, *That Happy Road*, 28.

17 LAC, Hooper Fonds, Vol. 1, No. 6, Hooper, "The Afro-American Folk Song: Its Origin and Evolution," honors thesis, Detroit Conservatory of Music, 1920.

18 Concordia University Special Collections, Gilmore Fonds, Interview with Lou Hooper Jr, 1 September 1982.

19 Hooper, *That Happy Road*, 61.

20 LAC, Hooper Fonds, Vol. 1, No. 11, Frank Rasky, "Homage to Hooper – Jazzman for Nearly 80 years," *Canadian Panorama, Star Weekly*, 21 July 1973.

21 LAC, Hooper Fonds, Vol. 1, No. 9. Dane Lanken, letter of reference, 5 May 1972.

22 The "young fellow" appears in the closing paragraphs of *That Happy Road*.

23 For books on the aesthetics and politics of free jazz, see Jost, *Free Jazz*; and Anderson, *This Is Our Music*.

24 Mills, *A Place in the Sun*, 82–9.

25 For example, see Préfontaine, "Musicojazz," 672–4; Straram, "Les divertissements," 55–7; Gervais, "Black Music," 34–42.

26 See Fillion, *JAZZ LIBRE et la révolution québécoise*.

27 See Lapointe, *Nettoyer Montréal*; Caron, "Dissipating Darkness."

28 See Gilmore, *Swinging in Paradise*.

29 Ibid. See also Miller, *Such Melodious Racket*; Gilmore, *Who's Who of Jazz in Montreal*; and Miller, *The Miller Companion to Jazz in Canada*.

30 Tamboukou, "Relational Narratives," 171.

31 See Beissenhirtz, *Affirmation and Resistance*; Heble, *Landing on the Wrong Note*, 89–116. William Howland Kenney reflects on the complexity of autobi-

ography for jazz musicians in his work on Louis Armstrong, noting that the famed trumpeter and vocalist used his private correspondence and other private archives to chronicle his experiences and perspectives on race and racism in America. This theme is also explored in Sacha Jenkins's 2022 documentary, *Louis Armstrong's Black & Blues*. See Kenney, "'Going to Meet the Man,'" 40.

32 Many scholars have written on the question of the visibility/invisibility of Blackness in the Canadian context: Hay, "Blacks in Canada," 14–17; Walcott, "'Who Is She and What Is She to You?,'" 137–46; Mensah, *Black Canadians*. See also Nelson, ed., *Ebony Roots, Northern Soil*; and Currie-Williams, "Life after Demolition," 56–75.

33 Williams, "Sankofa." On the same subject, see Thompson, "Searching for Black Voices in Canada's Archives."

34 On the notion of "absented presence," see McKittrick in Hudson, "The Geographies of Blackness and Anti-Blackness," 235. On the question of anti-colonialism and social movements, see Mills, *The Empire Within*. Some scholars have, of course, sought to read the history of Black Montreal back into the history of the period. See, for example, Cummings and Mohabir, eds, *Fire That Time*; Austin, *Fear of a Black Nation*; Williams, *The Road to Now*.

35 Ketelaar, "Cultivating Archives," 29–30. See also Ketelaar, "Archives as Spaces of Memory"; and Fuhrer, *Cultivating Minds*.

36 For the programs of these concerts, see LAC, Hooper Fonds, Vol. 1, Nos. 4–5.

37 We borrow the image of "fingerprints" from Ketelaar, "Cultivating Archives," 29.

38 There is no substantial discussion of jazz, for example, in Vance, *A History of Canadian Culture*.

39 In recent years, an increasing number of scholars have explored the ways in which people and music travelled across borders during the Jazz Age and beyond. In particular, see Putnam, *Radical Moves*; Denning, *Noise Uprising*; Von Eschen, *Satchmo Blows Up the World*; Jackson, *Making Jazz French*; Feld, *Jazz Cosmopolitanism in Accra*; Kelley, *Africa Speaks, America Answers*; Monson, *Freedom Sounds*; Heffley, *Northern Sun / Southern Moon*; Bohlman and Plastino, eds, *Jazz Worlds / World Jazz*; and Saito, *The Global Politics of Jazz in the Twentieth Century*.

40 Broyld, *Borderland Blacks*; Broyld, "'Justice Was Refused Me, I Resolved to Free Myself'"; and Broyld, "Harriet Tubman." See also Adjetey, *Cross-Border Cosmopolitans*; Adjetey, "From the North Star to the Black Star"; Cooper,

"The Fluid Frontier"; Thompson, *The Long Road Home*; as well as Smardz Frost and Tucker, eds, *Fluid Frontier*. For a look at Buxton in particular, see Hepburn, *Crossing the Border*.

41 Tamboukou, "Archival Rhythms," 79.

42 Breakell and Worsley, "Collecting the Traces," 179.

43 MacDonald, "Louis Hooper's Musical Career Spans 70 Years," 2.

44 Buxton National Historic Site and Museum, Hooper Collection, publicity for event, 1976.

45 LAC, Hooper Fonds, Vol. 1, No. 11, "Anglican Church Plans Supper with Difference"; "Professional Music Career Provides Exciting Highlights"; Murphy, "Music Man, Island Style."

46 Buxton National Historic Site and Museum, Hooper Collection, Frank J. Storey to Barbara Hooper, 20 September 1977. The CBC series is mentioned in LAC, Hooper Fonds, Vol. 1, No. 11, "Anglican Church Plans Supper with Difference."

47 Buxton National Historic Site and Museum, Hooper Collection, *Island Anglican Church News*, December 1977.

48 Gaudet, "Town Talk," 3.

49 Tamboukou, "Relational Narratives," 170.

PART 1

Co-Editors' Note

The version of *That Happy Road* that follows is held in the Lou Hooper fonds at LAC. A copy is also available in the John Gilmore fonds at Concordia University Special Collections. Alice Margaret Hooper typed the manuscript using her husband's handwritten original (which is now part of their grandson Adam Barken's personal collection). Anonymous queries and annotations were subsequently added in the margins and throughout the text, with Hooper providing answers and suggesting additions in written form at the end of the typed manuscript.

We integrated this material in the transcribed version reproduced here. For ease of reading, we made some light edits in the text, correcting punctuation as well as misspelled words and names. Illegible words were inferred when possible and corrected. We also added chapter numbers where chapter titles were missing. Lastly, we, along with our research assistant Mayar Shahin, annotated the autobiography to provide additional context, clarify information in the text, or suggest additional readings. *That Happy Road* is dense with information about people that Hooper befriended or worked with, musical works that inspired him or that he composed himself, anecdotes that convey something about his experience of place and community. In preparing the endnotes, we focused on individuals who repeatedly entered Hooper's life or notable artists who have been largely forgotten today. We listened to some of the unfamiliar songs mentioned in the autobiography, sharing discographic details about them when possible.

We zoomed in on the key venues and locales that appear in the narrative, gathering and music-making places that carried special meaning. All our decisions were made with an attempt to respect Hooper's wishes of how he wanted the final product to appear.

1

THAT HAPPY ROAD

LOU HOOPER

I
Childhood

My musical career started at the age of three in Ypsilanti, Michigan, in the year 1897, at a Christmas concert at the Baptist Church. The family had moved to Michigan from Buxton, Ontario, in September of that year, and the songs in the concert I had learned from my older brothers and my sister Sarah, who were attending the Fifth Ward Public School. My singing was quite a hit, but the praise, though warm, meant nothing to me, as it was dwarfed by the gift I received off the Christmas tree.

It was a small air pistol with a rubber-tipped ramrod which, inserted into the barrel, was shot out by pressing the trigger. An older boy kept insisting on "trying it," which he did – and he broke it! Infuriated, I let out a flood of loud, uncomplimentary words: "That black nigger broke my gun!" And I began to cry; I cried all the way home and could not be comforted (I was to walk this same route – across the same river bridge – ten years later as a budding young orchestra pianist). The use of the word "nigger" was common in the home, as well as in friendly or unresolved situations. In social conversation, its use, in most cases, was intended to denote either warm familiarity or scorn, even when used only among Negroes. But for a white person to make use of the word "nigger" in any conversation directed to a black person could mean only one thing; flagrant discrimination and the intent to insult or degrade. Hence, the scorn intended in its use by one so very young.

I was born on a farm in the Bear Creek region between the 9th and 10th Concessions, Kent County, Ontario, 18 May 1894. My father was James Rouen Hooper. He was the son of a white southern planter and a slave woman. My mother, Sara Hutchison, was the daughter of a Cree Indian and a slave woman.[1]

My father was not, like many others, a veteran of the Civil War, and although we lived on a farm, he had only a slight knowledge of farming; he did play the violin well and was very popular. Mother ran the farm, though I have little recollection of life on our farm; I was much too young.[2]

The only tintype picture of my mother's father I ever saw shows that he wore his hair shoulder-length. My mother married my father at the age of sixteen and she bore him eleven children: six girls and five boys. The firstborn, a girl, died in infancy. I was the youngest of the eleven. My father died two months before I was born. Shortly after I was born, my mother married again, but we boys and girls retained the Hooper name.

Josiah James Anderson, who was also a Canadian and grew up with Mother's family, became our stepfather, and our half-sister from this marriage was named Mabel.[3]

Our stepfather, who had fought in the Civil War, was very good to us, a stubborn, hardworking man, cutting logs or working in the woods, as a gardener, or as a coachman (driving a horse and carriage), and also as the janitor of Ypsilanti Normal College. He owned a home in Ypsilanti.

Mother sold the farm in Canada, and we travelled to Ypsilanti by train. We were met by a hired man and taken on a hayrack to the house where our stepfather was waiting at our new home to welcome us. The property was a small garden farm on the edge of town with fruit trees, berries, and flowers. When we saw the fruit trees, we jumped off the hayrack and ran to pick some fruit: we had fallen in love with the place at sight!

My childhood was happy and full of music. I loved to sing and soon wanted so much to go to school that my sister Sarah had permission to take me to Grade 1 as a visitor. My visits soon became so frequent that I was admitted to school at the age of four; at that time, it was an integrated school. My teacher's name was Miss Steffy, a young woman who was a great favourite with all her pupils and their parents.

The distance from my home to school was not far, with a short cut through an orchard. One day after my mother had bought me a new ruler and pencil I was on my way to school – taking the short cuts as all the other children did. As I, with childish curiosity, poked the ruler into a hole in the ground that I knew bees lived in, the attack was so sudden (by a stream of the deadliest stinging yellow jackets) that I took off, howling, at a high speed, minus my precious new ruler, and, yelling louder than a normal four-year-old, I burst into the classroom. After Miss Steffy quieted me down and was sure I was alright, she sent me home with a boy named "Fudge" Pearce who was my neighbour and playmate. Mother was not too disturbed: she put damp baking soda on all the bumps, but at home I dodged every insect that flew, for days after. This incident is still in my mind as being the highlight of my first school year.

In spite of a sprightly nature, I was said to be a sober child, due to circumstances before my birth and I was soon to enjoy Sundays at the Baptist Church, listening to beautiful hymns led by the preacher and sung by a congregation that loved to sing; a special corner for the sisters and brothers was called the "Amen Corner," as often one or another answered the preacher with a lusty "Amen," or "Yes He Did," or "Praise His Name," and other replies.

I loved to stand beside my mother and hear her sing. We all went to church every Sunday with midweek prayer meetings too. I remember an elderly gentleman named Exlum Johnson in the "Amen Corner," who possessed a powerful singing voice which seemed to reach back into history for its strength and who, after he had answered "Amen" to the preacher, would laugh with a modulated chuckle – he was so happy!

I also remember some of the brothers and sisters: Mrs Eliza Harris; Mr Tree Brooks – a tall, rangy, strong man; Sister Norris; and Mr Thomas Roadman, cornetist, who led the Lincoln Colored Band.[4]

The Baptist Church held lawn socials at the Good Samaritan Hall in the summertime and possum dinners in the winter, prepared by the Ladies' Aid Society. My mother always helped at these functions, and we all went with her; we loved the food, the fun, and games and wished the day would never end. Alas, as the hour grew late, I would fall asleep and Mother would gently waken me and we would make the long two-mile walk home, where we would all fall into bed, tired but happy.

School continued to fascinate me, and I was soon a leader in the class, music being my first love and my number-one subject.

When I turned five, I was promoted to Grade 2 where we were taught tonic sol-fa music (solfège); this consisted of learning the names of the lines and spaces, the staff, treble clef, and notes of the music scale. The lines and spaces of the music staff were drawn upon an easel-like chart, I remember, which could be moved from classroom to classroom. Throughout the week, there was a daily music period supervised by our classroom teacher, while on one day a special music teacher visited each class.

My love of music added to my eagerness to learn, and by the age of seven I was able to read music well and had been promoted to Grade 3. One of my early experiences upon arrival in Grade 3 came about while taking time out from studying to throw small objects, big enough to alert my live target and disrupt his studies. Among these objects I threw happened to be a bean, which I found in my pocket. During a lull in the action, the teacher looked my way. I laid the bean in my right ear, expecting to lift it out, unobserved. To my great alarm, when I reached for the bean with the thumb and forefinger it moved, not out, but into the ear, and I soon discovered that special attention would be necessary.

My mother was away from home at day-work, and when I went home for the noonday lunch, I was afraid to tell my brothers and sister. I returned to school; then, at the end of the day, I was afraid not to tell. My mother had not come home yet, so I told my sister who was thirteen years old. She tried several ways which only drove the bean further into the ear and it held in the wax. Finally, Mother came home, and, after examining the situation, made an appointment with the doctor for the following day, and my sister took me. The doctor was very impatient with me, but the bean was so imbedded in the wax, that every effort of the doctor caused me terrible pain, and I was eventually "put to sleep" through the use of chloroform. Gauze, not a mask, was placed over the nose for this was the year 1901, and the doctor instructed my sister not to take me outside until he returned, as the air would cause me to be sick. My sister's fear was greater than mine, this being her first experience in such a situation, so as soon as the doctor had left the office and I was awake she took me off the table, whereupon I became so ill, I could not walk. The coloured attendant, Mr Austin Dew, carried me back inside and placed me again on the table. When the doctor returned, he scolded my sister so harshly that even now, as I think back, I feel very sorry for her as she was then, so young and so frightened. After another hour I was dismissed, and we walked home, a distance of one mile and a half. I was quite a hero in the neighbourhood and at school, but not at home!

Mr Maybee was our first special music teacher, and a year later Mr Arthur Bostick took over that post. This fine man was instrumental in paving the way for what proved to be a successful musical career for me. He was the director of the boys' and men's choir of St Luke's Episcopal Church in Ypsilanti, a predominantly white church.[5] He invited me, through a note to my mother, to join the choir. Needless to say, I was very happy but also very frightened at the idea of such a new experience. I was only seven years old! So, with trepidation and great enthusiasm I prepared myself for my first choir rehearsal.

I walked alone to the church house where I thought rehearsals were held, and, seeing none of the boys nor the choirmaster, I thought I had made a mistake about the time or the place for rehearsal. With some apprehension I returned home. As I told my mother of the incident, she, too, thought that I had made some mistake or that the invitation to join the choir was not sincere. I had missed my first rehearsal!

During the days that followed, Mr Bostick came to our classroom for the weekly music lesson at school and questioned my absence from the Wednesday choir practice. I told him my story and he reassured me that I had indeed been expected and encouraged me to try to be at the next rehearsal. This time, I heard the singing voices as I approached the church house, not the church, as I had mistakenly thought. I knew that my choir career had begun and went inside the hall with excitement.

I was aware by now that Wednesday afternoon rehearsal was for the boys only, Friday nights for the full choir. Afternoon rehearsals in the church house, with piano; Friday night rehearsal in the church with the organ.

I started in the preparatory choir, which did not rehearse with the full choir. After a year with this choir, sitting in the church every Sunday, I felt dissatisfied. I knew all of the music, I knew the Order of Service included in the Book of Common Prayer. I went to Mrs Gardham, the rector's wife and our choir-mother, and told her I wanted to quit, as I felt I had rehearsed long enough. By the next Friday, my dream was realized: I rehearsed in the church with the full choir. I was jubilant! This was where I belonged, and where I stayed until I was eighteen years of age.

The Reverend William H. Gardham, rector of St Luke's, was one of the finest men I have ever known; his kindness and great wisdom had a strong

Figure 3
The boys' and men's choir of St Luke's Episcopal Church in Ypsilanti, Michigan
(ca 1900s). Courtesy of Adam Barken.

influence upon my life and that of my family. He was a real English gentleman: and so, in this atmosphere, began what was to be ten valuable years of growing up with music.

On looking back, I can realize that our choirmaster and the organist were the finest, and that we had access to the very best church music available at that time. Some of the organ music that attracted me as a boy, and which I was later to learn and to play, was: a Wagner overture; Verdi's triumphal march from "Aida"; Mendelssohn's "Elijah"; and "Oh Rest in the Lord," which I later sang in St Luke's church choir as a solo for contralto.

At the present time, I was a boy soprano, and was soon to become soloist, until my voice lowered – then contralto soloist until my voice changed completely. I also had to fight with my fists with some of the boys to prove I could do something besides sing well.

Many pleasant events took place in our lives as choir boys, outstanding among them being two special choir dinners each year: one during the Easter season, the other in the Christmas season, with a Christmas tree and presents (I got a drum – my very first). At dinner, we were served "everything from soup to nuts": paper hats and so forth – "the works!" Dinners were always served by the Ladies' Auxiliary.

Then there was the church's annual picnic which took us to places outside Ypsilanti, such as Belle Isle or Wolf Lake, where there was boating, baseball, roller-coasting, and all "the fun of the fair." and which families of the boys usually attended.

Some of the boys were the younger sons of local merchants and college professors and, as choir boys, were paid fifty cents a month; I, as a soloist, was paid one dollar.

We received our pay from the office of Mr Wortley, who was a churchwarden and notary. Two other boys, also soloist, were members of wealthy families. All were nice fellows, showing no discrimination towards me – except one: John Jobson.

We were at rehearsal on Friday evening in the church and John was sitting in the choir stall behind me with some of the choir boys. I heard the remark spoken *sotto-voce*, "You damned nigger," and as I, always doubly alert to the sound of that word, looked up and, seeing the expressions on the faces of one or two boys, I turned around to face John. With real hate showing in his face, he repeated his remark, at the same time throwing a rolled-up ball of paper at me which luckily missed its mark, my face. In the general involvement of rehearsal, the incident seemed to pass, strangely unnoticed, I felt beat. When the practice ended, I spoke to John's older brother Claude about the incident. He was in the choir and was also president of our choir boys' club. He dismissed the whole thing all too lightly, laughingly saying, "Aw – he didn't mean anything." But I was mad and hurt and I told Claude if John ever used the "word" in speaking to, or about me there would be a real fight. Nothing further occurred except to say that John and I never became friends, although I had many in the choir.

The local opera house, restaurants, and confectionery parlours did discriminate, and one incident occurred when I was about twelve years old. Following a rehearsal for a show being organized by the city's local talent, Mr

Fred Daley, the new choirmaster of St Luke's, was directing the show and with other young boys I was in the cast. As it neared the time for the show's opening, rehearsals were held after school as well as in the evening. At the end of one of the rehearsals, there was not enough time for me to go home to supper and be back in time for the show. The father of one of the boys met him to take him to eat at one of the local restaurants; our two families being very good friends, the father invited me also; but, after we had found a place in the dining room, I started to sit down only to be told, by the father, "Oh no, you go in there." "In there" was the kitchen, and the policy of the restaurant was to serve Negroes in the kitchen. I was so ashamed as I sat on that stool with the awful clatter of dishes going on around me, and I cried. It was Louis Hooper's voice that they depended upon for "ear harmony" in the George M. Cohan songs, yet it was the nobody who sat in that noisy kitchen: I have thought of that incident often in the course of my life and have wondered who felt worse or who felt the greater shame, Mr Len Beatle the father of the boy, or twelve-year-old Louis Hooper.[6]

II
Family Life

While the family life in our home allowed a fair amount of free time for three growing boys, yet there were additional projects planned, and directed, by brother Arnold, that were not always above suspicion. He always knew where the best "cultivated" purple-grape vineyards were situated. We visited several outlying farms (always at night), often at considerable distances from our home and each bearing a "No Trespassing" sign; but the grapes were luscious, and anyway, none of the "take" reached the attention of our mother, thanks to our large barn with upstairs hayloft, and where Mother never ventured. The neighbourhood kids were no strangers to our place and often enjoyed the fruits of our nocturnal forays. But we had to be careful always of a dog or the farmer himself; but Arnold always did a good job "scouting," though I can remember more than one "close call." As daring and wrong as it all was, perhaps even then as now, it was a challenge to the young who have no thoughts of consequences.

Often a few boys in the fall of the year on weekends or after daily school would go to watch the threshing of grain – rye and wheat – which the workers put into large burlap bags. We would fill our pockets with wheat as we enjoyed eating it raw. Sometimes, of course, there were fights. One happened when a boy named Harry "Bump" Heath started an argument with our brother, Arnold, who would often run away until we boys began calling him a coward. This feud went on for over a year, but Arnold always told Fred and me that "Bump" could not beat him. Once, as they were scuffling and Arnold must have hurt "Bump" with a smack, Arnold ran and climbed up into one of the willow trees growing along the roadside. "Bump" chased up the tree and caught hold of Arnold's ankle and twisted it. Arnold finally was hurt and mad. He came down and proved to all of us, to our great surprise, what he had always said. No one was more surprised than "Bump" Heath who soon made an excuse: "Stop – I've got something in my eye" (we knew he was good at excuses). The fight was over. They became friends and there were no more fights. "Bump" had learned that what he had told himself all along was wrong. He could not whip Arnold. Maybe even Arnold didn't know that himself.

"Flowering" with sister Sarah, whom we called "Sade" was always fun, though one occasion nearly ended in tragedy. "Sade" was tall, rather jovial and could outwalk all of us. We always made these flowering trips on the day before Memorial Day (more often called Decoration Day then).[7] We knew the places where wild phlox grew along the borders of some farmlands. We always left long stems on each flower for carrying the long way home, where we distributed them among the neighbours. I can picture Sade now, a half-mile ahead of us, turning to look back with her head tilted upward, and we were completely tuckered out. On the way to one of these spots, we used to pass at the foot of a high sand cliff of about one hundred feet where sand swallows lived by tunnelling holes into the cliff to build their nests. At the foot of it the Huron River ran, while at the very top of the cliff lay the landscape of farmlands. Below, when we followed the river's edge, it was exciting and not without dangers of shifting sands, rocks, and the swift current of the river. Above the cliff was land and safety.

Sarah and I were following the river. I had travelled this way dozens of times with the bigger boys and my brothers. We would climb the cliff, then roll part of the way down. We knew this stretch of river and, though young, we could swim. We had confidence because we had been "taught" by smacks from the bigger boys ("You must be careful!!"). On this trip, Arnold and Fred were travelling above. Sarah was walking in front on the bank of the hill. It was a sand cliff gradually giving way to a high wall of earth, with tree shrubs and large rough stones near the foot, with a few small pockets of loose earth slides. The boys heard Sade cry out and knew she was in trouble; each move by her to reach a firm footing only caused her to slide more and with the slope of the bank, she edged nearer and nearer to the water. I called up to Arnold – he came cautiously holding on to small trees and stopped a few feet above Sade. We always carried bamboo fishing poles and bait in case we decided to fish. Arnold told Sade to catch hold of the pole and he could pull her up to solid ground, but she was now crying and afraid he could not do it.

I was urging and reassuring her of Arnold's strength and that he could, as she very slowly slid downward. I'm sure we thought of breaking that awful news at home, while I still urged her. Arnold was all action, giving a splendid display of courage and self-confidence, pushing the end of the pole into Sarah's hand. She must have realized, for a moment, that the only way to save her life, was to listen to us and be pulled up on to firm ground, for most certainly she would soon have slipped into the river. The strong current there prevented any possibility of rescue.

I do not remember just how we handled the details, if any, at home; I do know that until "flowering" was outgrown, we still returned to some of the same places each year.

III
Incidents

One incident stands out in my memory concerning one of the several choirmasters during my lengthy membership in the choir. Professor Ducomb was a kind, elderly man, though very inefficient. He wished to give me piano lessons and I was pleased, so he asked for permission from my mother. With her strong feeling of pride, though having a small purse and large family, she agreed and sent fifty cents for the first lesson. Professor Ducomb kindly refused with polite explanations, but Mother still insisted. The professor finally prevailed, and the lessons commenced. We had no piano at home, but I used one in the church house for practice. It was more than a mile from my home. As I look back to those days, everything you did was far away, with no transportation, so you walked! However, after a few lessons playing with hands alone, I asked the professor: "When am I going to play 'hands together?'" "Now – if you think you can," he answered, and turned to an exercise. I tried but could not play "hands together." I had no co-ordination. Needless to say, I was shocked and surprised. This was much different than just singing the single vocal line, I guess. My nose was put badly out of joint at the thought. I was NOT a good pupil! Soon came summer holidays and with them one church service on Sunday morning only, during the month of July, and piano lessons ended. However, when a piano was brought into our house, a big old square one, by my brother Arnold in the fall, I continued lessons with Miss Carrie Bergen. With more regular practice, I progressed. I have never considered my piano work to be outstanding, neither in the classical nor in the professional fields, but I worked very hard to make my performances adequate and to improve, and have enjoyed some moments of success in each field. During my third and fourth years, up to graduation at conservatory, I averaged eight to ten hours each day in practice. Any measure of achievement, I must attribute to strict application to basics: theory, technique (scales, chords, etc.), teaching, and accompanying also, along with the added value of a wide association with various interesting people and with my choir activity.

Each year, the circus visited our town. It was cause for great excitement and joy. On one such visit, my brother Fred and I and several other boys were given jobs helping with tents, carrying water for the elephants, and just about everything else. For this, we were to be allowed into the "big top" free at the afternoon and evening shows. However, it did not work out as we expected because, first, they took the coat of each boy to keep as security. We did not know when we would get them back; it was not soon! Roustabouts, as they are called, were in charge – they drove us, swore continually, and we were really frightened. The boys were twelve to thirteen years old, and we learned how much water an elephant can drink; also, we were to keep clear of all the cages with wild animals in them.

We began working in the morning, but the curiosity had worn off by noon. Each of us had brought his own lunch, fortunately; we kids always did when we went to a circus. We had no money for pink lemonade, boxes of popcorn, or sacks of peanuts that kids like. By the afternoon showtime we found, to our horror, that we would have to be sneaked in under the side edge of the tent, not the main entrance, and by the roustabout boss, two or three of us at a time. We had to stand under the long boards arranged as seats for people in the "big top" show side sections. We were beginning to be tired and were feeling sorry for ourselves! Little did we think it was not to end until midnight that night. Every tent, including the "big top," tent posts, buckets, and hand tools – we worked until all the canvas was rolled up. There were dozens of men working on takedown, but the jobs did not lighten that we were made to do before we finally got our coats back. No money was given to us. Fairchild's Field, where the circus had been, was as clean as though nothing had ever been there.

One bright spot of the afternoon came when I heard some great piano-playing. I sneaked away; outside the sideshow was a pianist playing ragtime tunes of the day: "Ponyboy," "Cheyenne," "Hiawatha," "Rainbow," etc.[8] I stood there transfixed; completely carried away at that great piano-playing of this man; also the songs he played. I didn't get caught either by the roustabout boss.

I guess that circus experience was not all bad for me. As my brother and I told our troubled story to our mother, who knew where we were but not of our involvement, as always, we knew she would be very understanding, even with penalties. As we started up to bed, dog-tired but not punished, I thought I noticed a faint smile on my mother's face.

My feelings were always easily hurt and being highly sensitive, I cried too easily, even to the point of embarrassment to myself.

My two older brothers worked during the week, and on occasions I took care of some phases of their banking. One incident was the withdrawal of funds and required my brother Arnold's signature, as it was his bank account. The bank teller, Don Braisted, knew me well as he too was a member of St Luke's church choir. I explained to him what I wished to do: he answered simply, and very kindly, "No Louis, you are not allowed to sign your brother's name." Immediately I was in tears, and couldn't say anything more, but turned away and left the bank. I was thirteen years old then, in first year High School and this disturbed me so badly that I was frightened for myself; but I resolved then and there that this must be stopped, and I had to do it! It was then that I spoke to my brother Fred, two years older than me and my very close pal. He explained that the bank teller had had to tell me "No"; it was a rule of the bank and I must speak up for myself, politely but not afraid: especially to adults, because they understood. And no more crying! Don Braisted, whose younger brother Roy was also in the choir, never spoke to me of the incident further, and with my brother's help that harmful affliction finally disappeared.

IV

As I have mentioned, the area in which we lived was adjacent to several small fruit and vegetable farms and in mid-June each crop, as it ripened, needed to be harvested. Entire families would go into the fields in the morning, on foot, with their babies in carriages, and carrying lunches.

We spent the whole day in the fields. It was a community attitude; we all needed money and we earned it together – hardworking, poor, honest people.

During the month of August, we boys would collect our old tents and with a home-made wagon and the family dog we were free to go camping for two weeks; and that meant overnight too – no running home for even the youngest of us!

Often, we pitched our tents on the banks of the river which ran through the country farms and woods, about three or four miles from town. Our mothers would walk out on at least one Sunday with pies, fresh cookies, and other goodies; our vegetables, sweet corn, potatoes, our milk and butter, we got from the farmer; also, spring water for drinking and for cooking.

When winter came, we went skating together on the river and the mill-ponds, as there were no formal rinks at that time; also, there were no hockey skates on special boots such as boys have today; we just walked to the pond and put on our skates over our ordinary shoes and secured them with straps; they were the clamp-on type and you were darned lucky if they stayed on!

Skaters from all sections of the city came here, with few signs of segregation in their behaviour, although as a rule the coloured usually skated with each other, and the white did the same. There were few troubles, probably because all the men and boys played hard "skating games." Fellows did not seem to skate much with girls; they skated too swiftly and too hard; also racing against each other.

On one occasion when I was about ten years old, I was skating with my brothers and the kids on the river, which was not completely frozen across, because the current was too swift. We were playing "shinny" with a block of wood and as I was skating for it, I was carried by my momentum too close to the still unfrozen edge and I broke through the ice.[9] I managed to hold on at the elbows until the fellows pushed sticks towards me, which I grabbed and they were able to pull me out.

It was Christmas Eve, and the annual midnight service was to be sung that night. We didn't go home at once; there was a lumber yard nearby from which the fellows picked up small pieces of wood to start a fire. I did not take off my clothes, but dried out for two or three hours. When we went home for supper, I wanted none, but went directly into the front room where there was a big box stove, and took off my shoes and stockings. We did not tell Mother the story until years later; but I went to the service and never did experience a cold or any ill effect from my unexpected dousing.

My Christmas gift that year was a pair of knickers and a new pullover sweater; and we were allowed to go skating for a while on Christmas Day.

It was the depression year of 1904, with mountainous snows and very little work for our stepfather.[10] I had taken a newspaper-selling job on the streets, which I used to do daily after school. One very blustery, snowy night as I was running and calling "paper," I saw the Reverend Gardham coming towards me. (I was not at all interested in seeing the reverend at this point, because some time after Christmas I had left the choir, at the suggestion of several older boys who said "there were too many little kids" in the choir.) I heard him call "Louis" and stopped at once. When he asked, "Why have you not been to choir?," my answer was "Too many little kids." He seemed a little surprised at my reply, but his gentle reminder rather shamed me: "Don't forget Louis, you came to us when you were so small you could hardly toddle." I answered, "Yes sir" and started away, as the reverend said, "I expect to see you in the choir on Sunday." Something told me I was glad; when I told my mother she too, as calm and unruffled as ever, said she was very glad. Thus ended my participation in the "too big for their britches brigade."

Since I had attended Sunday school regularly at St Luke's, Reverend Gardham spoke to my mother regarding my confirmation. I was baptized on a Sunday morning, so as to be confirmed at the annual afternoon service by the visiting bishop – Charles Williams; I still recall his rich bass voice as he joined in the hymns. My mother was unable to attend my baptism, which took place when I was nine years old (1903), and a lady parishioner was my witness.[11]

The previous year, the rector presented me with an autographed copy of the *Book of Common Prayer* for my regular attendance at Sunday school; I still have the book, which is dated 1902.

Three years later, Reverend Gardham passed away. I was one of the few who were privileged to visit him until his death.

As time passed, my brothers and I bought cheap instruments: Arnold, a violin from Sears Roebuck; Fred, a cornet from a musician who later became his teacher; and for myself, an extra-large slide trombone which my mother bought for $3.50 from the local barber, Mr Burtis, whose son also sang with me in the choir. Arnold was four years my senior, Fred two years, and I was now twelve years old.

I left the choir temporarily in 1908 at the age of fourteen, as my voice was changing then; however, I visited St Luke's Church often during the following two years.

We formed the Hooper Brothers' Orchestra: Miss Ozzie Gough, pianist, brother Fred on cornet, Arnold on violin, and I playing slide trombone. We did not use a drummer. On one night of each week, we played for a dance at the Good Samaritan Hall.[12]

Fred and I later joined the Lincoln Colored Band in Ypsilanti, playing at lawn socials given by the church, and we made a trip to Sandwich in Ontario on 1 August, at which time Emancipation Day, commemorating Lincoln's Emancipation Proclamation, which freed the slaves, was celebrated.[13]

I soon started taking piano lessons and later became pianist for the orchestra, reading chords from orchestral arrangements which Arnold had bought. We were paid strictly according to "the gate" and sometimes received the large sum of fifteen cents each on a bad night. Our salary increased by stages from twenty-five, thirty-five, fifty, and on up to the astonishing amount of seventy-five cents each; but this was the real beginning of Hooper Brothers' Orchestra – and our baptism by fire. Many nights, we played until 2 a.m., but even the fact that I had to get up at 7 a.m. to go to school was no deterrent to my intense desire to be part of this orchestra.

Over the years, we gained experience and popularity, accomplishing much on our way to the new Koppin Theatre, Gratiot Avenue, Detroit, as its first orchestra.

Back at our home in Ypsilanti, our neighbourhood was fully integrated. There were some poor whites and a few fairly well-to-do; on one side of us lived the Lawsons with two girls and one boy; and on the other side lived Miss Caroline Hill (or Davis), a former slave woman.[14] We lived on the opposite side of town from the section where most Negroes (always referred to as the "coloured people") lived, which was called "Hungry Hill."[15]

The word "black" at that time represented something bad, scorned, and was used to injure one's feelings; it did not possess the dignity it has acquired today.

Most of our neighbours there were descended from Bohemian, Polish, German, and English stock. We knew and had many close friends among coloured and white, including the family of the Negro inventor, Elijah McCoy. This was a family of brilliant people; the wife was a schoolteacher and public speaker, with a flair for the theatrical, while son George was a singer and "buck-and-wing" dancer.

Mr McCoy had a small office in the Michigan Manufacturing Company (machine shop), alongside which ran the Michigan Central Railroad, and where one of his earliest inventions was employed; a lubricating device used while the train was in motion. I can see Mr McCoy now on his way to the office; flowing white beard Prince Albert coat, hatless and carrying a walking stick. He looked grand![16]

Then there was uptown, the main business section which was divided from our section of the town by the Huron River, spanned by an open wooden bridge.

The big dances which were held were not mixed racially, though all of them were held in the Light Guard Armory and an orchestra led by Tony Whitmire played for all of them in turn, coloured or white. Whitmire gave music lessons to a number of the neighbourhood boys (including my brother Fred on cornet), who in turn tried to start up an orchestra of their own, but finding a place to practice became so difficult, that the idea had to be abandoned. Two other boys, one being my brother Arnold, studied violin under Whitmire, the other, Frank Panek, continued his violin studies and eventually became director of the orchestra of the local opera house.

Since my brothers and I were taking lessons on our instruments, we rehearsed regularly and long hours, mainly on Saturdays (at that time, my brothers worked in the Michigan Pressed Steel & Die Co. with Saturdays off). Arnold used to buy folios containing excerpts from the operas, Viennese waltzes, and standard overtures.

We played at church socials and concerts, and soon were playing school dances in the surrounding villages – and we were paid! Our repertoire consisted of music for square dances, waltzes, and two-steps.

Two years before and while I was still playing trombone only, we would go sometimes to our sister Fanny's home – usually on a Saturday; we always took our instruments and there was great fun and lots of good food; a highlight of our visit was her new Edison phonograph with its cylinder records and "morning glory horn."[17]

It was there that we first heard the overture from Mozart's opera *The Marriage of Figaro*; a military band march "Call of the Wild"; comic songs by the great Negro comedian Bert Williams; songs with such titles as "Nobody" and "That's Gratitude."[18] All of this proved to be an interesting, pleasant prelude to the later, successful Hooper Brothers' Orchestra.

Having two older brothers was an advantage to me; it meant I could go to the big public dances right along with them and sometimes to the public pool hall, without worrying Mother. While attending these dances, we would make a note of the titles of the music being played and try to buy the tunes for our own repertoire, through the facilities of the local drug store; the owner, Mr Kilian, was the violinist-leader of the pit orchestra of the Ypsilanti opera house. The pianist in the orchestra which played for the public dances later became a teacher on the faculty of the Detroit Conservatory of Music where I subsequently attended.

An especially happy throwback to my choir days was the annual service of the local unit of Knights of Pythias, held on Easter Sunday. The most thrilling highlight was the procession into the church under the crossed swords of the knights, which parted as the choir, led by the cross, passed through. The processional hymn was always the well-known "Onward Christian Soldiers" and each choirboy wore a spring flower which was pinned to his white surplice by a choir mother.

I was also a member of the Grade 8 mixed chorus – Miss Loretta Hughes was our director. Among the musical works performed were a sacred cantata entitled "Ruth," Mendelssohn's "Italia," and other fine compositions. On numerous occasions, I sang solos both secular and sacred; some of them chosen by Miss Hughes, for which she played the piano accompaniment for me. I once sang the alto part in a duet from an operetta with a girl of my own age; the title of the operetta was "Who Killed Cock Robin?" The girl sang the soprano role of the dove, while I sang the role of the beetle. The local press made a most favourable comment on the singing. Strangely, though just as well, no doubt, I never personally assessed my voice – whether I was a good singer or not. I just never thought of it at all. Children at that age simply can't be bothered, I guess. Now, no doubt, had it been about ice-skating or another sport, I could have reported the comment verbatim!

In two years, I left High School, completing my sophomore year (Grade 10), and although I was still in the church choir, I had the feeling of having been there too long – my voice was changing and sometimes I felt embarrassed.

V

I was the first of the three brothers to go away from home to work, having reached the age of fourteen years; with my mother's consent I went to Detroit, returning home each weekend. My stepfather, a good man and provider, being of an older school of reasoning, considered eight grades of school to be enough for a girl or boy; this did not include High School, of course. My mother was not of like mind and found this situation extremely unpleasant. However, by the time my stepsister Mabel (his own daughter) reached High School age, his opinion had altered completely, and she finished High School.

It was decided I was to live at my sister Sarah's house in Detroit, which I did; Sarah was twenty and married to Frank Gatliff, who was a hotel dining-room waiter; they had one son, Clarence. I lived with them for about two years.

Within one week of my arrival in Detroit, I had a job shining shoes in the barber shop of Mr McFadden at a salary of $1 a week, plus tips. I left the job after one week, and the boss was so mad he would not pay me that big $1. I already had another job, anyway, through the help of an elderly, wealthy gentleman whose shoes I had often shined; this was a delivery job, and he was instrumental in helping me obtain the bicycle which was needed for my deliveries.

After buying a bicycle, I had several jobs in quick succession, one week apart, each paying $1 more than the last. My first parcel-delivery job was for a dry-cleaning firm at $6 a week. Then the Detroit Valet Company paid $7.

Figure 4
Portrait of Lou Hooper (n.d.). Buxton National Historic Site and Museum,
Hooper Collection.

Then Kaufmanns, the largest dry cleaner in Detroit; finally, the Detroit Photographic Company, where I stayed over one year, my salary increasing from $9 to $10 a week over that period.[19]

Next, my friend, Mr Allie Smith got me a job in the Woodward Arcade Building, where I drove my first automobile, a Hupmobile IV; it was at an electrical firm, the Duntley Manufacturing Company, which sold and serviced Duntley Vacuum Cleaners and Hurley Washing Machines, for which I was a repair man.

After I had been there for one year, the firm purchased the Flanders XX, a new automobile by Studebaker; a light model four-cylinder job, with a dray back to which was added a detachable wooden platform for carrying the washing machines.

My employer, Mr Meeker, took a partner, a Mr Keenan, who was part-owner of Keenan Furniture Company, and whom I thoroughly disliked as he expected me to do at least three different jobs for one salary, including taking care of the furnace in his home, giving driving lessons to his spoiled daughter, as well as the job at the Arcade. This was definitely not to my liking! The inevitable happened in the form of a favour from Keenan, who by now had become the senior partner in the firm; he fired me!

Prior to this happening and for the first time, a young man rode with me daily; this was, no doubt, to report on my driving behaviour (I was very wild at times). He also wanted the job himself, so I was discharged before my driving could cause injury to me or someone else.

On thinking back, this has been my opinion, though I may not have had the same feeling at the time it happened. Anyway, from my first encounter with my employer, I objected to his loud, gruff manner in speaking to me; however, I always replied in like manner, which did not sit well with him at all. I could almost hear him thinking, "Who is this young brat?"

Following my discharge, I returned home to Ypsilanti, remaining there for six months, where I worked as a cupola tender in a factory which produced iron castings from smelted iron-ore.[20] One day while preparing the fire for a routine pour-off, I was badly burned; the fire was always started in the cupola, a stack about four feet in diameter. I stood upon a platform eight feet above. As I poured the lighted kindling into the cupola from a metal bushel basket, the wind caught the shavings, causing the flames to shoot up into my face and inflicting burns, the marks of which I carry today.

Six months later, I returned to Detroit where, with the help of a friend, I was hired as an elevator operator in the Healy Linen shops on Woodward Avenue. My friend, whose name was Don Bryant, held a similar job in this very exclusive linen shop.

During my two-year stay at my sister's house, I continued with private piano lessons, but had to practice at home on a harmonium – an organ which I had to pedal to produce the sound, and because of the mechanical difference between the instruments, I experienced much difficulty in practicing: this was often the subject of great amusement to my sister and myself. This monstrosity was, in due course of time, replaced by a piano, which I was able to rent at $3 a month.

At the age of sixteen, I became a professional musician, joining the musicians' union, the American Federation of Musicians (AFM), Local 5. This enabled me to play for Fred Stone, the leader of Stone's Famous Orchestra.[21]

In this period, quadrilles, lancers, square dances, and so forth formed an important part in the music of the day, especially in the rural areas, and music for these dances was carried by all bands as part of their repertoire; occasionally, we would be asked for a straight waltz or a two-step. The pianist bought and carried music parts for all the players, so consequently, he owned the entire library. Every musician was schooled to read music at sight.

Detroit boasted a field of Negro musicians – some of the best to be found anywhere. There were excellent orchestras, some playing in the hotels, some on the Detroit River boats, between points such as Belle Isle and Boblo; Negro musicians were popular and highly respected. Famous names such as Finney, Stone, Ben Shook, violinist and leader of a very popular hotel orchestra, all figured prominently during this era.[22]

The obvious occurred when white women began to express too great a public interest; the scene changed, and Negro popularity declined. There was no integration at all in the orchestras of that period.

Although living in Detroit, I still used to return to Ypsilanti to play dances with my brothers who had not, as yet, come to Detroit. The Hooper Brothers' Orchestra had become quite successful and popular, playing engagements in and around Ypsilanti in the normal school gym, and in small towns such as Sheldon and Belleville, Michigan, which I was able to do by interurban travel.

After working at Healy's for a few months, I tried my hand at making electric table lamps which were also sold in the shops. The eldest son was pleased, so I asked for and was granted a chance at the job of house electrician. I was not a success!

Late one Saturday afternoon, having hung a large light globe suspended on a chandelier on the exclusive second-floor shop, I was surprised to learn on the following Monday that I had tightened the screws into the holding metal band so tightly that the opposite side buckled, and the globe had fallen, barely missing a shopper. So I was back on the elevator, and lucky too! That was really where I belonged, as I was not a qualified electrician, for sure!

VI

Soon after my eighteenth birthday, I enrolled in the Detroit Conservatory of Music, happy at last to be in my world; I knew it and progressed rapidly.[23] I completed a regular four-year graduation course in three and a half years, and was vice-president and valedictorian of my graduating class of 1916.[24]

During the course of my studies at the conservatory, I had my own third-year junior recital, together with an assisting artist, Mr Tom Johnson, baritone, with accompanist Miss Lorrainetta Henderson, herself an alumnus of the conservatory.

At the graduation ceremony which followed in due time, I gave a recital at which I played the first movement of the Beethoven "Piano Concerto No. 5 (Emperor)" with organ accompaniment by my teacher, Francis L. York. This was followed by a dozen other numbers, entirely from memory. This was "par for the course" – then for graduation.

Before graduation and while in college, I left my employment at Healy's to devote my full time to music, teaching at home, playing and doing some composing. My two brothers were now in Detroit and since none of us was married at the time, we three bachelors took up housekeeping together; each was studying music privately and was allotted certain hours of practice; at this point I was practicing eight to ten hours a day, six days a week. My brother Fred was studying trumpet with Earl VanAmberg, lieutenant musical-director of the Detroit Police Band; Arnold was studying violin with Mr Henri Mattheys.[25]

Dancing schools were popular at this time and public dances were held two evenings a week with special group instruction, the better dancers giving

Figure 5
The Hooper Brothers' Orchestra in Detroit, Michigan (ca 1910s). Photo by
Harvey C. Jackson. LAC, Lou Hooper Fonds, Vol. 13, No. 1.

personal help to anybody needing it. A straight admission was charged and
the director, called "Fess" (for professor), always hired an orchestra. The
Hooper Brothers' Orchestra of four musicians then played for "Fess" Montgomery at the Elks Hall on Gratiot Avenue, upstairs. The orchestra consisted
of violin, cornet, piano, and drums. "Tacky" (for Tackhead) Madison was
the drummer.

There were other dance professors: "Fess" Edwards, Lou Hunter, and his
wife, both of whom conducted more of a society school; but these society
schools sold "class." "Fess" Montgomery's school sold "colour."

"Fess," a man of forty or forty-five years, in his own words "had been everywhere and seen everything" and was really colourful. Being a professional
dancer, his school "really jumped"; it was in the heart of Black Bottom.[26]

"Fess" was a working man with a good day job, married to a handsome woman who also worked downtown in the business area. At dancing school, he was very strict, and everyone knew it and liked him, or stayed away.

Young, would-be pimps, shady ladies, and young working-class men and women all met and danced together here – and how they danced! Led by Bob Elder, the number one instructor who was a great dancer, they did the "Texas Tommy," a very lively skipping sort of dance; the couples would hold one hand, skip and come together, then apart, executing intricate dance steps in swift flight across the floor; we musicians often marvelled at those uninhibited, joyous happy dancers. All of the currently popular dances were taught and danced here and also some specialties.

Earl Johnson, the number two instructor, and Bob Elder loved our orchestra; fortunately, for it created a pleasant atmosphere between the hirer, the hired, and the dancers; and many of them were our own personal friends.

I had bought the orchestration of a new tune called "Round-up Rag," a catchy, lively tune, very popular with the dancers at the "Fess" school and especially Bob Elder, and it was often requested. One night, having played "Round-up Rag" several times, Bob walked to the bandstand smiling and said, "Louis, they want Round-up Rag" (it did seem especially suited to the "Texas Tommy"). This sometimes happens, with no planning. I may have been tired, physically, or perhaps from repetition of the tune: I said "Please – not again" or some such remark. Bob, who was now laughing out loud said, "Well Louis, you introduced us to it, we love it, it's a red-hot tune, and everybody wants it again – so play." So, with Bob still laughing, Earl and a few dancers went into the "Texas Tommy" routine as we played it (one more time).[27]

I was not the orchestra leader: Arnold the older brother was. I was manager for engagements, fees, and general business, while Arnold was responsible for musical performance, rehearsals, and was generally known as musical director. Years later, when the orchestra was augmented for the theatre, playing for silent films with cue sheets, Arnold was always violinist-leader. Fred assisted in an overall capacity, being responsible that nothing was overlooked, forgotten or broken. We three worked closely together and when cue sheets preceded the arrival of a new "silent," Arnold and I set up the music score, selecting appropriate music from his large library.[28]

There were also dancing schools for white dancers in the city; some engaged Negro orchestras; ours was one. One such school was operated by Mr

Tom O'Neil and his lady friend whose name was Irene. These were two white, very liberal-minded persons, entirely devoid of colour consciousness.

Tom hailed from Australia though he seemed to be more Irish. He was not a good dancer, nor was Irene; but being such fine people, they attracted nice clients, mostly young and a few middle-aged. Arnold and I played for that school, just violin and piano.

A rare incident took place while we were playing for Tom's dancing school, which will bear retelling; it all started after Tom had taken over a sort of pavilion dancehall, a semi-open-air place in a suburb of Detroit named Mount Clemens. For this engagement, we had added three men: trombonist Warren Lewis from Buxton; drummer "Tacky" Madison; and our brother Fred on trumpet.

Two claims to success in this city were sulphur baths and mineral water. Not claimed but practiced, were prejudice and segregation.[29]

Tom's idea was this – and, I believe, innocently enough planned: we were billed as a Hawaiian band. We Hoopers, with our strong Indian ancestry showing in our features, could make it, especially with the inevitable leis around our necks. Not so trombonist Lewis, nor drummer Madison. The hotel in which we were registered was, ironically, called the White House, and we were received royally. After playing our first night at the pavilion, when we returned to the hotel, we found our luggage had not only been removed from our rooms, but had been put outside on the front gallery. Tom O'Neil launched a vigorous objection to such treatment and was simply told, "There's been a mistake." This has to be the oldest excuse ever used – still used at times, even today. It was about 2 a.m. when Fred and myself ended up in the city's lone black hotel, with its complete lack of facilities. Tom was absolutely furious, but he had had his baptism in "That's the way it is, mister." The engagement ended then and there, and we returned to Detroit later that day; but we continued to work with Tom just the same; he was, indeed, a real man. And this was nearly sixty years ago.[30]

In the course of time, Tom left the country.

I had now become organist of St Matthew's Episcopal Church in Detroit, continuing my studies at the conservatory towards graduation. Our orchestra played miscellaneous engagements with other orchestras, singly and collectively. Arnold and Fred each married following a summer-season engagement in Chicago's Riverview Park, under the direction of Charles "Doc" Cook, a

great pianist, composer, and conductor, who was later to receive the degree
of Doctor of Music from Northwestern University. I first met Cook in Detroit,
when he was pianist-leader for the Ben Shook Orchestra enterprise.[31] He was
highly respected and very popular in musical circles but when in 1918 he left
for Chicago and I for France, I never saw him again.

In looking back, I can recall the names of many excellent pianists whom I
met in Detroit, some great and many who were also my personal friends:
George Golden who died in his early thirties, a very tall fellow with very long
fingers, an exciting player, well-schooled; Bart Howard, a session and cabaret
pianist, not only a fine accompanist for vocalists but also a commanding
soloist, with even then a jazz-influenced sound; Dr Sylvester (Syl) Smith, a
professional dentist, scholarly, gruff and not young, but with a highly finished
technique; Earl Conway, who read and transposed music at sight in an amazing manner; Fred Anderson, who also possessed a fine tenor voice, and who
travelled throughout Europe in the concert field, his return to America being
brought about by the approach of World War I; and Johnny Waters, a pianist
from Toledo and the brother of the famous Ethel Waters, although I did not
know this at the time. I would be remiss in not mentioning Fred Peters, Oscar
Solomon, Harry P. Guy, and Billy Adams; among these were arrangers, composers, organists, hotel orchestra musicians and the younger ones coming up;
all these were architects of the world of music.[32]

VII

The military draft law called up those in the age bracket of twenty-one to
thirty-one for induction into the service. I was class 1-A and unmarried. Having kept company for over two years with Miss Cecilia Johnson from Sarnia,
Ontario, we were married on 1 February 1918. I left for military service in the
US Army on 1 August 1918.

Our first army camp was Camp-Custer in Michigan, then south to Alexandria, Virginia, where we were organized into an engineer battalion. Following
a two-week training period, we left one night to board a troop transport for
France. While most of our duties were performed with pickaxe, shovel, and
wheelbarrow, we still found time for some singing and dancing. Finally, and
before too long a time, what had started as some vocal-harmonizing and a

"buck-and-wing" dance step or two soon became a small but organized entertaining unit under my direction. We were able to give two concerts in the area, one in a small French village and one in our YMCA but this was my first soldier concert party.

After a short time in France, I returned to Detroit and was discharged in July 1919.

Then commenced my rehabilitation into civilian life, the most important phase of which was the construction of the Koppin Theatre, by Henry S. Koppin, a leading building contractor.[33] Presenting live stage performances and the latest in films, this theatre was soon to host such names as: Ma Rainey, Paramount Recording artist and pioneer blues singer, famous for her necklace of gold pieces; the wonderful Ethel Waters, recording star, who later established her name forever in the Broadway theatre of drama; Butterbeans and Susie, that lovable, laughable team of song and black comedy. I can recall so vividly a comic line delivered by "Butter," who always worked under cork, in one of his monologues to the audience describing his family.[34] He said, "To look at me you wouldn't believe it, but I'm from a big family; the young'r they is the blacker they is, and I'm the lightest; the little one runnin' around the house – we don't see him a'tall – we just hear him cryin'!"

Here an amusing incident comes to mind and which I consider worth the telling. When Ma Rainey's roadshow was travelling on the Theatre Owners Booking Agency circuit, Ma's Company was booked into the Koppin Theatre where I was the pianist in the pit orchestra of which my brother was leader-violinist. I, as pianist, was responsible for getting the music and any special "cues" from the director of all shows appearing in our theatre. On this occasion and after the first three daily performances had been given, I went backstage to check on any possible connections; this, of course, I always did. Following the usual suggestions of tempos of one musical number or another from the director, Ma Rainey joined in a conversation with me. It was then I noticed this fabulously attractive necklace of gold pieces, of varying denominations which she was wearing. Ma was not a real beauty of face nor figure, but her warm personality certainly made up for any other shortcomings in her personal appearance. I was young and, never having seen gold money worn in such a fashion, I was fascinated, to say the least, and expressed my admiration saying, "Miss Rainey, your necklace is simply beautiful and very valuable," to which she replied quietly, "Yes and you could be spending some of this money if you know how to act right." But she was indeed a great singer and interpreter of the blues, a big bosomy woman who when she sang of the "rains in the delta," you listened! It was a poignant history you were hearing! Ma always made her stage entrance stepping out of a kiosk, which was on-stage, and had the letters P A R A M O U N T emblazoned on it. Paramount was the name of a recording company at that time and Ma Rainey was one of its artists. From the moment she stepped out on stage, she was the "take charge" blues shouter and you just didn't forget it. I still remember it with great pleasure.[35]

Then there was Irving Miller, a theatrical producer of such Broadway productions as *Brown Skin Models* and *Blue Baby Company*; also drama with the brilliant and intellectual Clarence Muse; Laura Bowman, Andrew Bishop, Sunshine Sammy, the juvenile star of the original Our Gang comedies produced by Snub Pollard; also the lively Whitman Sisters' company, and so on. It would appear that I have mentioned too many names; but there were just so very many engaged in black theatre in some form at that time; beautiful, earthy, sincere, laugh-provoking, from musical comedy to moving drama.[36]

Mrs Martha White, a gracious woman, widow of an Ohio church minister, now living in Detroit, contributed greatly to the social and musical life of the city along with her son Luther, a professional dining room waiter. Luther could always "dish the dirt," as he referred to it, on what was happening in the street; while adroit and amusing, he also possessed a rich baritone voice. In fact, his voice attracted me most through his singing in harmony with a few of his friends who often came to the house.

Mrs White, with the help of "Lute" as she called him, presided over a spacious and comfortable rooming house, where one could obtain meals if desired. Only permanent lodgers – no transients – was the policy of this home. To this place came musicians, politicians, doctors, day job workers, and railway porters; all people both interesting and influential. Over the years, Mrs White and Luther moved to different locations, and each time I moved with them as a member of the family. Since there was no piano in the household and since I was engaged in a conservatory course, I rented my own, and special consideration was given to my hours of practice. This situation was accepted by all, musical and non-musical alike. As a student engaged in the pursuit of learning, in the midst of such a wide variety of interests and outlooks, this was a priceless association for me.

There were open discussions on many subjects between residents and visitors. At times Luther and his mother could cut me down to size when I spoke out of turn; the doing of a thing in the right way and at the right time influenced my life at that important period more than I could ever put into words.

Among the lodgers was a young Pullman car porter, Alvin Drayton by name. We were roommates sleeping in the same bed, and I remember well our both being in bed at the same time, stricken with measles. Needless to say, this situation was a joke to every visitor as well as the other lodgers. However, there was a bright side to all this; we had many visits to our sick room from a lovely young lady named Georgia Alford (a fellow boarder) who eventually, after her tender ministrations, became Mrs Alvin Drayton.

Two years prior to my own marriage, I had moved with the household of Mrs White to another house, at which time I bought a grand piano. I was given a large front room as I was then accepting pupils in piano instruction. Sharing the room with me was a great little guy named Mac McCage who, at my request, gave up the comfort of the big bed in which we slept, for a foldaway settee with a very thin mattress, just so the propriety of the room as a studio might be maintained.

The day of my marriage, I moved into the house next door where my sister Sarah was now living. On our wedding night, through a conspiracy between my sister and Mac, my wife and I were awakened around 3 or 4 a.m. by the sound of an alarm clock which had been tied to the springs of the bed! For days, we two wondered who could have committed this foul deed, until one day Mac confessed to the intrigue between my sister and himself.

September of the year 1919 saw the completion of the Koppin Theatre in Detroit, which was to mean the rise to the highest degree of success in popularity and performance of the Hooper Brothers' Orchestra. Unfortunately, there were no local facilities for recording at that time, so my brother Arnold and myself, the only two surviving members of that orchestra, will never know just how we may have sounded to others.

(Our brother Fred died during World War II: I was away in that war also; "Tacky" Madison our great drummer died in hospital just after the war; Warren Lewis, our trombonist, also passed away a few years ago in his native Canada; Arnold is now 81 years old and living in Detroit.)

Koppin Theatre contracts, awarded from 1 September to 31 August each year, changed periodically, as did the leader-contractors. My brother held contracts several times between the years 1919–29; eventually, the theatre fell to a street widening project (Gratiot Avenue) and, along with many established businesses, disappeared.[37] Though I was to go to New York later (1921) and though I remained nearly eight years, I always returned to the Koppin at my brother's request.

The next important phase in my life was my visit to New York and the then-fantastic, flamboyant, beautiful, artistic Harlem. Everyone seemed to be learning or putting to practice the results of having already learned; and many were also earning!

The Renaissance Theatre, an all-black movie theatre owned by the Charity Brothers, was one unit in a complete business block comprising a general merchandising store, a beauty salon, and a spacious upstairs auditorium. It was here that I first heard the incomparable Marian Anderson, then a mere nineteen years old, in a full-length song recital; where, on a later occasion, I played in a dance band in which the famous Coleman Hawkins, sometimes called "Bean," was the saxophonist.[38]

However, this experience was not my initial introduction to New York. In spite of Harlem's flamboyance, my real introduction to New York was, in fact, a quiet one. A friend, William Service Bell, whom I had met in France during the war, and who later had suggested my coming to New York, had actually met me at the train, and during the remainder of the day had introduced me to many students, writers, and musicians. Bell himself possessed a fine baritone voice.[39]

On that Sunday morning, 19 April 1921, as my train moved along the Hudson River with the beautiful view of the Catskill Mountains, the Pullman porter in talking to me asked, "Is this your first trip to the Big Apple?" I answered, "Yes," to which he replied, "Well, when you get a drink of this water, you'll stay!" I did, for eight years.

It had all begun when I arranged a recital for Bell in Detroit, with a concert pianist, Hazel Harrison, before I had ever considered a New York trip. Bell stayed at our home in Detroit and since my contract at the Koppin Theatre had expired about that time, he offered the suggestion that I go to New York. Shortly after his return there (in April 1921) I decided to visit the Big City. I have never regretted the decision.

Among my new acquaintances soon after arrival that day, was an organist of the local church which would celebrate its anniversary the next week. He

Figure 6
The Renaissance Movie Theatre Orchestra in Harlem, New York (1925–26). From
left to right: Geo Haywood, "Ernie" Bullock, Felix Wier, Don David, "Jap" Foster,
Benj. Mitchel, and Carl "Battle-Axe" Kenney, with Lou Hooper seated in the
middle. LAC, Hooper Fonds, Vol. 13, No. 1.

engaged me to play in a trio for the occasion – violin Felix Weir, cello Marion
Cumbo, piano, myself. A few years later I played in the Renaissance Theatre
under the direction of Felix Weir.[40]

Here begins a strange phase in my introduction to a man who shall be
nameless. He was a homosexual, the fact of which I was totally ignorant, but
was later to learn much. Several of the men to whom I was introduced were
also "queer" including the aforementioned organist. This nameless man was
also a fine musician.[41]

He and I roomed together, even slept in the same bed; still I knew nothing
aside from his feminine behaviour, in spite of his "Dance of the Seven Veils"

(which he took great delight in performing for my benefit) and other peculiarities.[42] He made me so furious, and I cussed him out more than once about it. Later, I was "awakened" by a friend who had questioned him concerning our relationship. He told him, "I never interfere with married people." This was a colossal revelation for me, following which I saw and learned plenty.[43]

During the week following my Sunday arrival in New York, my friend took me to the Martin-Smith Musical School on 137th Street between 7th and Lennox Avenue where I later taught pianoforte and history of music.[44] Mr David Martin, director of the school, was a prominent violinist and the father of three highly gifted children: Eugene, the eldest, violinist, pianist, and conductor; David Jr celloist and pianist; Gertrude, the youngest, a violinist and pianist. Each possessed the gift of perfect pitch, while the father and mother, also musicians, did not.

I should mention here that I had obtained a degree of Bachelor of Music from the Detroit Conservatory, which combined well with a good knowledge in the field of popular and dance music. I had played for the silent movies and had composed considerably. All this helped much in my making new acquaintances and the securing of professional engagements which I needed. I had written a thesis on Afro-American folk music which, at that time, was a requirement for a bachelor's degree. My oratorio *Ruth* fulfilled yet another requirement of the course. This segment consisted of a work of my (our) own choice, sacred or secular, for mixed voices and with full orchestral accompaniment: I chose the Old Testament life story of Ruth. (My version was recently given a successful public performance. This presentation, after fifty years, gave strong evidence of the audience appeal in this work.)[45]

In the professional field, I met numerous influential people, many from the Amsterdam Musical Association. Among numerous others, both men and women, I met and worked with: William Grant Still, now a famous composer in Hollywood; Hall Johnson, founder of the famed Hall Johnson Singers; Mildred Franklin, violinist and leader of the Lafayette Theatre Pit Band of which I was a member; Ford Dabney, former associate of James Reese Europe, who earlier led orchestras for Irene and Vernon Castle at the famous Castle House; Fletcher Henderson and his Band; Bill Elkins, vocal teacher; and Carroll Clark, a truly great baritone with whom I later formed a vaudeville team which opened at Proctor's 14th Street in lower New York.[46]

It was through the contact of the Martin-Smith Music School that I entered the recording field as the professional piano man for the Joe Davis Music Publishing Company.[47] Here, I was to be associated with musicians and singers, men and women, some who have gone on to great popularity and fame. There was the late, great Rex Stewart, trumpet-man with the famous Duke Ellington Orchestra and an earlier Fletcher Henderson Band. Another Ellington alumnus was Bubber Miley, the first horn-man I recorded with, and one of the greats. Then there were Bob Fuller (sax and clarinet), Elmer Snowden (banjo), Louis Metcalfe (trumpet),[48] Tommy Morris (trumpet), Jake Frazier, and J. Green (trombones), and others. We played under some of the following names: Three Hot Eskimos; Three Monkey Chasers; Kansas City Five; Choo-Choo-Jazzers; but the name best known is perhaps the Three Jolly Miners, who were Fuller, Snowden, and Hooper, and who later developed into a solo instrumental group, cutting many records.

An LP album now exists under the Historical Records Label, produced in New Jersey.[49] This album lists several numbers bearing composer credits of "Fuller and Hooper" and originally published by Triangle Music Publishing Co. from which we received royalties. Bob Fuller and I would compose some of the tunes during rehearsal and I made short music notations for us to follow while recording the number. After the record was released with Fuller's special fill-ins and technical antics, and if Joe Davis liked what he heard, I would then copy the finished solo clarinet part by listening to the record. I always wrote a piano part, and this (over) complete arrangement went to the publisher as a special novelty jazz clarinet solo with piano accompaniment. I received no regular contract for these tunes but occasionally some royalties were received on Joe Davis personal cheques. I did compose and record some original numbers with the trio, "Grand Opera Blues," to name only one, which was released with composer-credits upon the record.[50]

The singers for whom I played included Rosa Henderson, Josie and Lizzie Miles, Viola McCoy, the team of George Williams and Bessie Brown, Billy Higgins with Alberta Perkins, also Art Gillam, a white vocalist. Then there were Monette Moore, who later appeared in the Broadway production *As Thousands Cheer*, and Maggie Jones, who later appeared in the same production of Lew Leslie's *Blackbirds* as I played (1928–29). Our recordings were known in the record catalogues as "race records."[51]

Very often the "man–woman" recordings ended with spoken dialogue between the two artists, as in the case of the one titled "Hit Me but Don't Quit Me" by George Williams and Bessie Brown. Sometimes this practice led to amusing and occasional harsh repartee which, to me, sounded very comical. As the singing on the record ends, Bessie says to George (pleadingly) "Baby, you can't quit me." George replies sharply – "I've done quit you and when we 'get' over past 8th Avenue I'm 'gonna' hit you!"[52]

A similar situation occurred when Billy and Alberta were recording the song "I'm Tired of Begging You to Treat Me Right." At the end of the song, Alberta says to Billy "I don't have to beg you to treat me right, I'm a perfect thirty-six" (a remark of the day meaning neat, chic). Billy replied, disgusted – "'A perfect thirty-six?' Just look at you, standin' there lookin' like the backend of a taxicab."[53]

One recording that I particularly remember involved Shelton Brooks, the Canadian composer of "Some of These Days"; Ethel Waters, who a few years later won a drama award for her role in the Broadway success *Mamba's Daughters*; and myself, as staff pianist for the Joe Davis Music Publishing Company.

While looking through the mail one morning, Mr Davis noticed a manuscript (and in pencil) of a song entitled "Refrigeratin' Papa." After I had played it over a few times Joe said, "I've got a hunch; I'm going to see if I can get Ethel Waters to record this song." He did get her and soon we two were together in Davis's music room working out a musical arrangement for the recording. When we were satisfied with our efforts, we left at once for the Columbia Phonograph Recording studios nearby on 7th Avenue. Shelton Brooks was to play for Ethel on a recording of a composition of his own, "Throw Dirt in Your Face," and I played for her for "Refigeratin' Papa." Columbia had progressed to electrical from acoustical and the result was a great recording; I still have a copy of that original 78 rpm of about 1925.[54] Playing by myself and on a Steinway grand piano, I felt confident and relaxed, all of which resulted in, perhaps, one of my best recordings.

I was also brought into touch professionally with such prominent members of the music scene as Cliff Edwards (Ukelele Ike); Andy Razaf (lyricist extraordinaire) who teamed with the inimitable Thomas "Fats" Waller; the affable Paul Whiteman, known to all as "The King of Jazz"; Rube Bloom (pianist-composer); Peggy English (vocalist); Joe Tarto (composer and one-time tuba player with the Vincent Lopez Band).

Much of our rehearsing was done in Joe Davis's music room; it was in this room that The Three Jolly Miners was started and quickly matured; also other larger units *viz*: Choo-Choo Jazzers, Five Musical Blackbirds, and Kansas City Five. Rehearsing was also done in the recording studios, especially at Ajax, occasionally: Mr Berliner was the owner and often we cut twelve or fifteen records during a one-month period. I remember one session when we recorded eight numbers in one day at Ajax; Monette Moore was the vocalist for all the numbers and we were all dead tired, believe me![55]

VIII

This being my first visit to New York, I gradually absorbed the Harlem of the twenties, enjoying and being employed in it. There was so much and all so beautifully 99 per cent Negro; highly professional people involved in business, politics, etc. Everywhere there seemed to be poets and writers.

The social life and extravagance of Negro Harlem was perhaps best shown in the novel with the then shocking title, *Nigger Heaven* by Carl Van Vechten, a white man. It spoke of the rent parties and "chit'lin suppers" to pay the rent; it also exposed other "up-stage" activities of some of the "dicty" snobbish chorus-chicks from the black musicals on Broadway. This exposé was, at least, a healthy one; whether accepted or rejected, personally, that is![56]

The potential greats and near-greats; Claude Mckay the noted poet who left Harlem to live in the USSR; Essie and Paul Robeson, she to become successful novelist and student of anthropology, and he the world's greatest bass-baritone. They were all there, and were part of the tapestry of my life.

One acquaintance I made while in Harlem and of special importance and interest to me, was that of Paul Robeson. I had met Paul, by chance, at a Sunday afternoon impromptu musicale in Harlem. I, along with my wife and son, had called at the home of a new acquaintance of ours. I was to discover a pleasant musical atmosphere prevailing, though ours was just a social call and not associated with an artistic event. So, once inside and following the usual introductions, I was invited to play the piano, and after I had been playing for a while, Paul and his wife came in to join us. I had known each of them earlier, but as Paul Robeson and Essie Goode, not as Mr and Mrs Paul Robeson. Essie was director of the Harlem YWCA.

When I had finished playing, Paul and I started up a conversation, during which he asked me if I would be interested in being his accompanist; at this point Mrs Robeson jokingly remarked, "He even has the clothes for it!" I was wearing an afternoon walking-suit: grey cut-away coat, striped trousers and vest, spats, derby hat, and walking stick. This was the normal dress of many for Sunday wear. It was then agreed that plans would be finalized by Paul's visit to our apartment during the next week.

My subsequent association with him as accompanist at his first song recital in New York in Sherry's Park Avenue Hotel is still one of my pleasantest rec-ollections. A magnificent giant in stature, Paul was a retiring man and very shy. In conversation, every word was cherished by his friends. Paul sang mostly spirituals that evening. As his rich voice filled the room with its velvety warmth, a new hope sang again in these ancient and sincere expressions of a people.

It was only after persistent urging by friends and theatrical associates that Paul finally consented to sing at all. He did not think he could sing, and he once told me just that, but Paul could sing and was blessed with a matchless voice to aid him.[57]

Other concerts followed – at each concert I played a piano solo – at Rutgers University, Paul's alma mater, where he had dominated classroom studies with the highest grades and excelled in track and field sports. Then there was a concert at the Long Island estate of the Pells (a socially prominent family of the time), a return to a New Brunswick (New Jersey) church concert, and our final recital on a Sunday afternoon at the Copley Plaza Hotel in Boston.[58] Here, we were turned away with the suggestion that we try the Copley Annex for accommodations, but while we were leaving, somebody, somewhere, must have "got the message" that it was Paul Robeson they had turned away. At any rate, upon our arrival at the Annex, and after a few whispered comments be-hind the counter, we were escorted to a waiting taxi which took us back at full speed to the Plaza, where we were shown to our luxurious suite. It may be that the sudden about-face was made when someone looked at the list of patrons on the official program for the concert; at the head of the list was the governor of Massachusetts, Lieutenant Governor Cox. This was in 1925.[59]

A short while after this engagement, Paul came to see me at our apartment: I could see that he was a little uneasy and wondered what was to come.

He told me that he had been approached by the Victor Phonograph Recording Co. to record with a second singer, in the person of H. Lawrence Brown, who was also a pianist and who had recently come to New York. Paul was most apologetic and very disturbed, even though he and I had only a gentleman's agreement, and I had been handsomely paid for each concert. We soon reached agreement, however, as I had no wish to travel, leaving my home and my family in New York.[60]

Thus ended, amicably, my six months' association as accompanist to Paul Robeson, a great artist and brilliant scholar. I have met Paul in Montreal twice since in his recitals and was able, in the short time at our disposal, to reminisce a little with him and his now well-known accompanist, H. Lawrence Brown.[61]

IX

Miller, Lyles, Sissle, and Blake were collaborators in the hit success *Shuffle Along*, which ran for four years on Broadway. The Lafayette Theatre was home to some of the greatest artists, black and white, in the world.[62]

I often wonder, with so much to be enjoyed and learned, if I fully grasped the pulse of that exciting experience; since growing up as I had in Ypsilanti knowing and feeling the ever-present discrimination, I nevertheless spent an integrated life, at school and socially to a great degree. My day-to-day playmates were my brothers and the whites where we lived, and I was soloist in the wealthy St Luke's Church.

In Detroit, I had noted more colour-consciousness: here I had learned and played St Louis and Memphis blues; heard Negro spirituals etc. These were played and taken more or less for granted, not as basic expression of black culture. Harlem displayed far greater awareness – a "doing something about it" attitude; surely an increasing show of togetherness for that time. Negroes were striving for an identity and were less than sure which they wanted to be – black or white – from long being compelled to ape "Mr Charlie," they were now emerging from an era in which "Uncle Toming" (acting in a servile manner to whites) was all too well known.

I was gradually learning to look more deeply into the source of things, literary, musical, theatrical, and social. My recording experiences played a helpful role in part with all the race-recording movement being centred around "blues" – largely the twelve-bar variety. The recording companies were getting as much of that sound – coupled with the strange "word-story" – as they possibly could, and were being harried, urged, and practically browbeaten by such great pioneers of promotion as Perry "Mule" Bradford and Clarence Williams, to mention only two of the foremost.[63]

Thus was created this new, lucrative, market in the Deep South and Chicago, and as black people heard their own music sung by their own black artists, this same music gradually emerged as a basic folk music of America. Millions of blacks felt lifted up. That was Harlem! Where it all began for me![64]

My strictly professional work took me into various fields of performance, much of which was along Tin Pan Alley. The Joe Davis Music Publishing Company, where I was staff pianist, had offices in the Broadway Central Building, which opened onto Broadway on one side and 7th Avenue on the other side, either avenue easily reached by a spacious ground floor arcade.[65]

Other tenants in this building were the radio team of Billie Jones and Ernie Hare, and Philadelphia Jack O'Brien, who at that time was world light-heavyweight boxing champion and had a gymnasium on the fifth floor. Our offices were on the seventh. The popular Roseland Ballroom adjoined our building and was home to the Fletcher Henderson Band with its many stars, not the least of whom was Louis "Satchmo" Armstrong, for a brief engagement.[66]

My activities took me to Paul Whiteman's office one day and to radio station WOR another day, where I must have been a "first," as I played "sustaining music," for which I had been sent there by my boss. Other celebrities came to the office: Phil Edwards, Bessie Smith, Art Gillham, Spencer Williams, and W.C. Handy (composer of "St Louis Blues").[67]

I had played club dates in a dozen cities in New Jersey, Long Island, Washington, DC, and, of course, the hotels and clubs of Manhattan and Brooklyn; Waldorf-Astoria, Brevoort, and Astor hotels; New York Athletic Club and Friar's Club, and sophisticated Delmonico's. I played in small "combos" and for different bookers in most cases, including many one-nighters in Harlem and with musicians of varying degrees of popularity and ability. I was pianist with the twenty-five-man Clef Club Orchestra at Manhattan Casino, where between three and four hundred dancers attended the colourful Annual Spring Frolic.

Back on Tin Pan Alley again and Broadway, it was an important part of my job to know some of the staff members of other publishing companies, which I gradually did, from Thomas B. Harms Music Publishing Company (near 6th Avenue) to Irving Berlin Pub. Co and Marks & Co., one on 51st and Broadway, the other on 47th Street.[68] I enjoyed the exhilaration of Manhattan in those earlier years of my life. They were hardworking, satisfying years.

Harlem! Fashionable St Philip's Church (strictly establishment!), Lincoln Theatre near 5th Avenue, where one midnight show found me in the pit orchestra playing for Allie Ross – who later was to conduct the orchestra of Lew Leslie's *Blackbirds* 1928–29 of which I was pianist.[69]

On stage that night, among many others, were George M. Cohan and Eddie Cantor.[70] They put on a skit (believe it or not) with each trying to convince the other that his style of presenting a song was the most popular with the audience. Cohan's accompanist played on a stage for both of them. It ended in a "draw" with both at centre stage, shaking hands and being equally accepted amid thunderous applause.

Also on the bill was America's foremost female impersonator of theatre, Julian Eltinge.[71] I was asked to play on stage for him, alone, and was graciously thanked by him, to the applause of the audience. That's called "The Big Time."

A few acts "got the hook" that night; i.e., they were pulled offstage politely but firmly with a large padded hook. Any act that could make it at the Lincoln was safe on any vaudeville bill, anywhere. As a rule, the audiences were not rough, nor unkind; they simply knew what was not a good performance and management acted accordingly!

As each act on the bill was ready to go on stage, their music was passed up to us through the door of the pit, with whispered cues (we had had no rehearsals) and we were on our own, sink or swim, reading at sight. That's showbiz!

My former classical training proved very helpful on many occasions but may have caused some lack of real abandon in my interpretation of the genuine black music; then too, I was teaching the classics daily. I was thrilled by it though and realized I needed to know more about it.

I was seeing, from time to time, important men; composers and performers who represented the merging of the eras, ragtime and popular: William H. Tyers, who composed "Maori"; Tim Brymn ("Ghost of Blues"); Will Marion Cook ("Exhortation"); Bert Williams of the theatrical team of Williams & Walker, Williams later on as a blackface comic starred in the *Ziegfeld Follies*.[72]

Harlem!! Yes – it had them all. Newspaper publishers, politicians, all caught up in the same search for an identity, moving ever so slowly, closer to and needing each other.

My wife and son arrived in the late summer and we happily set up house in "Strivers Row" – 139th Street – where I was already lodged.[73] Our boy was now walking. The street was a row of fashionable houses built by the architect Stanfield White, who was later shot and killed by Harry K. Thaw.[74] Thaw was the husband of Evelyn Nesbit, who had become involved with White, and this event rocked the entire social world. Thaw was pronounced insane and confined for several years, but was later released.[75]

On this 139th Street (between 7th and 8th Avenues) lived the vaudeville team of Moss & Frye (Keith Circuit headliner). At No. 219, we lived in the home of a chiropractor, Dr Willis by name. Also living here were Mother Liza, a huge, lovable mammy-type; Aunt Dee and Aunt Kate, her sisters; they were all expert cooks. Our son Lou Jr needless to say, at the age of four, had the run of the house, and how they loved him. Mrs Willis, wife of the owner, was a most pleasant person and a schoolteacher, as was her sister. They were all highly intellectual people.

These houses each had three floors, plus basement and attic. I and my family occupied the second floor with the reception foyer and had use of the kitchen. It was a happy, busy, place indeed.

William Tandy, an architect, lived two doors away; sharing his home were Mr & Mrs "Slim" Thompson; she was the lovely Florence Mills, star of several Lew Leslie Broadway productions, among numerous others.[76]

Dr Louise Wright, a police surgeon, lived across the street and had as his neighbour Dr W.E.B. Du Bois, the brilliant educator, lecturer, author, and editor of *The Crisis* – official magazine of the NAACP.[77]

These people I used to see every day.

The Landlords' Association was determined to maintain the high standard which then prevailed among the tenants who willingly agreed to display cards in their windows bearing the word "Vacancy" instead of the more common "Room to Let." All of this was Harlem lifting its head a little higher, but together and trusting each other, determined not to forget that outrageous housing "rental rape" which accompanied the trend to Upper Harlem's fashionable and fragile Sugar Hill; that brand of vicious exploitation of which the Negro has always been the innocent victim.[78]

I continued teaching music and was still engaged in phonograph recording until August 1927, when I returned to Detroit; my wife and son remained for the fall opening of school, but rejoined me in December of that year. We had a joyous Christmas together, then, tragically in February 1928, during a cold snap of sub-zero weather, my wife was stricken with lobar pneumonia and died within two weeks.

The attack had occurred to my wife on a Sunday night, as we were on our way home and the weather was viciously cold. My wife had spent the evening at the apartment of our sister, as she often did, waiting for me to finish my last show at 11 p.m. after which we made the trip home by streetcar (surface trolley). On the car my wife spoke of her back being cold, though she was dressed extra warmly, as she always was very careful about. Our arrival at home was as usual, with my wife going to bed after having a hot drink. The following morning upon arriving at the theatre for rehearsal, I learned that, as often happened, the incoming show carried its own musical-director-pianist, thus giving me a two-week holiday with pay. When I telephoned this information home, my wife's mother, who was visiting us at the time, came downtown bringing our eight-year-old son Louis to meet me. I had promised to take him to see a Charlie Chaplin film, *The Circus*. With the situation seemingly not serious at home, we went to see the film, which was hilarious and very enjoyable. When we reached home later, however, my wife's condition had worsened, and the doctor was at the house. Then began the vigil which was to end with her death two weeks later in Providence Hospital with her mother and myself at her bedside, as consciousness remained to the end.

X

After completing another year in the orchestra of the Koppin Theatre I joined Lew Leslie's *Blackbirds* revue in Boston, as pianist in the orchestra. I continued for a full season, the show closing in Montreal in June 1929.[79] That was the most enjoyable lesson in learning and experience I had had as yet in the profession. True, I had done pit work in the Lafayette Theatre in New York and the Koppin Theatre in Detroit, played "tab" shows, vaudeville, and for the silent movies, but *Blackbirds*, a colourful revue with beautiful tunes expertly arranged for orchestra by Bill Vodery, a former arranger for Flo Ziegfeld and now Leslie's personal arranger, and played by our own nine-man orchestra augmented by some of the finest artist-musicians in the world, was entertainment at its best. Musicians from the symphonies of Boston, Philadelphia, Baltimore, Rochester, Buffalo, Toronto, and Montreal were added to the orchestra as we played in their city; these orchestras supplied the strings and woodwind to our brass, reeds, percussion, and timpani. At times, I felt I was enjoying the ultimate. The tour ended in Montreal, and we returned to New York. Then I went to Detroit, and after a short vacation I spent two years doing summer band work at Pleasant Lake, near Jackson, and in Flint, Michigan.

Following the engagements, I returned to Canada with my two brothers, my son, and three other musicians. It was 1932.

After an unsuccessful year in Toronto, the other musicians returned to Detroit, but I stayed in Toronto and joined Myron Sutton's Canadian Ambassadors band, which was to come to Montreal in the Spring of 1933.[80] We were booked to play at Connie's Inn, now a nightclub, but formerly known as The Frolics, when the fabulous Texas Guinan was its hostess. Many Montrealers would remember her famous greeting, "Hello Sucker!" Of course, the policy was changed to an all-Negro show, with a producer and entire cast from New York and Sutton's all-Canadian band. Each show played for two weeks; then the format was changed, although the cast remained the same.[81]

Headlining the regular cast were such stars as Johnny and Victoria Vigile, Dewey Wineglass, Johnny Hudgins (prince of pantomime), Dr Jazz, and the immortal Billie Holiday, then a mere sixteen or seventeen years old.[82] Her fame of later years was to rename her "Lady Day."

A top star of the plush jazz spots of New York and other leading cities as well as band vocalist with the Artie Shaw and Count Basie orchestras, she also cut many records with small bands, some led by Teddy Wilson and including such stars as Roy Eldridge, Benny Goodman, Lester "Prez" Young, Charlie Shavers, and numerous others. Lady Day, with her unique rhythmic treatment of the lyrical sentence, influenced the entire vocal jazz scene. One time, when Billie Holiday was starring in Connie's Inn and I was piano man in the band, I asked her about the backing of the band to her unusual style of singing. She answered me saying "That's alright baby, you just play like you're playin' and everything will come out together." Billie was then about nineteen years old, in 1934.

Neither must I overlook our chorus of hand-picked multi-complexioned dancing dolls. That's where it was at. Real class!![83]

XI

Before I enter Canadian life permanently, let me return to New York which I left rather abruptly in this narrative.

In New York, my wife and I were living in what was regarded as a preferred social setting and which was 99 per cent Negro. Our son won scholarships to a private school of ethical culture, which was 99 per cent white. If it were now, he would have been in a public school, learning about people and knowing how to meet daily situations, instead of aspiring to attendance at a white private school, as did the sons of so many well-educated middle-class Negroes. All my pupils were Negro, neat, well dressed, and intelligent; we saw no sordid side of life, though there was a section known as San Juan Hill just a stone's throw over the Harlem River, where poorer blacks and South Americans lived.[84] We were always invited to the "right" homes and fancy balls and we read good books.

Harlem saw two race riots and taxi disorders. Marcus Garvey led a parade for the United Negro Improvement Association (UNIA) along 7th Avenue and many of us laughed, but I wonder now if his "vision" for blacks was not without some merit.[85] The *New York News*, the *Pittsburgh Courier*, the *Chicago Defender*, and other papers printed crime stories and tales of oppression, while black voices often criticized that "alarmist element" which was really trying to awaken Negroes to the subtle intimidation against black men.[86]

My family left New York in its state of progressive change which, judged by conditions there now seems to have collapsed.[87]

<u>1927.</u> Having returned to Detroit, I spent one year at the Koppin Theatre followed by a year and a half in Flint. In a four-man group I played in a small but attractive Chinese dine-and-dance restaurant, The Teaco Inn. We played light classics as dinner music and popular tunes for dancing. Harry Bradley,

now deceased, was the drummer, xylophone soloist, and leader; Emmett Adams was guitarist and vocalist; Ben Richardson played saxophone and clarinet, and also sang; I played piano and also did vocals. We had a singing trio within the group. I also taught piano in Flint and had a few radio half-hour spots but work was far from plentiful because of the Depression, which had started in 1929. Because of this and also because of the death of my wife, I decided to return permanently to Canada.

XII

From Detroit, I came to Toronto, Ontario, with my brothers' own band. I had been in Toronto with the *Blackbirds* company in 1929, when I had roomed at 198 Beverley Street, the home of "Tobacco Brown," a professional wrestler. Since my son was with me (he had never been left alone since the death of his mother), I returned to the same rooming house and received a great welcome. There were two sons and a daughter; the youngest son, nine-year-old Bobby, was great company for Lou Jr. Their mother was a large, pleasant, very strict, Italian lady known as "Mama Marietta." During my stay, Lou Jr was enrolled in school, as always.

An all-black theatrical company arrived in town hoping for an extended run in Toronto's Princess Theatre, which had been "dark" (not in regular use) for many weeks. In the company were many stars: Laura Bowman, Rose McClendon, Leigh Whipper, and Juano Hernandez. The company produced such dramas as *Porgy*, *In Abraham's Bosom*, and others. (Bobby and Lou Jr each had parts in this play.)

Several of the cast stayed at the Browns' home, but after about three or four weeks the entire company returned to New York; the tour had not been a success.[88]

The band we had brought into Canada from Detroit had seven men, retaining the original name of Hooper Brothers' Orchestra. The AFM in Toronto prohibited the acceptance of steady engagements for a period of six months; we could play only "club dates." So, we engaged a business agent, added an attractive girl vocalist, and were booked into theatres and occasional dances, but the jobs were not regular enough so, after six months, the men in the band were forced to return home to Detroit, stopping on the way in Toronto; the band was breaking up. We were in the far north in Rouyn-Noranda during the Christmas week of 1932. At that time, Rouyn was a duck-board, dog-sled, "native-Indians-and-miner's" town, with a fair hotel and Chinese restaurant. There was also a very nice snack bar, with private booths and fully licensed. It was also forty-five degrees below zero![89]

With our drummer and sax man, I played at the snack bar on Christmas Eve; on Christmas Day we three made the trip back to Toronto by train and had a "ball" all the way, marching the length of the train, playing our instruments and singing holiday songs. When we arrived in Toronto, we found the other members of the band preparing to return to Detroit.

We had had lots of fun together with many varied kinds of musical entertainment. We had sung spirituals, done some outdoor concerts in the summer, and played in dancehalls. We had been personal friends for years and although we split up with real regret, everyone understood and accepted the situation.

In the fall of 1932, I played at the Canadian National Exhibition (CNE) for two weeks from late August up to and including Labour Day. It was on the midway – for a "music-by-ear" show; their regular pianist could not make the trip from Buffalo. It was very, very, hard work, playing alone from 9 a.m. to 10 p.m. daily, except Sunday.

There were comedians, skits, dancing girls, and singers; all in all a fast-moving and exciting show – but that was *really* "making a buck the hard way" as far as I was concerned.[90]

During the spring of 1933, I played at an attractive Southern Fried Chicken place in town, near College Avenue. This place had been opened by a member of the former show which had appeared at the Princess Theatre, and he had remained after the show tour ended in 1932.

By April of 1933, my brother Arnold, leader of our band still in Toronto, had been keeping in touch with Myron Sutton and his Canadian Ambassadors, and had learned that they would be coming to Toronto for a one-nighter; they needed a pianist and expected that I would join them. Their former pianist, who was leaving to go to Montreal, was none other than the talented young Buster Harding of Buxton, already a promising piano man in the Earl "Fatha" Hines tradition. He soon became a sensation in Montreal and later left for the US, finally becoming a leading big-band arranger for Benny Goodman, Count Basie, the Dorsey Brothers, Woody Herman, and many others of that great musical era.[91]

When I joined Myron Sutton, I found my cousin, Terry Hooper, was the drummer and we were contracted to open at Connie's Inn in Montreal. Terry and I have worked at many jobs together since, and over the years we had not a few laughs at some of the situations we found ourselves in. Unhappily, Terry passed away in March of 1972.

I have described this glamorous spot (Connie's Inn) in earlier pages; the owners were "Charlie the Chauffeur," Eli Hill, Mr Ellis, and Mr Barr. It was considered an "Establishment" at that time in the nightclub world. Others were the famed Standard Club, a favourite after-hours spot in Black Bottom[92] (the St Antoine at Mountain Street area) which was later renamed the Terminal Club.

Then there were the cabarets: Chez Maurice, El Morocco (a white-only place) – George Dewey Washington, a great baritone, was a favourite there. Montreal was a wide-open city with the flourishing red-light district, booze unlimited; no labour strikes, and no bank robberies.[93] I enjoyed our band life very much, playing the floor shows and for the special female soloists between shows (we did two a night) and then for the dancing. Three or four times a week, some of the band and show personnel would go, after our own work, to a few other clubs (we called this cabar-eh-in). One club about two blocks from Connie's Inn was The Paramount Grill, and the sensational Buster Harding ("88'er extraordinaire") played – and how he played. One of our chorus gals after one visit to that club renamed it "Rabbitville" – and that name stuck.

The personnel of our show company (one of the best in town) changed very little in the year and a half that our band was there; every two to four weeks, a new "star act" would be the principal change, other than new costumes for each new show and new musical arrangements which I made for the band.

One "star-act" change was to bring our show the then under twenty-year-old Billie Holiday, who later went on to become the toast of the plush nightspots in downtown New York and other leading cities throughout the US. Her distinct style of off-beat singing was one of the varied and natural attractions of her artistry, but playing for this type of singing was a new experience for me and our band.

Following its stay at Connie's Inn, the band moved to another spot in the same area, named the Hollywood Club, also with a fantastic floor show starring Emmett "Babe" Wallace, who later had a leading role in the film *Stormy Weather* with Bill "Bojangles" Robinson and Lena Horne. Also playing at this club were such artists as Marcia Marquez, Myra Johnson (a positively great singer). Another male star attraction was Ralph Brown, later a Cotton Club tap dancer deluxe.[94]

It was here that Babe Wallace introduced "Minnie-the-Moocher" (à la Cab Calloway) to Montreal. Our band and the cast of the show got along splendidly – offstage and on. In our free time, we went to the beaches to swim and we even had our own baseball team; also by now we had weekly broadcasts (remote-control) direct from the club, not to mention the numerous jam sessions that had a way of materializing, mostly at the black clubs or bootleg joints (in Black Bottom), but attended by white musicians too. The AFM was segregated then and only "emancipated" itself during World War II. Now, there is one union "local" for all and free integration is practiced (to some degree) at work.[95]

XIII

<u>1935.</u> My son was with me now, following a short stay with some friends in Toronto. I had found a place for the two of us in Montreal and so we settled in with a fine Italian family – the Baris, father, mother, two teenage girls, and two younger boys, who all spoke Italian, French, and English. There was a splendid home atmosphere for Lou Jr, and he profited from it greatly.

Along with my musical arrangements for orchestra, I began giving piano lessons and also organized a group of nine male singers whom I called the Hooper Southern Singers. We enjoyed a high degree of success via church, public school, and radio appearances and even made a news film for United Theatres, under the title *May We Present*. Though we were given a private preview, I could never learn of its showing publicly in Montreal.[96]

Figure 7
A baseball team comprising waiters and some musicians from the Hollywood
Club in Montreal, Quebec (1934). Concordia University Special Collections,
John Gilmore Fonds, P004-02-032.

<u>1936.</u> Of more than passing interest to me was the happening which
brought a very young Oscar Peterson to my attention, via a telephone call
from his father, requesting that I accept Oscar as a piano pupil. He was
eleven years old at the time and I was not fully aware of his playing ability,
nor the theoretical knowledge he already possessed. Suffice to say, I was in
for a startlingly delightful surprise when, as had been arranged, I arrived at
the Peterson home for the first lesson.

I met Oscar, a rather plump eleven-year-old, looking very neat in an overly
snug dark suit, buttoned up to the top and with knee pants, not today's man-
nish-looking slacks. My first pleasant experience came when I was presented
to Oscar, in his polite manner and the pleasantly modulated voice in which
he replied. Even today, this has altered little through the years when we occa-

sionally meet, and as I came to know the parents and other members of the family at that time, I discovered this kind of courteous dignity to be a strong characteristic of all of them.

When, on that first day, I asked Oscar to play for me, I was indeed astonished, not only at what I was hearing but at the intelligent interpretation; the easy and adequate technique while playing entirely from memory; and this from a boy of eleven was, to say the least, unusual. Then followed a short period of basics – scales, arpeggi, keys, chords, minor vs. major. He knew them all, as well as possessing nature's gift of perfect pitch, which I observed and "tested" fully.

The Petersons were a family of six; all of them performed music well. The father was a one-time horn player. Charlie, the eldest boy, played trumpet and piano until he met with a tragic accident in which he lost one hand, amputated at the wrist. But, with indomitable courage and an artificial hand-in-a-glove, he continues to play fine horn, using only his one hand. Daisy, the eldest girl, herself a qualified pianist, has her own private studio as well as giving instruction in piano at the Negro Community Centre here in Montreal.[97] Another younger sister, May, has also played piano well.

Following a few lessons with young Oscar and realizing his outstanding potential, I advised Mr Peterson that, in view of Oscar's present ability, I had decided to select only such musical pieces as would challenge to the utmost his musicianship, leaving him to deal with them in his own way. As I observed the results through bi-weekly visits to his home, I was satisfied that this practice was proving satisfactory: it freed young Oscar to forge his own illustrious way, which he has since done with such brilliant success. Eventually we parted, I to leave Canada for six years of military service, and Oscar to pursue his music diligently with the help of understanding parents.

When I returned to civilian life in October 1945, I soon began to hear the name of Oscar Peterson always in words of highest praise, and during a subsequent visit to his home, hearing him play I quickly understood and agreed. His playing that day was to me an experience in controlled power, facility, and gentleness. I heard Oscar from time to time following this meeting, and learned he was doing some studying with Paul de Marky, the European pianist-teacher whom I heard often on Sunday mornings in thirty-minute recitals of the classics, over a Montreal radio station.[98]

Oscar appeared for a season at Victoria Hall with the Johnny Holmes band as featured pianist; then followed a lengthy engagement of the Oscar Peterson Trio at the Alberta Lounge on Osborne Street in Montreal.

He was a star anywhere and everywhere he performed, and I recall one night, during a period when name bands were being booked into the former night spot called Chez Maurice, that the Dizzy Gillespie Band was the current attraction. My son, Lou Jr and I were there as we both "dug" Diz's playing but good! Oscar had finished his appearance at the lounge and had come into the hall while the band was playing a set; his name was immediately spread by the "real cats" via the grapevine through the hall, on its way to the band-stand. Evidently, Dizzy had not heard Oscar play and invited him to join the band for a set. The look of sheer disbelief on Diz's face when Oscar took his special "spot" in the number with a display of solid dance-band piano which, even in its great rhythm, did sound here and there as though four or even six hands may have combined in the performance, was something to see!

Naturally, the house "caved in" (professionally speaking) not only for the hometown boy, but as much in the knowledge that here was indeed already a truly great artist, barely twenty years old.

The next time I heard Oscar (Dizzy had wanted him for his band) was at His Majesty's Theatre in Montreal; he was one of a group of "greats" who made up one of the various units of Norman Granz's Jazz at the Philharmonic (JATP) – Flip Phillips, Ella Fitzgerald, Coleman Hawkins, Trummy Young, Buddy Rich – to name a few.[99]

During an interval away from JATP, Oscar toured with his own trio in which he had Herb Ellis on guitar and the fine bassist Ray Brown.

In this period of activity, Oscar was living in their home (he was now married with two girls and a boy in family) on West Broadway in Notre-Dame-de-Grâce. His fame spread as the *DownBeat* music biweekly's winner of the Annual Jazz Poll among the pianists. His trio discs and popular public appearances in North America and abroad were sound proof of his success. Later, he had moved with his family to an apartment on Linton Avenue, where again I visited him following his return from Italy, where he had been presented with a motor scooter. In this Linton Avenue apartment, Oscar, who by the way is also an expert photographer, had built a complete stereo-amplifying system which my friend and I were privileged to hear and marvel at its performance.

Oscar eventually moved to Toronto where he now makes his home, and it was there that he established a music school for the instruction and performance of basically jazz "charts" and literature. Ably assisted by Ray Brown, his bassist, and Ed Thigpen, his drummer, who replaced the original guitarist, Oscar and his all-star assistants soon established an internationally known school, with students from various countries of the world numbered in its classes. And finally, it was the continued pressure of road travel for personal appearances, recording sessions in various cities, and the general fatigue of it all, which made continuance of the school an impossibility; after about three years of great popularity, it closed its doors.[100]

I often have news of Oscar, and in a recent issue of the AFM's *International Musician* his smiling "chops" were riding the cover page with an excellent life story on him in the issue.

I last saw Oscar about three years ago when his new trio was appearing at Place des Arts (Montreal) with JATP and, as usual, he was with the real "High Society" of jazz; to name just a few – Duke Ellington and his band; Ella Fitzgerald; the Jimmy Jones Trio; the one and only Coleman "Bean" Hawkins; Benny Carter; Zoot Sims; Clark Terry. And when the Duke introduced Montrealer Oscar Peterson to take over the piano in Duke's own band (I remember they were playing "Take the A Train") and when Oscar really "started to take that 'A' train" – the house simply caved in, man![101] It was another day, you might say, or right then, "we was really livin!" And that was that! Oscar Peterson continues to dominate the field of jazz piano virtuosity year after year.

XIV

Another popular club in Black Bottom, the Monte Carlo, had recently come under new management and among other changes being made, I was engaged as director of entertainment. I was asked to engage a band, which I did, a combo of piano, sax, bass, and drums, and supervise the floor shows and their personnel. My long-time friend, John Madison, was general manager, and, at the time, a valuable member and second tenor of my vocal group the Hooper Southern Singers.

The Monte Carlo was a happy place with some great floor shows; featured among its artists were the highly versatile team of the Spencer Sisters, Olga and Minerva, both of whom were local Montreal girls. Olga was a solid tap-dancing star and possessed a fine alto voice. Minerva, who was also a fair dancer when called upon, was a soprano with a voice of rare quality and beauty; her solos were always a highlight of every show, and singing together the girls "stopped" many a show.[102]

There were also Russell Lee with a fine baritone voice and a still finer repertoire of great songs; Georgie Staton, the diminutive, five-foot tall, Russian-born dancer and singer; Cliff Bookman, a "symphony in rhythm" on tap; Bernice Jordan, a small cute, saucy entertainer, whose very vivacity and high-speed dancing made her an all-time favourite; Frenchie Mendez, the African tribal dancer with elegant, "New World" class; then Larry and Eleanore Washington, two of the loveliest people, who to see in performance was an experience in "all-out" comedy.[103]

One visitor, a guest of the management for nearly a month, was the popular songwriter Shelton Brooks, who occasionally honoured the numerous requests from guests to sing and play (he was not a member of the show) with some of his own songs: "Darktown Strutters' Ball" and "Hole in the Wall," among others. He delighted the audience with his performances and humorous personality.[104]

In the checkroom, Lou Jr was helper to an attractive young lady, Miss Marie Wright, who had a real crush on my cousin Terry. So, when Terry and I were not visiting our dentists (both of us experiencing painful bouts with our teeth), he began to take Marie seriously, and so – well now she is Mrs Terry Hooper and a dear friend of our family.

To round out our staff we had Vic Bonner, head waiter, Charlie Gordon (second in charge), Jacklin (chef), and Thomas, our uniformed doorman. The late Al Palmer (deceased 1971), my good friend and very popular newspaper man at that time, was our publicity man for the club.[105]

The living was good with literally dozens of nightclubs in operation; burlesque and neo-burlesque shows daily from 1 p.m. to midnight; tab-shows and complete stock company stage plays and comedies.[106] Midnight shows on New Year's Eve, when regular nightclub acts were booked for three and four spots at different theatres in one night, would prove a bonanza for taxi drivers. Performers would hire a cab to drive them to each theatre and wait for them. A fifteen-minute act was not long, and they were making the dollars to pay the fare easily.

The musicians' Local was not very strong then, and musicians were forced to work very long hours; many nights, our band has played from 9 p.m. to 7 a.m. the following morning. Gradually, the musicians' union broke that underworld control of numerous clubs and by 1938 a minimum-hours nightly limit was established which appeared in writing in all contracts made with employers, AND contracts were compulsory on ALL engagements, as is the case today.

XV
Summer 1937 – Chambly Basin Hotel

One day nearing the middle of June of 1937, I had a visit from a musician I knew but with whom I had never played before. He was a native Cuban named Mario Cummano, a splendid musician in the classical tradition and who played saxophone and clarinet, though his conception of the rhythms of the dance music then being played left something to be desired. However, he spoke about an engagement soon to be starting in Chambly Basin, Quebec, and for which he already held a contract; he asked me to accept the position of pianist in his five-man band. After discussing the more important details of such an engagement, *viz.* board and lodging (we would live on the premises), hours of playing, salary, and dress, I agreed to the terms and signed my name. We opened the job on a Saturday night, the weekend including 1 July, Dominion Day. I had learned that my friend, Frank Johnson, trombonist extraordinaire, and a good vocalist, was also in the band; Eddie, whom I had not known, was the drummer and number one vocalist, and there was a young tenor sax player named Leo Alarie who spoke little English at the time, and we others were not fluent in his "langue canadienne française" either. He was very shy at first, but our common love of all sports gradually helped to create a friendship between us, which still continues to this date, January 1972. Chambly Basin then was a small town where the provincial locks of the waterway up to the five Great Lakes via the St Lawrence River were situated; that waterway continued down to the Atlantic Ocean via Lake Champlain and New York. The Chambly Hotel was a rather attractive building, spacious and sprawling over a fairly wide area; its inviting verandahs ran nearly all the way around it at two separate levels and were ideal for reading in the late afternoon or even for letter writing.

Owned and operated by Mr and Mrs Maw, the hotel was quite comfortable and the food not bad.

The dancehall section provided ample space for dancing, with tables seating twos and fours set up all around the dancing space, where beverages were served. The bandstand, situated at one end of the room, was not too large but more intimately arranged, and built around a medium-height stage with the end wall in back of us serving as a sounding board, thus improving the blend of our music.

The crowds were large, especially on the weekend, but since we played each night until 1 a.m., in the time of one week the attendance had increased noticeably and our music had improved too. We were becoming more used to each other's style of playing. Our normal dance program for an evening included tunes and songs of varying speeds, from the slower ballads and waltzes to medium tempo swing fox-trots, with a few of the livelier Latin numbers and some fast pieces for the exceptionally good dancer. The guests ranged from teenagers to middle-aged men and women with a few "oldies" so there was very little problem at any time concerning the type of number we played during an evening. Then too, there were always the requests of dancers, which the band welcomed; they usually meant something special to someone.

The townspeople were very friendly and numbered about 95 per cent French-speaking residents; the remaining 5 per cent living in the town spoke at least some French. I found it very interesting living among so many non-English and to observe their customs and habits "at home." The hotel's bathing facilities, which everyone used, included a high-diving tower with two diving boards; also various fun crafts such as row boats, canoes, and a deep-water float. There were many excellent swimmers in Chambly: some were experts who even qualified for and entered the CNE swim during the annual fair in August.

Many of these young athletes welcomed us, made friends and invited us as guests to their local tennis club and baseball team. There were the Charron Brothers, Bert and George; Frank Pope, whom I later met in Bordon, England, in the uniform of the Dragoons; Tony Demers, an amateur golf champ and "Tarzan," his brother; also Jean Pusey, a professional wrestler. Some of the women were Ruth Phillips; "Sunny" Ross (a high school teacher); Marthe Gauthier (clerk at Montreal's juvenile court); and others. I was unmarried then and we all enjoyed tennis competitions, softball, and swimming together in that spacious body of water, Chambly Basin. I used to swim early in the morning with my "trainer" rowing and coaching me until I swam nearly the mile across – not exactly an Olympic feat but it did contribute to my general fitness.

Situated in this beautiful area was an island accessible only by boat or by swimming; there, during the weeks of summer, many a young man and his girlfriend, both from the town, would enjoy a primitive life in premarital bliss. No doubt, they eventually married, and though a seemingly strange practice at the time, this may have been the start of bringing that practice into the open as now.

As the days grew into weeks, I came to realize that regular rehearsal of the band, a customary practice on such engagements, was simply not to be, as more than one attempt to hold a rehearsal failed because Mario, our leader, preferred to "go fishing." So that chapter was closed, though among the other members we always found time to work over a new song for our vocalist, Eddie, or maybe a new musical arrangement of Frankie Johnson's, our trombonist.

Leo, our sax man, and I had each been improving his swimming, and often, along with Ruth Phillips and George Charron, when a boat of size had gone through the locks coming into our basin, we would hurry around to the high retaining wall and leap down the twenty or twenty-five feet into the turbulent water caused by the passing of perhaps an expensive, privately owned yacht en route to New York.

The tennis club held its annual tournament, and we took part, but neither Frank, Leo, nor myself reached the finals, although our own playing had improved somewhat.

And then, one day, we had two visitors from Montreal. My son Lou Jr and his teenage friend Art Ryan had hitchhiked to Chambly, each bringing along a model airplane he had built; a rubber-powered job which flew by the power of the rubber bands and the grace of God. Needless to say, the manoeuvres of these graceful ships flying upward and away to great distances amazed the adults while fully delighting the children. And no one was to know that by 1944 both Art and Lou Jr would each win his wings and a commission as fighter-pilot in the Royal Canadian Air Force. Many happy events

Figure 8
Lou Hooper and his son, Lou Hooper Jr, in Chambly, Quebec
(1937). Courtesy of Adam Barken.

had contributed to a successful summer season – the improved performance
of our band, the sports, the new friendships made, and, in general, the opportunity of just being outdoors.

Labour Day finally arrived; our contract expired, and that entire scene
changed completely, as each one concerned himself with the approaching fall
season.

Leo Alarie has often confessed to me that the experience of that summer changed his life profoundly, coming as it did at a critical time and when he was about nineteen years old. Musically, it caused him to immediately buy a new and better saxophone, which, while improving his playing, also increased his value to the band leaders, thus producing added engagements. Socially, by his own admission today, he was taught his greatest lesson in tolerance; a complete reversal from earlier thinking, and for which he, even more now, feels the change was like a miracle.

Leo today is an interesting, sincere, honest young man who, in spite of aggravating attacks of ill health, still maintains a pleasant sense of humour, including a very logical concern for the present problems of society. He and myself are in constant touch, meeting often somewhere just for a walk around; perhaps Place Ville Marie or the new Radio-Canada building. A really gracious man, he is well-travelled, and I, though older than he, am proud to call him my friend, and am deeply grateful for the chance meeting in Chambly that summer of 1937.

XVI

As sometimes happens, signs of the coming depression were beginning to appear; a change in the political party took place, with a "new-broom-sweeps-clean" attitude very much in evidence; this, in turn, led to the closing of many nightclubs.[107]

Soon, our band [the Canadian Ambassadors] made plans to take off for the Gatineau Country Club, a beautiful and spacious private club situated in Hull, Quebec. However, I did not wish to leave my pupils in Montreal, my singing group, and, more importantly, my son who was still in school. I found a replacement piano-man from Windsor, Ontario, and thus officially severed permanent contact with Sutton's Canadian Ambassadors, although I did make one barnstorming summer tour with the band (altered to a smaller combo) when they returned from Hull. That "tour" was for kicks and finally ended in Toronto.

We had played North Bay, Timmins, Callender, Rouyn-Noranda, Orillia, and a few other towns; just having a good time and finishing the last three weeks at the Ridley Lodge in the picturesque Muskoka district.[108]

Figure 9
The Canadian Ambassadors and Bernice "Bunny" Jordan Whims in North Bay, Ontario, during a summer tour (ca mid- to late 1930s). Concordia University Special Collections, John Gilmore Fonds, P004-02-016.

We had met many of the local musicians from town to town that summer and had enjoyed several good jam sessions, and a few booze-ups as well. This was my first time visiting those areas of Canada.

It was while we were at Ridge Lodge that war was declared on Germany and I, along with thousands of others from the area, went to the CNE recruiting centre in Toronto to enlist. Here, I was interviewed by personnel of the 48th Highlanders, and was given a card of application enlistment, which I duly filled out. I handed it in, but never heard further; perhaps they felt that a black man would look a little strange in kilts.[109]

Several days later, I started to hitchhike to Montreal, but after the first hundred and fifty miles I found myself without a ride. Luckily, it was September and the days were warm, sometimes too warm, and the nights were cold. After a few short "pick-ups" and with a night coming on, I was only too glad to find myself a large haystack in a nearby field and burrow into it.

When I reached Kingston (halfway point between Toronto and Montreal), I was so tired from walking nearly all the day until nightfall without a pick-up, that I went to the Kingston jail and asked to spend the night; after a real display of suspicion by the desk sergeant and, oh yes, taking my fingerprints. Even though I showed the enlistment application, he took my belongings and put me in a cell with two real rubby-dub bums, judging from the smell.[110] This was my first and only experience of being in a "civvy" jail – I was in "the digger" (jail) for an hour and a half once while in the army, because I neglected to read daily orders (I was at the time a trumpeter in my unit and had failed to parade with the daily guard).

I was really afraid, and soon called out and rattled the cell door asking to be let out into God's fresh air. The sergeant didn't deign to even answer my call. At 7 a.m. the next day we were let out, I with a warning of a vagrancy charge if I remained in town; if he only knew how badly I wanted to be out in the country again and how much I despised him and his breed!

The day proved to be long and hot, so once out of town I sat down to rest beside the highway and had not been there very long when a car whizzed by, stopping well down the road because of its speed. I had given up thumbing, but as I watched, a young man got out of the car and started towards me: I immediately recognized him a personal friend of mine and a fellow musician from Montreal, Hugh Sealey. He, with his wife Margaret and some friends, were returning from visiting relatives in Gaspé and had been amazed to see me sitting by the roadside.[111] Boy! was I glad to see them. We christened their car "Sweet Chariot" – she was swingin' low and had come to carry me home; back to Montreal. But, best of all, they had FOOD in the car. Man – I ate! We were still about fifty miles from Montreal and we all laughed and joked about the incident in genuine and friendly manner; but I was really much too "beat" to appreciate the jokes.

When we finally reached Montreal and I was once more in my own room, my first thought was of a hot bath, giving special loving care to my poor aching feet; my second thought to sleep-around-the-clock, which I did.

I was soon myself again, and next day immediately set about furthering my army enlistment. I finally joined the Royal Canadian Artillery (RCA), which was recruiting in Craig St Drill Hall; the complete, war story with my concert-party involvement, etc., I will deal with in the next chapters.

XVII

It was late in September 1939 when I became D-9151-Gunner L.S. Hooper, and again my music had played a part in my early acceptance into this 7th Medium Battery, where I was soon to become battery trumpeter, similar to the bugler in some other military units. For a period of four months, we were busy with the many things that go into the training of an army recruit; namely, general discipline, physical training, route marches, social activities, and such. I had formed a small dance band made up of members from several units based in Craig St Drill Hall (which has since been demolished) and we played for army dances at the Red Triangle Canteen in Phillips Square. We stayed at our own homes and reported at 9 a.m. each morning to the drill hall for daily parades and other training. Each day, we were given tickets for our meals, which we ate in the North Eastern restaurant. When we moved into the Place Viger later on, our own cook-kitchen was set up, where we ate all meals and occupied a large section of the hotel as full-time barracks and also slept there.

Under this arrangement, the men soon began to know each other better and some amusing things started to happen, some of which occasionally called for disciplinary action.

One prank, which was all in good fun, happened to me (or nearly did) when four or five fellows who had got hold of a tin of white paint grabbed me, and were about to paint my testicles white; but I was rescued just in time. Don't forget, I was the trumpeter! They never forgave me that first a.m. "get-up" call (Reveille).

So, work and play went on until late in January 1940, when our final orders came through and we left Craig St Drill Hall and entrained to our port of embarkation at Halifax, Nova Scotia. Following a restless 48-hour wait aboard ship, we sailed. Our ship was HMS *Aquitania*, famed commander.

On 10 February, we landed in Greenock, Scotland, without incident. I had played my way over, on piano along with a few other musicians aboard ship, for the impromptu entertainment of all personnel; this included playing for church services each Sunday during the Atlantic crossing. Arriving in Greenock we entertained on the long, slow journey to "we knew not where." Our destination was in Hampshire County; it was very cold and the camp we

Figure 10
Portrait of Lou Hooper in the Royal Canadian Artillery, Montreal,
Quebec (1939). Courtesy of Adam Barken.

occupied was in horrible condition – with broken water pipes, water-soaked
palliasse mattresses, and biscuit pillows; it was far from a "warm welcome."

Our base was in the south of England, in Bordon, Hampshire, and once
arrived I was first introduced to the Soldier's Canteen or Navy, Army and Air
Force Institutes (NAAFI). This is the place where military personnel of all
branches of services may purchase tea and cakes, cigarettes, beer and soft

drinks (no liquor), boot laces, etc. There is always the slightly out-of-tune piano for anyone who can play it; needless to say, I played it! Here began what was to prove one of the most fulfilling phases of my entire army life: that of bringing a bit of music and a few laughs to troops; in hospitals or on the field of action in some faraway theatre of war outside the UK. Soon followed the regular courses in basic training: parade square and battle schemes, one of which took us to a shooting range at Redesdale, Northumberland.

This was to be our first real "shoot" using live ammunition; I was signaller-trumpeter. As is often the case in artillery exercises, injuries occur, sometimes fatal. One such injury, though fortunately not fatal, sent one of our dispatch riders to hospital suffering from severe concussion, when his motorcycle was upset in a collision. A good friend of mine then as now, Allan Glass, lay unconscious in hospital in Newcastle upon Tyne, which was not far from our tent-camp unit. During our two weeks' stay in Redesdale, we visited the hospital daily hoping to awaken a spark of recall in Allan, but without success, and the unit returned to Bordon without him. But Allan, it developed, had other ideas, for finally waking one morning several weeks later, he saw his nurse for the first time, liked what he saw and proposed marriage to her; she accepted. This happy ending continues through the years, in Montreal.

Newcastle, that great, friendly city! So convenient too; we visited it often, even without benefit of pass. Finally, on the Saturday prior to our unit leaving the area, Gus Bouchard, trumpeter, Eddie Wilcox, mechanic and I, had weekend passes to visit Hawick, a town in Scotland, twenty-five miles away. We had been invited to a party at the home of Mr and Mrs Johnson, friends we had met during our stay in Redesdale. So, depending upon the usual mode of free transportation, hitchhiking, we set out, failing to heed the nationwide broadcast of Prime Minister Churchill in which he asked car owners not to use their cars and so help to conserve petrol. Not one civilian car was on that highway all day, and by nightfall we had walked fourteen miles, arriving at the Carter Bar, a northernmost boundary between England and Scotland. Since we had travelled uphill all the way, by now the temperature was near freezing.

A telephone kiosk, perched on top of this famous bar, which runs through the Cheviot Hills, was a most welcome sight for us as it represented a shelter from the cold wind and the possibility of phoning ahead to Jedburgh eleven miles away, in the hope of engaging a taxi there.

Figure 11
Sunday church parade in Bordon, England (ca early 1940s). LAC, Lou Hooper Fonds,
Vol. 13, No. 2.

We did call and the telephone operators tried their best to help us, but to no avail. The time passed with the three of us crowded together in the telephone kiosk until about 3 a.m. when a farmer with a horse-drawn hay wagon delivering milk to Jedburgh took us the remaining miles into town. We went into the first large building we saw. Steps led downstairs, so we followed them, not caring where they went; we were too tired to care. We found ourselves in a room full of army blankets and other equipment and we knew we were in a military billet. A sound sleep refreshed us, of course, and though we felt a bit unsure about breakfast next morning, we nevertheless were made very welcome by these English sappers. One young headquarters driver was given the use of a car and drove us into Hawick; late, but we did at least visit our friends. It was now Sunday afternoon and we spent the night in Hawick with our friends, who drove us back to camp Monday morning. We learned later that we had made the news headlines – "Three Canadians marooned in a telephone kiosk on The Carter Bar!!"

XVIII

Following the return of the regiment to Bordon, we soon moved to Ash Vale Camp. From here, I went to hospital, the victim of an eye infection contracted from sun glare on the water during our ocean crossing, and aggravated by the tightly blacked-out, smoke-filled barrack rooms. Nevertheless, all this proved to be a blessing in disguise. Because my regiment had moved out to the field by the time I returned from hospital, I was sent to a new Canadian Artillery Holding Unit (CAHU) based in Bordon.

My inability to join my regiment later provided the opportunity for starting what quickly developed into a well-known and very popular concert party. We gave performances throughout the UK and on the BBC radio with shortwave broadcasts to Canada and Malta.

One such broadcast was a celebration of the mass on Christmas Eve, during which the Glee Club section of our concert party sang carols at intervals throughout the service, accompanied by the famed string quartet from the London Philharmonic Orchestra. This was one of the highlights of our work in the UK, which also included an appearance at the Cambridge Theatre in London's West End, for the top brass from the Canadian Military Headquarters (CMHQ).

This was, in fact, a complete "show" by theatrical standards and had as its M.C. (compère in Britain) Mr Gerry Wilmot, who by now held the rank of war correspondent.[112] There was a strong possibility of keeping our concert party in Britain, but I have always been thankful that this did not work out. I liked Britain and the people very much, but our real fulfillment was to be realized in other theatres of war.

I recall with equal pleasure two other happy events; the first involving the band of my CAHU concert party, and the second a radio broadcast by members of the Glee Club section and for which I retain the radio script of the entire program.[113]

Details of the first event, which was not a radio broadcast, by the way, were conveyed to Colonel Roberts, our OC, via an invitation for my band to play at the Annual Hunt Ball, to be held in Grosvenor House in London. Our unit auxiliary officer accepted and special orchestral music soon arrived in camp to be rehearsed and learned; our present band was to be augmented. Two violins were added to our original eight members. There was to be a floor show, and the special music necessitated a larger orchestra, as the ballroom was vast.

The evening was most enjoyable, to say the least, and was a huge success; as I listened to the words of the master of ceremonies before each dance: "My Lords and My Ladies" … I realized that we were playing for one of the leading social events of the season. The second event reads:

"Greetings Canada – and good wishes from the Beaver Club"[114]
Mother's Day Broadcast
From the Beaver Club
Sunday, 11 May 1941
5:00 to 5:30 B.S.T.

That was the voice of Gerry Wilmot, Canadian radio news commentator and good friend of all Canadian servicemen in Britain, heralding another "back to Canada" broadcast, featuring Sergeant Bill Moskalyk, Sergeant Bert Churchill, accompanist, and Gunner Harold Taylor, tenor, from Toronto, and assisted by the concert party choir. Also appearing were two distinguished guests: the first, and I quote "and so it's with extra special pleasure that I introduce Mrs Vincent Massey who has a few words for you back home"; a song by Gunner Taylor and the choir, entitled "Little Mother of Mine," brings Gerry back to announce "The Mother for the day" to the Canadians in London – "Someone who has taken on this role on several previous occasions, Lady Polson!" "Now, of course," Gerry continued, "a greeting from the lads who've been singing for us today. First we'll call on Bombadier Lou Hooper, who is to a great extent responsible for this grand choir of ours – Lou." Messaging back to Canada, Gerry: "Thanks again fellas and our best wishes to you at home."

XIX

Day-to-day living in the unit had its bad times and its good times, from without and within. Situated as our barracks were on the air route often used by enemy aircraft returning from strikes on London (only forty minutes away), we were visited several times by machine gun strafing attacks. One all-out dive-bombing attack on all Canadian units closely concentrated in this area proved fatal to several soldiers and civilians. Incendiary bombs made hits on buildings, setting fire to the post office and many unit huts. A young officer with his men, manning a machine gun sandbagged post, was cut in half by a bomb which exploded nearby. The "bomber" then crossed over our area, flying so low (and possibly wounded himself) that our riflemen who were deployed around the parade square, shot him down and I saw him go down in the trees near camp. The home guard took charge of the enemy fliers involved, and the CAHU received credit for downing one plane.

But rumblings from within came from some of the NCOs about the way our concert party time was spent on rehearsals and shows outside the camp. However, my men stood guard duty in their turns, one of them invariably winning the baton for the best turned-out guardsman. We went on leave only in our turn and our practices for show and band were considered "Parades" under my very strict supervision, followed up by a report made to battery headquarters by me. But one sergeant found it so distasteful seeing for the first time my new sergeant's stripes and (with gun) for a "trade" other than gunnery, that he decided one New Year's Day in the sergeants' mess to show his displeasure towards me by jumping down on me from a table upon which he was standing. He had run the length of the room towards me, and I heard someone call "Look out Lou!" I realized that I was in for trouble since "Moose" Gordon (that was the culprit's name) had been drinking. I don't know what gave me the strength to do what I did, but I reached up and caught him in mid-air, clutching his tunic at the throat determined to crash his head against the wall as he fell. A few folding chairs lying on the floor foiled my plan and, as his heels struck the chairs (I was pushing him backwards), he crashed with me on top. The other NCOs ran over to us, many of them my good friends, who liked me and knew I always tried to remember I was a sergeant and acted accordingly. So I stood up, considering the incident at an end, but they did not know this and a crowd surrounded him; some of them really punched him solidly as they hustled him out of the mess.

But Moose still tried to make life miserable for me, assisted by his "shadow" Sergeant Davis who followed him everywhere, until the RSM discussed the matter with me one day. I suggested a boxing match in our gym, under regular army rules, the RSM to be the referee; though I was twice the age of my antagonist, I knew I was not afraid of him. But when I gave RSM "Bull" Wharton my opinion, his answer was: "Oh no! I'll have no fighting in the camp. I'll call him into my office and tell him that any more of this behaviour and loudmouth language would end in his being sent out to the field." I don't think the Moose wanted that at all. Anyway, my transfer to the Canadian Army Shows (CAS) came through and I left Bordon, returning for a visit two years later.

I was now a Senior NCO WO II, having served in Italian and European campaigns, 1944 and 1945 respectively.[115]

Moose was still a sergeant; we sat at the same table in the "pub," but we didn't speak.

Before leaving Bordon members of my band, for obvious reasons, went on leave at the same time, but each to a place of his own choosing, Scotland being most popular. We did go to Bognor Regis together once, as we had been engaged in advance to play for dancing several nights in the auditorium. This was at the time of the Dieppe landings, and troops of the Second Canadian Division were returning to the UK at this point.

A year later the entire concert party was dissolved.

XX

In 1943 all Canadian concert party personnel were absorbed by the CAS and came under the jurisdiction of the Canadian government; Captain Frank Anders was named director of all activities, with Sergeant Stan Sheddon as his assistant. The eight-piece band from my Canadian Army Reinforcement Unit (CARU) concert party, about which I have written, was taken over by the Artillery Base Band, Canadian Government. The entire CARU concert party existed by military permission and the great support of our OC, Colonel Jack Roberts, who had previously decided, from medical officer reports, that my health would be best served in barracks, not the field. Hence, I was permanent director of the unit's concert party from its founding to its dissolution by CAS.

Following the transfer of my band to the Artillery Base Band, which was in Bordon, I was called up to the headquarters of CAS in Aldershot. For a period of fully two years prior to this break-up, my band had played dances for

Figure 12
Lou Hooper entertaining friends and fellow soldiers during wartime (ca early 1940s).
Courtesy of Adam Barken.

all ranks, including staff officers and nursing sister officers, both English and
Canadian; dances were played outside the barracks as well as within our unit,
for all branches of services, including US naval and air forces.

Among the earliest guests of our unit, through the courtesy of our auxiliary
services officer who promoted all social activities, were the girls of the Auxiliary Territorial Service (ATS), a company attached to the British No. 1 Railway Training Centre (Royal Engineers) at Longmoor, Hants.

These young women were invited to attend the dances for the men of our
unit, which were held, at first, in the social area of the NAAFI. Later, it was
arranged for them to take place in the huge gymnasium of our auxiliary services. These social activities formed a vital part of army service, promoting
as they did the boy-meets-girl aspect so healthy and leisurely, in spite of the
war. I met my future wife at a social evening in the NCOS mess one Sunday.
She was a WOII (Sergeant Major), I was a bombardier with two hooks. But

music was the keynote of these Sunday parties, with the singing of several fine soloists, along with dancing, all of which helped my cause.

Our guests, of all ranks, were transported to and from these events in the auxiliary-supervised vehicles of the unit (usually trucks) and sing-songs often developed on the return journeys. I had come to know many of these interesting congenial English folks from the surrounding countryside, as well as the girls from ATS and when I finally left No.1 CARU for Aldershot and my next concert company, I felt rather sad.

Shortly after my arrival at CAS headquarters, I was sometimes sent out with one party or another (there were always several here at headquarters) as a substitute pianist or drummer or sometimes as a vocalist in a singing group. I was subsequently assigned to The Bandoliers (No. 9 Detachment, CAS), not as director, though that did come later, but as a regular pianist. Then, when a change of personnel became necessary in the Kit-Bags show, I, to my great surprise, was named leader of this show. This unit numbered in its membership a sixteen-piece band, and a great pianist from Montreal, Jean Forget, who played the classics, with band or as soloist, with delicate artistry. As director, I conducted the band and sang in a group of six men for whom I also wrote music; it was also my job to conduct rehearsals. Our show, known as a Canadian Army Soldier concert party, was one of five such shows, composed entirely of active combatant personnel and contained no females. We did have female impersonators, though, many of them terrific artists.[116]

I enjoyed the large company well enough and there were some fine guys and performers in it, but then some "voice" from outside the party began to question my decisions concerning the show's format and regarding disciplinary measures (*viz.* handing out fatigues as punishment, etc.). Not only did I object strenuously to the interference, but I made a request through proper channels to surrender my sergeant's hooks (chevrons). However, before anything further could transpire, I received orders to report to the Bandoliers again; they were now in London preparing to go to Italy. My guardian angel had done it again and I could scarcely contain my joy. True, I had enjoyed the weekly BBC radio broadcast of the band on *Johnny Canuck*'s revue and I missed the musicians especially, but I hated that lack of confidence in my integrity, which I knew was unjustified.[117] And I was returning to a show with people I liked even more and with whom, though I was not to know it then, I was to go through the remainder of the war, live through several dangerous incidents under fire, and finally become leader of these fine men and pianist for the show when our next tour took us through the Netherlands, France, Knokke-sur-Mer (Belgium), and Germany. (I then held the rank of BSM woII.)

The V-I's. (buzz-bombs) had appeared over London at the time our party was preparing to embark for Italy, numbers of these infernal things doubling daily and wreaking great destruction and demoralization on city and people. After we had sailed and been at sea for two or three days, we still received the BBC daily news report saying, "Our interceptor planes are meeting these new buzz-bombs at the coast and shooting them down at the rate of two per minute." These unmanned bomb-planes were so fast in flight that no "plane" (even the splendid Spitfire) could overtake them, so interception was the only answer. Also assisting in this interception was the balloon barrage, consisting of hundreds of balloons strung close together, each attached to a wire cable anchored to the ground.

En route to Italy one night, travelling as did all troop-ships in strict blackout, we saw the lights of far-distant Algiers and later made a brief daytime stop at Gibraltar. Still later as we approached Naples, our destination, we passed the Isle of Capri with Vesuvius in the background, mildly erupting.

Upon disembarkation, we were met by the officer in charge of the concert party, which had just completed a tour of Italy and would soon be homeward-bound for England. We were transported by trucks to our quarters, where we met and were happy to see the members of the "Forage Caps" party whom we knew, of course, and they showed us around the town a bit before they were to sail.

We were based in Avellino, southern Italy, a rather hot and very dirty town where the animals also lived in parts of the house with the family. There in Avellino, we were introduced immediately to the world's bitterest, though effective, meppachrine[118] tablet at each meal every day and at night, to the caressing bite of bed lice (fleas) in our beds. We visited the busy marketplace by day, with its exciting throngs of expressive Latins. I also met a good friend from the 1st Division RCA, Flip Filmore, who, when he worked in the kitchen in Bordon often squeezed an extra ration or two in my haversack for my English hosts, who were entertaining me while on leave.

We did not stop in Avellino longer than one week, fortunately, as we were scheduled to leave for Rome so, while giving shows en route, in hospitals and in barbed-wire enclosed detention camps, where some of our more "difficult" lads spent some time, we moved along that hot, dusty, troop-clogged road. We were soon having our first encounter with the majestic Apennine Mountains, as we spiralled around, up, and even higher, with the panorama of olive and orange groves at last left miles below.

Out onto the level once more, our climb ended, we were again among the troops. Here we saw our first group of "holy men" (monks) with their donkey-drawn carts bearing kegs of wine (the popular vino rosa), cupfuls of which we bought from them to assuage our thirst of the moment, and then filling our water canteens too, in the hope of adding a little joy to the eating of the cold food, which we carried with us and which would be our next meal.

On we went, on past historic Monte Cassino, where my own regiment had taken part in the seventy-two-hour, non-stop artillery barrage before the mountaintop monastery fell to the Allies. And on towards that great river, famed in song and story, the Tiber. The Tiber of brave Horatius, stout Lartius, strong Herminius, the three who held the Tiber bridge against a host of thousands on that only passage into Rome.

I was now viewing history which before had been only words in books to me. I was deeply thrilled as we crossed this great river, because I had once read a fine poem which uncovered the politics and intrigue that finally made necessary the defence of the proud city – Rome.

Our stay was about four days during which we gave a performance in the Maple Leaf Club. I still have the news item from *Red Patch*, the official paper of Canadian Expeditionary Forces; it gave an excellent review, and we were well-satisfied.[119]

On our return trip we played to some units in the field, approximately ten to twenty-five miles outside of Rome; we also performed in Pesaro, Fano, Perugia, and Jesi; our No. 1 Canadian General Hospital was located here and we gave a lively, happy show (some are better than others, you know!) and the patients loved it. The chief staff orderly gave several of us a pair of hospital pyjamas. I still have part of mine, considerably the worse for wear, but full of memories.

On our way to the next performance – some forty-eight hours' travelling away – and driving from sundown, throughout the night without lights, one of our trucks struck a cement archway extending over the road, injuring one of our men, Garfield White of Vancouver, who had to be hospitalized. He was a female impersonator, extremely funny and one of the stars of our show. His absence hurt the show quite badly for a while, until we were able to change its format. But the accident was instrumental in causing some important changes to be made for the safety of the men; greater care was to be observed en route by our young driver of the equipment vehicle, where some of us always rode, and closer supervision of the loading so that no "shifting" of the equipment could occur.

The injury sustained by Garfield on that night in the blackout was a dislocated shoulder and he was away from us for several weeks, thus affecting the tempo and general balance of our show. So, when one day as we were moving along the military road the traffic stopped to unravel itself and in a vehicle headed in the opposite direction from us, we saw Garfield with full pack and, as he later told us, on his way to join us. Without benefit of signature from the "powers that be," we simply hauled him, bag and baggage into one of our vehicles and went on our happy way.

It was summer and, of course, fruit was plentiful; plums, grapes, oranges, etc., and someone was always suffering from dysentery. The urge to eat and enjoy these luscious fruits growing in abundance seemingly everywhere was simply overpowering; so we ate and ate, and were often very sick.

We lived almost entirely under canvas, a small one-man (pup) tent being part of standard soldier equipment. In Italy, a net canopy was added as protection, along with the neppachrine[120] tablet, against the deadly malaria mosquito. We did most of our shows in the open on this segment of the six-month tour, slept in the open and had our meals with the unit which hosted us for the length of our stay in the area. Sometimes we gave shows within a radius of fifteen to twenty-five miles from our base, always returning after the show. It was during one such stopover that I incurred one of the most serious accidents to befall me up to this point of my military service.

A small stream ran not far from our campsite and several of us, anxious for a swim, took off to this small paradise to enjoy our first dip since heaven knows when. Upon nearing the water, undressing as we ran, I took one look; it looked safe, so in I went with my best dive. Paul Cassidy had beaten me in and as I went down from the momentum of the dive, I felt something strike my forehead; I quickly surfaced, the blood streaming down my face and was quickly taken in hand by our medical corporal (who was also our trumpet man). Thus ended, nearly in disaster, my first swim in Italy. I should have known better, and I bear the scar today.

We did, however, swim often after that in the Adriatic Sea, near our base, watching as we did so, the Allied planes in strikes on the stubbornly resisting city of Rimini, where we were later posted.

This diving mishap proved not only weakening to me, but highly inconvenient as well, as I sat slightly dizzy and unprotected from the blistering Italian August sun, playing piano for performers on a stage put up in a farmer's field where troops were stationed. My only head covering was a crushed-in satin-covered opera top hat which I had scrounged somewhere, and which was perched on top of my bandaged head. I must have presented anything but a happy picture to the audience, and to put it mildly, I didn't feel very happy.

We next made our near-longest haul, not broken by performances, to Borgo San Lorenzo, situated north of the romantic city of Florence. In San Lorenzo, which was suffering from bad flooding conditions at the time, a few of our men, including myself, one day came face to face with Sir Anthony Eden and his party as we came out of the NAAFI canteen.[121] An unusually tall man, he was wearing a pilot's leather jacket and flight boots. He was most congenial and spoke several minutes with us before taking his leave.

Unable to give any shows at all in the Borgo military area because of the flooding conditions and being rather fearful of land cave-ins with possible loss of a vehicle and perhaps personnel, we withdrew to a base in Florence, which was also very hard hit by the flooding of the Arno River. It had overflowed its banks, resulting in heavy damage to property and priceless works of art for which this beautiful city is world-renowned.

We gave one show in the Canada Club, had some fisticuffs between two of our cast behind the scenes, and after the show, as I was having a cup of coffee at the snack bar, I found myself sitting beside a friend of mine from Verdun, Quebec: Johnny Kelso, who was in the armoured division (tanks). His brother Jimmy was in my battery in Montreal's Craig St Drill Hall, where we joined up. Jimmy was a wizard on the signals key and had helped several of us in the early days.

Our tour now continued back towards southern Italy and eventually to our permanent base, Avellino. Among the stops along the return route was, first, a Canadian General Hospital in Arezzo; next at Caserta, was the 14th Canadian General hospital, where I met three buddies from my regiment, 1st Medium Regt, RCA: Fred Greenshields, Alex Milne, and Ack-Ack Etienne. The ship on which this hospital unit originally sailed to Italy, the *Elena*, was dive-bombed and, I believe, sank with considerable loss of equipment, but, fortunately, no loss of life.

Our concert party arrived at the hospital in Caserta on the anniversary of the loss of their ship, and they were to celebrate and give thanks for just about everything, I suppose.

We did our full show that night, enjoying the special dinner prepared for the occasion, and following a rather sober, thoughtful, beginning, a carnival-like spirit took over and joy was, indeed, unconfined. The next day, prior to our tardy departure, we were privileged to visit the wounded "troops surgery" in this seven-storey hotel-turned-hospital – those men whose condition had kept them from seeing our show the night before. Going from ward to ward and floor after floor as we did, by an ancient elevator which was still operating, we saw many examples of great fortitude. Despite the numerous and varied disabilities from which these men were suffering, they repeatedly thanked us for bringing these excerpts from our show to them in the privacy of their own ward. Finally, having taken our leave from this scene, and as we again rolled along in that endless military stream, the question we asked of ourselves was, "Who should be thanking whom?" A man does his job in his own way, asking no praise; but that visit of ours to the wounded guys gave us considerable food for thought.

We continued our journey into the later October afternoon, finally sighting the city of our destination, Avellino, from which only one hill of moderate height separated us. But our poor, tired equipment truck was not equal to the climb, so after several attempts, our driver decided to "let the old girl cool off" while we awaited some kind of assistance. It soon arrived in the form of a passing American truck, equipped with the latest hauling and pushing devices. Its driver, seeing our plight, stopped and after a short consultation with our driver, pulled up to the rear of our vehicle. He began to push and soon had the truck topping that last hill, from which we coasted downhill to our base.[122]

We were now due for a rest, and though we could not leave the area entirely, our going and coming was greatly relaxed. Mail for us had accumulated considerably, with letters from my wife, cartons of cigarettes, and other goodies from Canada. It was here I had a letter from my son, Lou Jr, now in Canada, where he had been posted after three years in the UK and was now a cadet-airman in the Commonwealth Training Scheme. His letter contained a picture postcard of him looking very casual in a RCAF officer's uniform.

He had won his wings: I was happy.

I gave two cartons of cigarettes from several that I had received to our capable, dependable truck drivers, whose work seemed to grow increasingly difficult as the war continued, with its blackout restrictions. We were soon to leave these fine men, who were not to return with us to the UK but remain to meet and transport the next concert party, soon to arrive in Italy.

Our sailing day finally arrived in early December; so, leaving the new concert party to carry on, we bade *arrivederci* to Italia and embarked for England, the ship carrying many military personnel who had already seen long and fierce combat action. Among those making up this notable passenger list were veterans of the famous British "Desert Rats" who, led by Field Marshal Alexander and later by General Montgomery (Monty), had chased the German Marshal Rommel ("The Desert Fox") and his hard-fighting Afrika Korps halfway across the African desert to his final defeat (Hollywood movies notwithstanding).[123]

Added to this list were the Canadian "tri-wounds" veterans from the First, Second, and Third Army Brigades who, after fierce combat in the Italian campaign from Sicily up to the siege of Rimini, were now being returned to the UK and to Canada, having been wounded a third time.

Life aboard ship was worse than hectic at times, with the pent-up tensions of long periods of front-line action without the benefit of relief, because of a shortage of troops in this theatre of war in 1944.

Spending one's sleeping hours in a ship's hammock while being a most comfortable way to make an ocean crossing, did, however, create considerable confusion when breakfast time arrived and some of the late sleepers had not disposed of their hammocks. Orders were that at night we slung our hammocks in the same area where we ate in the daytime, and so they were fastened, hanging in mid-air from the ceiling. In the morning, if they were not stowed away on time, it delayed the breakfast meal and that meant real trouble, more than one fight resulting among the able-bodied men. We were seated on either side of small fifteen-foot-long tables where we were assigned an NCO and two helpers, all of whom were changed daily. It was their responsibility to bring food for the some-twenty men at our table, placing some items of food on the table, and serving that part of the meal which needed to be served. After each of the three meals was over, the men washed dishes and pans and returned all utensils to the ship's galley, after making certain that our table (which was our sort of a home away from home) was spic and span for ship's inspection. Here, we had to spend many of our waking hours playing cards, shooting craps, relating some incident or just grabbing forty winks on the table! Yes, the men griped and fought and some of us even sang, but I'll wager there wasn't one among us who was not happy that our port of call was the UK or Canada.

We sailed in a convoy of several ships with all orders of procedure being issued from the flagship leading the convoy; there was no destroyer-escort. After about three days at sea and shortly after the midday meal, it was remarked that our ship's speed was slowed down considerably. Immediately, speculation became rife among the troops as to the cause. We soon learned, as the flags on all ships were lowered to half-mast, that a soldier had died, and we already could observe preparations being made for a burial at sea. A sergeant from my own regiment, Jimmy Allen, 1st Med. RCA and who was returning to the UK to take an officer's training course, was NCO of the firing squad of honour. The body was wrapped in a strong tarpaulin, which was sewn tight, and covered by the Union Jack.[124] The honour-bearers moved in a short procession along the deck to the platform on which the body was placed and beside which the chaplain would read the burial service. When the final words committing the body were read and the rifle salute was fired, the broad wooden slab was slowly titled towards the ship's side, the flag was removed, and the body slowly slid down into the depths. One moment to look and perhaps to feel, as I felt, a vast loneliness for another soldier never to see his home again. But reality quickly returned as we realized our ship was rapidly regaining its original speed. We were still at war, we reminded ourselves, and the enemy lurked in the sea and the sky, ever watchful. Our orders from the flagship, "Keep up or be left behind," were followed to the letter.

We were expected to regain the time we had lost, and when later, for some reason, our ship was experiencing engine failure and we lost our place in the convoy for a short while, there were grave looks of apprehension on the faces of many of us. However, the difficulty was eventually overcome, and we were able to again take our position and keep it. So, aside from the daily firing practice of the ship's anti-aircraft gun crews, the trip continued uneventfully.

The weather being favourable most days, our Bandoliers concert party was able to present a show on the outer deck occasionally, this being the only space large enough to gather the troops in greater numbers than inside. En route, we stopped for diesel oil at the port of Algiers; this being in African coastal waters, we realized we were in yet another theatre of war and so were identified with the Allied 8th Army while in those waters. As the convoy continued through the remaining days, we began to realize that very soon we would sight Scotland's coastline. When that thin line finally came clearly into view, I saw tears in the eyes of more than one seasoned veteran of three- or four-year desert warfare, and heard one lad say to another, "Well, I never expected to see the old girl again." (I presume he meant his wife!)

The remaining time aboard ship was spent in boat drills, inoculations, and other necessary preparations for leaving the ship. We disembarked at Greenock, Scotland, immediately entraining for our respective military bases.

<u>1944.</u> It was late in December, and as we were soon off on long leave for Christmas to our dear friends and loved ones, I say, even now, in the words of the good old army "prayer" – "Bless 'em all, the long and the short and the tall!"

For my part, I enjoyed a real old-fashioned Christmas at home with my family; wife, sons Lou Jr and Paul, baby daughter Barbara, and my newly acquired relatives and friends. This Christmas meant a tree, with its decorations and tinsel trimmings strung around and round among the boughs, the whole fragrant picture crowned by the Star of Bethlehem. The dinner table boasted, in the absence of turkey, roast chicken, baked ham, sweet potatoes, and other vegetables; the meal was, of course, climaxed by the serving of – you guessed it – plum puddin'. It was truly a joyous time, with carols and other appropriate Christmas music pealing out from a little table radio. I've often wondered how many homes were as happy as that little cottage in Petersfield, Hampshire, where my wife and her mother and aunt were sheltering, following the savage bombing of their home in London.

During this army leave, I was to learn through the mail that my rank of sergeant had been raised to that of wo II (Sergeant Major); that I was to return at once to my base in Guildford, Surrey, and to prepare for a tour of the Netherlands and Germany in charge of my own concert party (Detachment No. 9 CAS), The Bandoliers. After considerable thought and discussions with my wife (I was now eligible, due to my length of service outside Canada, for return to Canada if declared physically unfit for further service, but being in sound physical condition and my promotion being now confirmed), I began rehearsals immediately, and by 25 January 1945, the revamped Bandoliers were en route to Tilbury Docks by truck, finally to proceed across the English Channel.

The weather was very cold at this date, and the crossing was made in an invasion craft, a Tank Landing Ship (TLS). It was only an overnight trip, but it carried us into the area of the German Flying Boats (E-Boat Alley), and though we made the run without incident, it was made at "All hands full alert at action stations." This caused most of us some anxious moments, since the Tin Hats No. 1 concert party were involved, a year previously, in a second channel crossing bedevilled by enemy naval action, causing them to lose three of their members, including their trumpeter-band director. All concert party personnel now carried a full complement of arms and ammunition at all times, either the .303 Enfield rifle, the Thompson sub-machine gun, or the Sten gun and, what's more, knew how to use them. (We had regular and recurring small arms training.)[125]

Thankfully, our journey progressed without incident, and we were landed at the port of Ostend, Belgium, proceeding to Ghent, the starting point of our European tour, officially named "Bronco." It was near Antwerp, and while en route to arrange for a "turn-in" of trucks as did each incoming concert party, that we heard the report of a bomb as we drove through the long tunnel leading into the city. When returning, after completing our business, we noticed at the exit of the tunnel through which we had not long since passed, the remnants of the bomb that had fallen, wreaking havoc on the wall of the tunnel. The V-I enemy rocket buzz-bomb, with launching pads spread well over the Netherlands, was in constant use now; we were to be made very aware of this wretched weapon later on in our tour.

As I now enter upon this stage of The Bandoliers in Europe, I will be aided by entries from my "War Diary," which begins a day-to-day report of our activities from 30 January 1945, at 10:30 a.m., to the end of hostilities.[126]

On arrival in Ghent where our headquarters was situated, I reported at once to the officer in charge of all concert party activities in Europe, Captain Day. He checked my party's equipment and personnel, giving instructions for the opening performance of our tour in five days, rehearsals, preparing the billets where we were to live (in a vacant civilian house); also ordering some necessary repairs to stage equipment.

<u>1945. 2 February:</u> Sunday – a free day, and since Canadian troops in previous combat throughout these areas had so endeared themselves to the townspeople, the day saw many friendly associations made and friendships which were to last throughout the war and well beyond, with frequent exchange of correspondence on both sides. This fact we observed at times when our itinerary would call for a return to their city; unfailingly, we would find the townspeople waiting in the streets to invite us into their home, if permission could be granted to us, which was not always possible.

<u>3 February:</u> This morning was spent transporting our stage and electrical equipment into the "Café Quebec" or Feestlokaal van Vooruit (I don't know if the renaming of this café was done out of love for the Canadian soldiers, but I think it quite likely was). Here, the afternoon was given over to rehearsal, as was the afternoon of the following day, 4 February.

<u>5 February:</u> Here, too, the Bandoliers gave their first performance on the continent and were very well received by an audience of about 450 soldiers and some local citizens. Refreshments after the performance provided in Canadian Legion Club by supervisor Ripley.

So began our tour officially.

During our crossing, I had developed a severe cold, as we had spent a night in tents with no heat other than a bale of straw and a small oil heater which was not in good repair, and which we feared to use in case it might cause the straw to catch fire and, possibly, the tent. As a result of the late January cold, my right eye was affected and became so inflamed it was necessary to keep it covered. Since our 2nd Canadian General Hospital was set up in Ghent, a few days after we were settled in there, I reported to the hospital for examination of my eye. A young officer with the rank of major, strict but sincere, told me the eye was abscessed and that I should return that afternoon prepared to be admitted to the hospital for two or three weeks' observation. I was shocked and explained my position clearly to him, to which he replied, "I'm sorry, but I am concerned only with the condition of your eye." I left the hospital with my mind made up; I was not going back. I was ready to risk arrest and its penalty for refusing medical attention, but I was not going back! I discussed the case with my two first sergeants, Richards and Cassidy, and it was decided that should the worst happen, Sergeant Richards (who played the accordion) would assume leadership and continue the tour of the party.

Sergeant Cassidy and I were now sharing a room in the home of Andre and Marie and their family of three, lovely and congenial civilians who insisted on washing and ironing any washable article of clothing AND polishing our boots every night unless we hid them. Nothing was too good for a Canadian, and these kind people wished to show their thanks. Then one day I told Paul Cassidy that I had something special I wished to do, and that I would like to be left alone in the room; he said "sure," and that was settled. After the noon meal in our own concert party kitchen, I went to my room and I prayed, silently and earnestly, several prayers on faith, the mind, and its healing powers, and eventually I fell asleep. Whatever name by which each individual may refer to that Power, be it God or any Other, my prayers were known only to that Power and myself. I can really say, in truth, that I did not return to the hospital; the supposed abscess did not (repeat NOT) develop in my eye, which actually healed rapidly. I was not apprehended for my act of disobedience by the military, and our party proceeded upon its proposed tour. (Moral: "Things ain't always what they seem.")

The waterway-canal flowed through this area at the foot of the street in which our mess kitchen was situated, and on the corner, where our street joined the bridge over the canal, was the Café des Alliés, owned and operated by a middle-aged man and his wife. It was a family-patronized café where all the members of the family came, especially on Sundays (from 4 to 8 p.m.). There were several other cafés in Ghent, one operated by a Canadian soldier and his Belgian wife; but our boys seemed to enjoy "des Alliés" because of its homelike atmosphere. I just remember too, a strange incident occurred to me later; after several weeks of touring through the Netherlands and Belgium, we had spent a week in Arnhem billeted in a German Oberschule for young officer training. It was an imposing, modern building, though bombed, with many rooms and there were in it five pianos in good condition; one was a small grand. Here I composed my "Victory Song," which we practised and performed.[127] We were reasonably comfortable, and as time came for us to leave, we were to return to Ghent for supplies. Would you believe – when my men checked the equipment there was an extra piano that had somehow "gotten on our truck" and I never learned just how. I did notice that night, in the Canadians' café, a very familiar-looking upright piano, and I noticed my sergeant seemed to be flashing a few extra guilders (money, gelt!), and I now remember I was slightly richer myself!

To return to the early part of our tour, my eye was improving rapidly, and we worked by the calendar date, depending upon assigned map references and road signs of special units and Canadian Provost Corp. My party consisted of one clerk, one cook, three 60 cwt. vehicles and drivers, 1 HUP (Mine) and driver, one generator, one electric panelboard, two attendants, two sergeants, two corporals, six musicians, and two female impersonators (Ronne White, M.C. and Chick Gardner; Billy Thompson, Chick Zamick, singer, dancer, and monologist).

At times, we were stationary with a host-unit, i.e. Third Canadian Division (Reichwald Forest). In Germany, or a Tank Corps Unit, where we lived under our own canvas, drew our own food rations from Quartermaster corps with beer and liquor ration at fifteen-day intervals; we ate our own rations prepared by our own cook. Our tour through Belgium included such towns as Bruges, Knokke-sur-Mer, North Sea Sector, Gijzenzele, and numerous others; playing to audiences of 450, 800, 300, 1,300 varying at each performance and almost entirely troops. We always returned to base in Ghent after each performance, night-driving accounting for perhaps 50 per cent of our travel.

<u>11 February</u>: Sunday – free day.

<u>12 February</u>: Our base was moved to Turnhout, Antwerp, and our first show, eighth of the tour, was given in a YMCA theatre for H.Q. No. 1 Canadian Army Troops Area, with an audience of four hundred; refreshments were served us by YMCA Supervisor McClaneghan.

<u>13 February</u>: Herentals, Antwerp. Evening show presented in the same theatre, but for No. 1 Cdn. transport Column. We were well received; I had called rehearsal that afternoon which improved the pace of the show over the performance of the previous night. Four hundred troops applauded us noisily and we enjoyed that. Lunch Y.M. (Mr McDuffee).

<u>14–17 February</u>: These four performances were given to audiences numbering 900, 900, 950, and 1,000 respectively; this area held many miscellaneous troops and, since we were billeted here in Turnhout, all of the last four shows we played in the YMCA theatre (the Lux). The auxiliary supervisor, Mr Baggette, did not arrange for refreshments as regulations clearly required; this necessitated rations being used from unit supplies, which arrangement should not have occurred. However, the shows went well, not having to tear

down after each performance, as when we were on the move to one-night stands; the troops enjoyed them.

<u>18 February:</u> Sunday – a free day.

Though we played shows in other towns, we were still billeted in Turnhout and returned there each night following the performance. This situation created difficulty at times for our courageous drivers who, some days, had to drive many miles, occasioned by our playing two shows on the same day, but in different places, returning in the strict blackout, driving without lights. The landscape by day was dreary and reflected the hardships through which this land and its people had passed and from which they were still not entirely liberated. But as the weeks passed and the Allies' successes proved more and more numerous, then spring began to appear on the land, and native costumes colourfully mingled with the native tulip; and we were now visiting towns in the home of the windmill, Netherlands.

Following our repeat performances in Turnhout's Lux theatre, we travelled to Schilde, Antwerp, for our fourteenth European show, 19 February, presented in the city hall for 65 General Transport Coy, RCASC and nearby troops. It was a good performance and well received by an audience of five hundred while V-bombs exploded in the vicinity; CLWS Supervisor provided tasty sandwiches and a beverage. The town of Gheel followed for No. 36 Composite Company, RCASC and held in the auditorium of St Aloysius College (audience four hundred); CLWS Mr Delaney. One more performance, this one in Tilburg, Netherlands, in a monastery auditorium for HQ 1st Canadian Main Army, audience three hundred, with K. of C. Mr Walsh, supervisor. We moved on the following day (22 February) from Turnhout to billets in the international casino in 's-Hertogenbosch, Netherlands. Gave performance at 7 p.m. in casino (huge auditorium) for four Canadian Armoured Div. The show was well attended (audience 1,100) but not up to our standard of performance, due to a number of small technical difficulties. Refreshments by the unit; no auxiliary officer.

The following day at 2 p.m., our show for miscellaneous troops was not well received, due to the small audience of one hundred in this huge auditorium. However, the evening performance was far better, both in attendance, reception and presentation, and our having a night's rest with no long day of travel, plus a show that same night, as happened the day before (attendance of one thousand).

Figure 13
Entertainment show for soldiers, near Emmerich, Germany (1945).
Courtesy of Adam Barken.

We found the townspeople very friendly and ready to welcome us, which they did, inviting us into their homes on days when our schedule permitted. Also, the young Dutch musicians, some of whom had met and played with members of jazz groups from the US on tour through Europe before the war, came to hear us and were eager to talk music with us; particularly jazz.[128] Also, the carillonneur who played in the city's large cathedral expressed a wish for the theme of our national anthem, "O Canada," which I wrote out for him; he played it each day at noon as a tribute to the hundreds of Canadians in the area.[129] It seemed, as our stay lengthened, that many V-bombs fell here too and within the city of 's-Hertogenbosch; many of the launching sites were erected in the Netherlands. The horrible noise of these V-I bombs with their time-keeping beat (there was a later series V-II) created intense fear and uncertainty; it was a demoralizing effect, its impact savage and devastating.

We remained ten more days, presenting afternoon and evening shows nearly every day, with civilians mingling in audience with Polish and Dutch troops, while our overall attendance for the twelve days was 9,175, among them numerous friends.

And so, less than a week after moving off and directed by a strange-looking map reference, we found ourselves in Germany's Klever-Reichswald forest, in tents, and putting the final touches to our adjoining foxholes. Through this forest ran the Siegfried Line, with its famed "Washing" of war song mention, which was hung on a short stretch of strong wire with the clothes fastened on it. This was displayed in a spot along the main road with an official signboard bearing the Canadian maple leaf and the words, "This is the Siegfried Line: This is the Washing." This objective was gained at a high price in Allied lives. It was here in the forest that several of my men and myself were looking around at the trenches and defences, where the terrain was literally covered with what appeared to be miles of M.G. ammo (live) in belts ready for the gun and firing. We came onto the body of a young German sniper lying at the foot of a tree from which he had fallen when he was hit by a round from a high-powered automatic weapon, having been killed instantly. We gave him an honourable burial and forwarded all his personal papers to the Commission for Enemy Dead.[130]

Our following assignments took us across the Rhine River and through varying degrees of enemy action; performances under fire in open air; air cover at times, but I do not recall one instance of cancelling or altering our schedule because of enemy action, and we've been "up there" mighty close, since our show included no females.

So, through many towns, from Nijmegen, Netherlands; Kleve, Goch, Emmerich, Germany; as far as Almelo and often being caught up in a victory celebration en route; as liberation increased, we were to see hundreds of collaborators behind the barbed-wire enclosures. We did a show for the victims of an enemy labour camp (twenty-four hours liberated). In fact, two Jerry snipers were hauled out from the belfry of the tall, spired church by townspeople, while our afternoon show was in progress. A grim visit indeed was the one to Vught concentration camp near Breda, Netherlands, where, in answer to a request, we arranged an extra show for the all-Allied staff members of the camp. And one incident much later on in our tour, following a tiring two-a-day schedule: our drivers (bless 'em) in the 100 per cent blackout lost their way. When stopped by an armoured scout car blocking the road, luckily, we learned from the young Canadian officer and driver, after the often used, "where the hell are you going?," that we were heading straight for the enemy lines, but fast, outside the city of Duisburg, Germany. Did we turn our vehicles

Figure 14
Lou Hooper and soldiers at the Siegfried Line, Reichwald Forest, Germany (1945).
Courtesy of Adam Barken.

Figure 15
Lou Hooper and soldiers in Germany (1945). Courtesy of Adam Barken.

(five of 'em) plus a heavy electric generator, around fast? We did, and took off for friendlier surroundings; so, what with one experience after another, we eventually were recalled to our base in Ghent and, in due time, we returned to the UK and to CAS headquarters in Guildford.

There was a happy round of homecoming greetings, a few extra glasses raised, I suppose, and eventually the much discussed "point system" as it applied to many of the 1939 and early 1940 arrivals in the UK. This could mean, for some, repatriation to Canada. Not, however, before all of our concert party personnel proceeded on a well-deserved leave during which we had the privilege of celebrating V.J. Day in "Blighty" and the joy of seeing the lights really "go on again all over the world."

My memory holds two special impressions of those courageous people of the Netherlands; one the new hope lighting their faces, following those awful years of occupation; the other being their sincere show of appreciation for their liberation through the very warm hospitality towards us.

XXI

After spending leave with my wife, son, and daughter in London, I was to report to repatriation depot at Crookham Crossroads, thus terminating my affiliation with CAS, and, after much preparation and briefing, I paid a visit to my Holding Unit in St Lucia Barracks. September had arrived and we were soon to embark for Canada. I could not know at the time that I would be returned to Canada, discharged from the army and back in Britain by Christmas 1945, but that's exactly what happened.

But I must recall our departure for Canada and that simply gorgeous Sunday sunset as we moved down the Clyde River and out to sea. We were aboard one of the grand old veterans of the war, HMS *Cameronia*, with a proud record against enemy action. I am fortunate in having a copy of the ship's paper bearing data of her noble behaviour in combat, and the name of her skipper.

I was to be responsible for all entertainment aboard, and with a few instrumentalists, singers, and others, we were able to present a ninety-minute show on deck and, at lunch time each day, a concert, sing-song, or jam session in the ship's lounge, with music for the church service each Sunday of the two-week crossing.

The show personnel were each mentioned under the caption "Orchids to" in the ship's paper.

There were Canadian nursing sisters among the passengers, and on the night before landing, a dance was held on deck and for our last time we, again, were the band. So, with comfortable quarters on this "crossing" in the senior NCOs section, good food, the chance sighting of an iceberg (my first), and several awe-inspiring sunrises, the comparatively pleasant crossing was made, ending in a Quebec port.

Upon arrival in Quebec City we entrained for Montreal and in two days were off on a thirty-day leave, complete with free travel warrant and a one-hundred-dollar cheque. I visited my brothers and sisters in the US (three had died while I was away – also my mother), many young relatives, some of whom I was seeing for the first time, and lifelong friends of our family in Ypsilanti. We were still in army uniform while on leave, and demobilization took three days after we had returned, I from a very happy holiday.

Gradually, the strangeness of new civilian suits and hats, hurriedly purchased, began to wear off and I became active in my profession, playing and teaching music, which kept me busy with not much time to miss the army routine. I did, however, miss my family in England, very much indeed; so much so, that early in the month of December, just prior to a business trip to Detroit, I obtained a passport, applied for passage to Britain, severed all ties (my air officer son was all I had here) and left by train for Detroit, where a telegram reached me from Montreal confirming my sailing on HMS *Mauretania*. I returned to Montreal at once, made hasty preparations, and the night I boarded the boat train for Halifax, I found at least half-a-dozen veterans making the return trip, some to remain there. What a ball we had! No one slept that night. On arrival in Halifax, we boarded straight away.

After an ice-covered crossing of five days to Liverpool, three of us travelled together right to London – again! Then, Christmas for me with my family and my "new" mom and pop; quite a happy achievement – rather – eh what? My wife and children would be brought to Canada with other war wives and families six months later by the government.

Early in 1946, we found a nice basement flat in the Kensington area for my family, and I began to rehearse a musical act (solo) for the clubs and music halls. I was making some progress, with an appearance at the Rainbow Club, which was predominantly American. I made a music-hall audition for the

BBC and had engaged an agent.[131] My plans were to remain in Britain, if successful, but the austerity picture being so very grim, and our children sometimes asking for more food which could not be had because of rationing, I thought of Canada, where nothing was rationed. I liked Britain so, considering the different aspects, my wife and I agreed upon a plan: I was to make an application for sailing to Canada or await acceptance of a musical contract, whichever came first. My agent was agreeable, but two weeks later my sailing came through to leave from Liverpool one week later.

The few intervening days were spent in having a number of strong wooden boxes made in different sizes for easier handling, and every household article that would not be needed was packed for the day my family would make the trip; we had no orders as to when that might be.

We spent many of the remaining days visiting beautiful Kensington Gardens, with its spacious lake sporting model sailing ships, and the Peter Pan statue and drinking fountain.

Finally, the day came for my leaving. After only three months, I was to make yet another Atlantic crossing, my sixth. (I sailed in April.) My family joined me three months later, in July 1946, having crossed on that great ship, the *Queen Mary*, now retired.

My crossing was made on an empty aircraft carrier, a cargo of wheat to be taken on at Montreal, our port of call. Travelling with almost no cargo, she was very high above the waterline and an easy prey to the Atlantic in April. An exceedingly rough crossing with severe stern conditions prevailed and we first-class passengers, having paid more (there were second-class below) had our meals at the officers' table and our chairs were always chained to the floor.

There were no female passengers aboard; in fact, I'm sure they would not be permitted on such a craft, especially at this season of the year.

We fellows entertained ourselves with numerous types of card games, the favourite being poker, and even put on a show in the lounge one night, without benefit of any musical instrument; only songs and jokes.

The chief steward was a very congenial young man, not too strict, and the entire voyage was really relaxed. One extra mild, calm day, we went outside on the top, flat deck, and while tossing around a small beachball with some of the crew, we were surprised to see a small school of whales at play. They seemed almost a mile (on water) away, but near enough that sometimes half of one's body could be seen as they spouted; they sounded and disappeared, only to appear again shortly.

And so the time passed, with arrival after ten days, at Montreal on a very snowy Easter Sunday; the snow had, in fact, slowed our carrier's speed so badly that it prevented our skipper from winning the gold-headed cane for first ship in port. A German ship was first in but our captain, a seasoned skipper, would not jeopardize the safety of his human cargo in that snow-blanketed stretch of the St Lawrence River.

As no one knew I was to arrive, no one met me, and since my son had acquired an attractive rooming house in my absence, I was not at a loss for a home.

The days following my return were given over largely to house-hunting where, I must admit, I experienced some discrimination, especially where apartment buildings were visited, although their signboards displayed a vacancy in large letters. Already, Canada was not extending the same welcome to all her returning sons, and my search continued for a few weeks, even after my family had arrived.[132]

My musical activities were divided between teaching piano at the Marrazza School of Music, plus a once-a-week radio broadcast originating at the school, with personnel selected from teachers and pupils.[133] I also played in a quintet and accompanied soloists, and made professional appearances in dance bands.

Needless to say, I kept in close contact with the government office for information upon the quota in which my family would be sailing; everything seemed to be moving so slowly. Finally, while speaking to one of my buddies from the regiment who already had a veteran's "pre-fab" house, I learned that his wife and son would be away for the months of July and August, and that I could rent his house. That meant I could be sure of a nice place to take my family, even if only temporary. They did arrive in the middle of July and remained at my friend's until his family returned.

My wife was not feeling too well, as our third child was on the way, and our next move, a single room for four of us, was most uncomfortable, to be sure. Luckily, we were there only two weeks (and, according to general practices, they charged us plenty), but I had been trying very hard always, through acquaintances at the music school, and, with the help of Mr Marrazza and a

Mr DeSerres, I finally got an option on a five-room house which, though I finally got it, presented strange and new financial problems. "Key-money" meant simply paying cash to a house owner for a key to the house you hoped to occupy. It was similar, in a way, to a sort of guarantee until the premises became available and, in some cases, the original amount asked was even increased and paid, so desperate was the need of so many veterans who, having gone overseas single, were returning with families, as in my case.

The house I finally got was furnished and I bought all of the furniture for $1,150 from the previous occupant who, as a middleman between the owner and myself, may have been the real cause of my "key-money" increasing on two occasions, before all transactions were completed. It was a known fact that overseas "vets" would be receiving money periodically for nearly a year, and they were easy prey to unkind practices.

It was October 1946 when we were finally able to take possession of the house and I was happy, for our new daughter was born on 6 December of that year at the Royal Victoria Hospital; we named her Marie-Terry.

Our son Paul and daughter Barbara were later enrolled in the Royal Arthur School, where immediately their British accent caused gales of laughter from many in the class and greatly confused Paul's teacher as to a logical solution. An incident that occurred one day accidentally supplied part of the cure; during a recitation period, Paul was asked to name the several Red Cross rules of hygiene as prescribed, and how he carried them out. He very innocently started by saying, "first I take a baa-th." Sudden pandemonium broke loose. I'm sure that was as far as he got on the subject. After quiet was finally restored, his very young teacher tried patiently to help Paul pronounce the words, bath, chance, and other like words, even to the point of (blushingly) requesting our help at home to remedy the situation, since half the kids in the class were trying to say baa-th now. We did not consider it to be that serious, though! True his mother spoke that way, and still does, and I like it. His sister Barbara spoke that way also, and though I regretted having to accept the disappearance of that sweet, childish, very clear speech, I of course, had no alternative.

I recall another occasion about six months later when my older brother George, who lived in Cleveland, Ohio, was visiting us. My wife had set up the dining room table and we had just started the meal. My wife passed a dish to

George asking, "would you like some butt-ah." He, not expecting that unusual sound, choked with glee, but controlled his mirth sufficiently to ask, "what did you say?" – only to hear the question repeated. My brother was simply unable to speak for his laughter, and it was some time before my wife "caught on" to the reason for his mirth; when she did – she thought it was funny too. George, though, was very fond of my wife, and thoroughly enjoyed hearing his new sister-in-law speak. When next he came to our new veterans duplex-dwelling a year later, he presented us with quite a large sum of money, equally divided between my wife and myself; he did the same for members of his wife's family in Cleveland. His wife was deceased.

During that winter of 1946, I was engaged by one of a chain of United Theatres in stage presentation, playing accompaniments for a young soprano from Greece, who sang some of the operatic arias and Cole Porter songs extremely well.[134] The language barrier proved to be a serious problem for her though, in learning English lyrics of the popular songs, so necessary in the repertoire of stage presentation of that time. Consequently, our rehearsals necessarily grew longer and longer, and inevitably defeated the entire purpose of the project, which was to make several appearances at various theatres in this chain, and which at the outset I had really enjoyed.

A second radio series of thirteen weeks with a trio followed; Paul Notar accordion, Phil Parizeau, guitar, and myself, piano. I still have some of those trio arrangements I wrote for us, and it was such fun working with those fellows.

Our first Canadian Christmas with my wife and children was a joyous one indeed, and included other veterans and their wives.

<u>1947.</u> This year, I spent my first summer playing in the Laurentian area north of Montreal, at a beautiful resort called Wooden Acres, owned by brothers Nat and Mac Cayne.[135] I was playing for a popular young orchestra leader-sax-man, Joey Kane, and with whom I remained for ten years. Here began an association and friendship (starting as a trio) and increasing to bands of varying numbers.

Following my first summer season at Wooden Acres, I returned to the city after Labour Day, the date when resort activities practically ended and staff personnel took off on brief holidays before the busy winter season arrived. I can recall the natural beauty of Wooden Acres, set as it was in a huge pine

Figure 16
Lou Hooper and his bandmates at Wooden Acres in Ste-Agathe, Quebec (1948).
Courtesy of Adam Barken.

grove with snug log cabins, appropriately called Spruce, Balsam, and Fir;
boasting a sparkling clear lake a mile in length only, but on which no mech-
anized boats were permitted. With excellent waterfront facilities, swimming
was always a happy and congenial experience, with special water shows as a
weekly feature, along with a water ballet and diving competitions. Swimming
had attracted a special "club" by this time, which included, among others,
certain guests, along with musicians, one of whom was Jack Orchard, a young
drummer of nineteen years, and myself.

Two of the regular guests were Jack and Bunny Jacobskind, he a barrister, she
a high school teacher, who lived in Brooklyn, New York. Miss Pearl Rosmarin,
of the musical Montreal family, was, and still is, a fine cellist; she was another
"club" member, and we met and swam together two sessions a day, forenoon
and afternoon, swimming as far as was considered wise and enjoyable.

A sound system was set up with loud speakers fixed in the trees, sending out the music of the classics, the new and popular *South Pacific*, Benny Goodman, Al Jolson, the Glenn Miller Orchestra, and many others.

In this happy atmosphere, I was inspired to write two songs; one titled "Wooden Acres," on which Bunny Jacobskind collaborated, and another end-of-the-season single effort called "Don't Let Old Acquaintance Be Forgot." Three of the above-mentioned "club" members are still personal friends of mine.[136]

There were, of course, dancing, with special instructors; tennis, with tournaments each week; ping-pong; shuffleboard; saddle horses for the riders among us; a golf course two miles away; and a Saturday night semi-pro show on the colourful sound-shell stage on the water. And one of our show producers was none other than the present popular Broadway stage and screen star, Lou Jacobi, who was also social director; we worked together for two summers.

Figure 17
Lou Hooper impersonating Bert Williams, a Duffy's Tavern production staged by "Lou Jacoby" at Wooden Acres in Ste-Agathe, Quebec (1948). Courtesy of Adam Barken.

Figure 18
Lou Hooper giving a lecture recital at Dawson College, Montreal, Quebec (1975).
Courtesy of Adam Barken.

So, at the end of four glorious seasons (1947–50) working with many famous personalities in many fields, the band returned to Montreal following a fire which destroyed the main buildings of the resort; but we stayed together, playing in the city while I opened my music studio for students of piano and voice, though I always took holidays the month of July and August playing with the band up north.

After a lapse of two years, Joey Kane placed the band in the Hotel Vermont, Sainte-Agathe-des-Monts, owned by Sonny Marcovitch, and a trumpet and bass fiddle were added to the band.

This new spot was also exciting, with interesting guests and many excellent dancers among them; the Latin rhythms were the craze at the time and, what with resident professional dance teams always on hand for private instruction, the atmosphere of the place was far from dull.

Among the guests who came regularly to the hotel was a young fellow who was a tennis expert, a good swimmer, and an enthusiastic dancer; he really "flipped" over the then one-and-only Glenn Miller sound. He and I had met on the tennis court as well as on the beach, and though we had become friends, we were not to know how our lives would become linked twenty years later; and in an even closer friendship today.[137]

This episode forms a vital link in my story and will be elaborated upon in later chapters. As for living in Sainte-Agathe, to which I had now moved my family, we were to spend the next fifteen years there and through many experiences, good and otherwise, among kind and unkind people, our children grew up in an atmosphere of natural beauty, with birds, lovely trees, lakes and mountains, while to my wife and myself, it was indeed, God's country. It was 1953.

Seventy-seven years have passed as I write, now in 1972.

NOTES

1 For copies of Hooper and Hutchinson family trees, as well as further information of relatives and descendants, see the collections at the Buxton National Historic Site and Museum.

2 Hooper was born in North Buxton, which formed part of the Elgin Settlement established in 1849 by Presbyterian minister Reverend William King from Louisiana, who came to Canada as a missionary along with fifteen people he had formerly enslaved. Initially, land was reserved for Black settlers, and many who came before the American Civil War did so fleeing the brutality of slavery. A community made up largely of Black agricultural families took shape. In the words of Sharon A. Roger Hepburn, "The community espoused freedom and hope for the future and accepted blacks who were single, married, and widowed; young and old; male and female; freeborn and fugitive." By the end of the nineteenth century, however, Buxton had undergone a significant shift. According to Shannon Prince, "Residents no longer relied on farming for their livelihood. While some residents maintained community businesses, others found work on the railroad. Many left their homes in search of employment in larger Canadian and American cities." See Hepburn, *Crossing the Border*, 1; and Prince, "Elgin Settlement."

3 Josiah James Anderson is listed as being buried in the Union-Udell Cemetery in Ypsilanti. He died in 1935, at the age of ninety-five.

4   Thomas Roadman was a respected member of Ypsilanti's community. He would have fought with (and performed music in) the 1st Infantry Colored Regiment Michigan during the Civil War, putting a band together after the conflict to mark yearly events such as Emancipation Day and Memorial Day. See Siegfried, "Emancipation Day." For a discussion of music making within the ranks of the United States Colored Troops, consult McWhirter, "The Civil War"; and Cornelius, *Music of the Civil War Era*.

5   In 1916, Ypsilanti librarian Genevieve Marie Julia Walton published a detailed chronicle of St Luke's parish, including its church and choir activities: Walton, *History of St Luke's Parish*.

6   Segregation was rampant in Ypsilanti. A quick glance over newspaper articles from the period demonstrates the widespread nature of segregation, and the various efforts to mobilize against racism. For an online archive of newspaper clippings on these topics in Ypsilanti between 1865 and 1920, see the South Adams Street @ 1900 website: https://southadamstreet1900.wordpress.com/.

7   The original name referred to the practice of decorating the graves of fallen soldiers with flowers.

8   The relationship between ragtime and Indigenous culture was at times fraught with tension, revealing an imperialist subtext that performers and audiences needed to contend with. For an illuminating discussion of the song "Hiawatha," read Schenker, "A Circuit Tour of the Globe." See also Hugues "Under One Big Tent."

9   Shinny is another name for the informal game of pond hockey.

10 The United States experienced an economic downturn from 1902 to 1904. Zarnowitz, *Business Cycles*, 228–9.

11 Hooper was not baptized until this point because the Baptist church (the church that he was raised in prior to joining St Luke's) did not baptize its members until they were old enough to consciously make "willful commitments of faith." The Episcopalian Church did believe in baptizing infants. At the time of Hooper's baptism (in 1903), Charles Williams was the dean of Trinity Cathedral in Cleveland, before being consecrated Bishop of Michigan three years later. Johnson, *A Global Introduction to Baptist Churches*, 393. See also Armentrout and Slocum, eds. *An Episcopal Dictionary of the Church*, 36, 558 (also available at www.episcopalchurch.org).

12 The Hooper Brothers appear to have overseen cultural evenings at the Good Samaritan Hall as early as 1907. See *Program 1* reprinted in this book.

13 Hooper is referring here to Emancipation Day, which celebrates the coming
    into force of Britain's Slavery Abolition Act on 1 August 1834 (and not Lin-
    coln's Emancipation Proclamation of 1863). The day had long been celebrated
    in Sandwich (now Windsor), just across the American border, and continues
    to be celebrated today (in 2021 the day was formally recognized by the Cana-
    dian government). See Henry, "Slavery Abolition Act, 1833."

14 Caroline Hill fled Alabama at the age of nineteen with her lover from a nearby
    plantation. He was to be relocated to another slave-owning farm in Missis-
    sippi. They eventually made it to Chatham, Ontario, where they raised a fam-
    ily. After losing both of her children and her husband, Hill remarried and
    moved to Ypsilanti. Her story is told in Mull, *The Underground Railroad in
    Michigan*, 116–21.

15 The 1900 US Federal Census showed that his family lived on Centre Street
    Alley, which was several blocks east of most of the other members of the
    African American community. See USNARA, 1900 US Census, Washtenaw
    Country, Michigan, population schedule, ward 6, enumeration district 114,
    sheet 13, families 23–32, Sarah Anderson; USNARA, Ancestry, NARA microfilm
    publication T623, roll 1854; Library of Congress, Sanborn Maps, "Sanborn Fire
    Insurance Map from Ypsilanti, Washtenaw County, Michigan, February 1909."
    For an outstanding interactive map of the 1910 African American community
    in Ypsilanti, see https://southadamstreet1900.wordpress.com/ypsilantis-
    african-american-community-1910/.

16 A renowned inventor, Elijah McCoy was born in Ontario in 1843 or 1844.
    McCoy was given the opportunity to pursue an apprenticeship in mechanical
    engineering in Scotland when he was sixteen years old. When he returned, he
    rejoined his family, which had now moved to Ypsilanti. Because of the racism
    that he faced, he was unable to find work as an engineer, and began working
    as a fireman and oiler for the Michigan Central Railroad. His job was to lubri-
    cate the train engines with oil, which was an inefficient process because it re-
    quired the vehicle to stop running for several minutes. McCoy invented a
    lubrication device (patented in 1872) that automatically applied oil to the en-
    gine, thus eliminating the need for constant train stops and manual lubrica-
    tion. In 1882, McCoy moved to Detroit and began working as a full-time
    inventor. Heppenheimer, "Elijah McCoy," 225–7.

17 Thomas Edison invented the cylinder phonograph in 1877 (a precursor to
    Emile Berliner's flat disc gramophone, patented a decade later). Music records

quickly became popular because they were portable, fairly affordable, and easily replayed (hearing the exact same song over again and having it sound exactly the same as the first time was a novelty). Gelatt, *The Fabulous Phonograph*, 20–1, 60; and Katz, *Capturing Sound*, 72–84.

18　Born in the Bahamas in 1874, Bert Williams emigrated to the United States with his family in his early teens. Often described as "the first Black 'superstar' of the twentieth century," he came to the attention of promoters and critics of minstrel shows, where he often performed in burnt-cork blackface. By 1907, he had achieved acclaim on Broadway stages and as a recording artist for Columbia Phonograph Company. The song "Nobody," which was featured in the show *Abyssinia*, was a best seller and became his signature work. Brooks, *Lost Sounds*, 105.

19　According to the US Bureau of Labor Statistics' inflation calculator, US$10 in 1913 (the first year for which data are available) had the same buying power as US$287 in 2022.

20　Hooper's responsibility consisted of operating the cupola, a melting device used in foundries.

21　Born in 1873, Frederick St Clair Stone was born in Chatham, Ontario. In Detroit, he asserted himself playing ragtime piano and helping unionize musicians, eventually taking the rein of one of city's most popular orchestras after the death of its founder, Theodore J. Finney. Beaulieu, "Fred S. Stone – Ma Ragtime Baby (1893)"; and Milan, *Detroit*, 15.

22　The rich tradition of African American music from this period is best captured in Björn and Gallert, *Before Motown*; Boggs, "Music Instruction in Detroit from 1874 to 1929"; and Björn, "From Hastings Street to the Blue Bird."

23　Established in 1874, the Detroit Conservatory of Music was "the first permanent institution of its kind in the city," marking an important moment in Detroit's musical development. By the early years of the twentieth century, there were at least six institutions like it, all training students in classical curriculum, and many other institutions offering musical education would soon follow. As Boggs explains, "During its first few years of operation the faculty and enrollment were small, but by the mid-twenties almost one hundred teachers were on the staff serving over a thousand students." Boggs, "Music Instruction in Detroit from 1874 to 1929," 2, 8.

24　As explained in the program for *Music through the Years* reproduced in this book, Hooper completed his studies in two parts: he graduated in pianoforte in 1916 and then, after serving overseas during the war, he submitted his thesis on the Afro-American folk song, which earned him a bachelor of music degree in 1920.

25 Henri Mattheys appears to have been a music educator and occasional composer.

26 Black Bottom was located on Detroit's Near East side, south of Gratiot Avenue and just east of Brush Street. The low-elevation area, stretching along the shores of the Detroit River, inherited its name from eighteenth-century French settlers who had taken note of its rich, dark topsoil. In the early decades of the twentieth century, Black Bottom became home to growing numbers of African Americans seeking to escape Jim Crowism. It quickly developed into a thriving centre of Black culture despite the poverty and persistent city-wide discrimination that many of its residents faced. In the 1920s, the term "Black Bottom" was also associated with a new dance form that originated from New Orleans and rivalled the Broadway-propelled Charleston. Both Jelly Roll Morton and Ma Rainey wrote songs inspired by the new dance craze: "Black Bottom Stomp" (1925) and "Ma Rainey's Black Bottom" (1928). Williams, *Detroit*; and Crease, "Jazz and Dance."

27 Con Conrad co-authored "Round Up Rag" with Bert Weedon in 1911. The "Texas Tommy," an early form of swing dance, travelled from San Francisco to New York that year, where it made a sensation in the Broadway revue *Ziegfeld Follies*. Jasen, *Ragtime*, 528; Conyers, "Texas Tommy."

28 The use of quotation marks here suggests that Hooper was very much aware of the important roles that musicians played during the pre-talkies era and that the term silent film was, even in his own time, very much a misnomer.

29 While Mount Clemens itself had a substantial Black population, the county of which it was a part (Macomb County) was known, according to BLAC *Detroit*, as "the historically 'Whitest' county in southeast Michigan with a history of racial intolerance." Its past, the magazine argues, "points to a clear unfriendliness toward Black residents." See "African-Americans Find Home in Macomb County from Detroit." For a discussion of how Macomb County was bound up in politics of racial segregation in the Detroit region following the Second World War, see Sugrue, *The Origins of Urban Crisis*, 266–7.

30 As Fiona Ngô writes, "One of the most recent US acquisitions, Hawaii took hold of the US imperial imagination, inspiring music, dances, and nightclub routines." Annexed by the United States in 1898, in the coming decades there

would be an increased demand for Hawaiian music, or music that claimed to be Hawaiian and played by Hawaiians. Many "Hawaiian Orchestras" played throughout the United States, something upon which Tom O'Neil attempted to capitalize. Ngô, *Imperial Blues*, 41–2. See also Carr, *Hawaiian Music in Motion*; and Imada, *Aloha America*.

31 Ben Shook, a violinist from Cleveland, had stepped into Theodore J. Finney's shoes after his death, joining Frederick St Clair Stone in the Finney orchestra. The two, however, promptly went their separate ways, leading to a fierce competition for dance jobs. Hailing from Louisville, Charles L. Cooke joined Stone's orchestra for a brief time before assuming a leadership role for Shook. He eventually settled in Chicago, where he led Black dance and theatre orchestras. Bjorn and Gallert, *Before Motown*, 14. See also Kenney, *Chicago Jazz*.

32 For histories of Detroit blues and jazz, with details pertaining to the artists and venues that Hooper mentions throughout the text, consult Duggan Murphy, "Detroit Blues Women"; Stryker, *Jazz from Detroit*; Milan, *Detroit*; and Bjorn and Gallert, *Before Motown*.

33 The Koppin Theatre opened in 1919, with a capacity of 1,500. It was located on the south side of Gratiot Avenue in Detroit, and in the coming decade it "was the single most important musical venue within the black community in the 1920s," and "the undisputed center of classic blues in Detroit." As *The Chicago Defender* would write in 1927, "Not in any theater the size of the Koppin can anyone find a more up-to-date musical organization than the one under the direction of Arnold Hooper, Louis Hooper, Ben Mitchell, and Harry Bradley." Björn and Gallert, *Before Motown*, 7, 11; "The Koppin Theatre," 6.

34 Jodie Edwards and Susie Edwards (born Hawthorne) formed the duo Butterbeans and Susie. "Butter," as Hooper calls him, and Bert Williams were among some of the African American entertainers who "worked under cork" to fulfill the expectations of – and subvert the modes of representations championed by – white audiences and promoters. See Berry, "When Black Celebrities Wore Blackface"; Lott, *Love and Theft*; and Roberts, *Blackface Nation*.

35 Writing about Ma Rainey, the political activist and scholar Angela Davis notes that "considering the cultural centrality of the blues during the formative decades of the construction of a 'free' African-American working-class community, it is significant that the most widely known blues performer – and defender of the blues – was a woman." Davis's study of Rainey, Bessie Smith, and Billie Holiday (three artists whom Hooper met during his career) under-

scores the centrality of a feminist consciousness in the making of Black popular culture. Davis, *Blues Legacies and Feminism*, 125.

36 Hooper is referring here to Irvin C. Miller. According to Elspeth Brown, Miller "had a long and illustrious history in African American variety theater as an actor, comedian, author, and producer. In the 1920s and 1930s, he was arguably the most well-established and successful producer of black musical comedy." Chapter 2 of her *Work!*, subtitled *A Queer History of Modeling*, provides an extensive look at the cultural politics of *Brownskin Models*, which opened in Washington, DC, in 1925 and then toured extensively in the coming decades. Brown, *Work!*, 88. For a brief discussion of many of the other figures that Hooper mentions, see Hill and Hatch, *A History of African American Theatre*.

37 The Koppin Theatre closed in 1931, marking the end of an era. The theatre had catered to an audience of working-class African Americans, many of whom had recently arrived in the city from the southern United States and lived nearby, and in particular in Black Bottom and Paradise Valley. Both neighbourhoods would themselves fall victim to urban renewal in the 1950s. See Bjorn and Gallert, *Before Motown*, 13; Conley, "Driven and Pursued"; Sugrue, *The Origins of Urban Crisis*.

38 The Renaissance was built in 1921, on what is now Adam Clayton Powell Jr Boulevard and West 137th Street. It was an iconic site of Black culture, entertainment, and sports. Born in 1897 in Philadelphia, Marian Anderson became a legendary vocalist who, although facing considerable racism, toured extensively at home and abroad. In 1939 she performed a massive concert at the Lincoln Memorial in Washington, DC, and later performed with the Metropolitan Opera Company in New York City. Coleman Hawkins, born in St Joseph, Missouri, in 1904, was, in the words of Ted Gioia, "destined to mature into one of the most important soloists in the history of jazz." Gioia, *The History of Jazz*, 129.

39 Originally based in Connecticut, where he was active in the local chapter of the National Association for the Advancement of Colored People (NAACP), William Service Bell relocated to New York after the First World War, making a living as a singer and staying socially active in artistic and literary organizations such as the Harlem Eclectic Club, of which he was the president. He kept an occasional correspondence with the likes of W.E.B. Du Bois and Claude McKay. The latter remembered Bell as a "cultivated artistic New

England Negro, who personally was very nice. He was precious as a jewel." McKay, *A Long Way from Home*, 114. See also Fearnley, "Eclectic Club," 327–8.

40   In the mid- to late 1920s, the Renaissance Theatre Concert Orchestra was considered to be "one of the most capable orchestras" in New York, thanks in part to the work of Felix Weir, an African American virtuoso violinist who had trained in Germany. "Much Expected of Orchestra," 10.

41   For a look at non-normative male sexuality in New York in the late nineteenth and early twentieth centuries, see Chauncey, *Gay New York*.

42   Salomé's "Dance of the Seven Veils" was an altered version of the biblical story of the killing of John the Baptist, a version that was made famous in an Oscar Wilde play in the late nineteenth century. It was an erotic dance of progressive unveiling.

43   The person who commented on the autobiography in 1972 told Hooper that "since you raise the subject of homosexuality, you ought to give some details about your experiences with them – either this, or leave out the whole subject altogether. If you include it, I suggest you do not mention any names." The name of the individual was subsequently crossed out. We therefore changed the name to a pronoun, to reflect Hooper's edits.

44   Incorporated in 1919, the Martin-Smith Music School (139 West on 136th Street, not 137th) had as its mission to "give all deserving children an opportunity regardless of their ability to pay for instruction, to train professional musicians as missionaries to work in conjunction with other educational institutions, and to make special provision for pupils of unusual aptitude and talent to continue their work in more advanced schools, after they have completed the Normal Couse." Cuney-Hare, *Negro Musicians and Their Music*, 256.

45   As Hooper mentioned earlier in this text, he had performed the Sacred Cantata "Ruth," composed by Alfred R. Gaul, in Grade 8 mixed chorus. When determining his composition for his bachelor of music degree, he decided to return to the story of Ruth for his oratorio. This oratorio, along with his other works, was performed in Montreal in the early 1970s. Right to the end of his life, Hooper remained proud of the work that he had originally composed at the Detroit Conservatory of Music in 1920. In 1973, he presented a copy of the oratorio to the people of North Buxton, referring to himself as a "native son." The oratorio would also be performed in Charlottetown, Prince Edward Island, on 30 October 1977, a little over a month after he died. See the copy of

Ruth, as well as the *Island Anglican Church News*, December 1977, both of which are held in the Buxton National Historic Site and Museum, Hooper Collection.

46 Could Hooper be referring to Tony Pastor's (not Proctor's) 14th Street Theatre, a leading venue for variety entertainment in New York? Although Pastor died in 1908 and the venue fell under new ownership, the name might have stuck among local and visiting artists. See Fields, *Tony Pastor*; and Snyder, *The Voice of the City*.

47 Born in New York City in 1896, Joseph Morton Davis began as a singer and a songwriter, but eventually expanded his activities to managing, broadcasting, and publishing. He was "a pioneer who unwittingly helped to break racial barriers in the music industry," writes Bruce Bastin. "Involved in such depth at an early period … effectively only with black artists, he stood out as an exception for the pre–World War II era." Bastin, *The Melody Man*, 3.

48 Louis Metcalf, whom Hooper first met and recorded with in New York in the 1920s, would go on to play an important role in Montreal jazz history. He lived and worked in Montreal for a year in the early 1930s, and then returned again in December 1946, when he formed the city's first bebop band, consisting of seven musicians from different racial and ethnic backgrounds. Mills, "Democracy in Music." For a discussion of Metcalf and Hooper recording together in 1920s New York, see Davis and Clarke, "Recordiana."

49 The Three Jolly Miners, *The Three Jolly Miners, 1925–1928*.

50 Credited to Hooper and Bob Fuller, the song was recorded in October of 1925 and had as its subtitle "Tristezas en la Gran Opera." Three Jolly Miners, "Grand Opera Blues" b/w "House Party Stomp."

51 Records recorded in New York were being pressed in Montreal for the "race records" of Ajax, but they were not distributed in Canada. Made in Montreal or in Lachine, they were sold to Black audiences throughout the United States. As John Gilmore explains, "Herbert Berliner elected to push Compo into the rapidly expanding race market. Herbert was no lover of black music, but he saw in the American race market an opportunity to expand his business horizons. In the summer of 1923, he launched his own race label at Compo, calling it Ajax. Herbert rented a studio on West 55th Street in New York City and began recording black musicians and singers there, including singer Mamie Smith, Fletcher Henderson's orchestra, and the Canadian-born pianist Lou Hooper. He transported the masters to Montreal, pressed them

into records at his Compo plant, and shipped the records back to the United States for distribution to stores in black neighbourhoods. The records sold for seventy-five cents each. Some were even shipped to the West Indies. But so specialized did Herbert consider the market for his Ajax race records that he didn't even bother to distribute them in Canada." He did release eight jazz records by Black Montrealers, although only one, a solo album by pianist Millard Thomas, was distributed domestically. This being said, some of the Compo records did find their way to the St Antoine district, with reports of them appearing in "a restaurant or tailor shop on Mountain Street." Gilmore, *Swinging in Paradise*, 36–9.

52 The two vaudeville blues singers recorded many duets together in the 1920s. The song that Hooper mentions was released on a 78 rpm disc by Columbia in 1926. Williams and Brown, "Hit Me But Don't Quit Me" b/w "You Can't Proposition Me."

53 Billy Higgins and Alberta Perkins recorded "I'm Tired of Begging You to Treat Me Right" with Hooper's Choo Choo Jazzers in March of 1925. Rust, *Jazz and Ragtime Records (1897–1942)*, 1325.

54 The session took place in February of 1926. Ethel Waters, "Refrigeratin' Papa (Mama's Gonna Warm You Up)" b/w "Throw Dirt in Your Face."

55 James Kidd, an Ajax Records enthusiast and member of the Montreal Vintage Music Society (a group of jazzophiles who collected 78 rpm phonograph records), compiled a detailed list of Hooper's remarkable output. Musicians were often not credited on recordings in the 1920s, so Kidd had to rely on the files of record companies and their studio logs when he decided to start piecing together the history of many of the decade's sessions. Through a stroke of luck, his path crossed that of Hooper in the early 1960s. The encounter led to multiple interviews from which emerged a discography that now includes dozens of titles on labels such as Ajax, Columbia, and Vocalion. In addition to recording with his groups (from Kansas City Five to Three Hot Eskimos, Five Musical Blackbirds, Six Black Diamonds, Three Monkey Chasers, Rocky Mountain Trio, Three Jolly Miners, and Three Blues Chaser), Hooper accompanied an impressive array of artists in New York studios during the 1920s: among others, Uncle Charlie Richards, Sis Quander, Kitty Waters, Rosa Henderson, Bob Fuller, Maggie Jones, Monette Moore, George Williams, Ethel Waters, Slim Perkins, Viola McCoy, Gladys Murray, Julia Moody, Kitty Brown, Lizzie Miles, Josie Miles, Louella Jones, Charlotte Evans, Sally Dale, Slim Jack-

son, and Blind Richard Yates. Kidd, "Louis Hooper Discography"; Lewis, *Louis Hooper*; and Bryant, *Ajax Records*. See also all three articles by Hitchens, "The Choo Choo Jazzers and Similar Groups," in *Vintage Jazz Mart*.

56 According to Alex Ross, Carl Van Vechten had started out as a reviewer of classical music, but began in the 1920s to become increasingly enamoured with blues and jazz. "Finally," Ross writes, "he pledged his allegiance to African-American culture, writing off concert music as a spent force. In the controversial 1926 novel … he observed that black artists were in composite possession of the 'primitive birthright … that all the civilized races were struggling to get back to – this fact explained the art of a Picasso or a Stravinsky.'" For Van Vechten and others, Ross explains, popular artists were not depicted "as entertainers but as major artists, modernists from the social margins." Van Vechten remains nonetheless a complex figure. Despite "helping the Harlem Renaissance … come to understand itself" and situating "blackness" as "a central feature of Americanness," Emily Bernard argues in her biography of Van Vechten, he also relied on sexual and primitivist tropes. Ross, *The Rest Is Noise*, 130–1; and Bernard, *Carl Van Vechten and the Harlem Renaissance*, 1–2. For a look at the polarized reception of Van Vechten's novel in Harlem, see Lewis, *When Harlem Was in Vogue*, 180–91.

57 Robeson was the second African American to graduate from Rutgers University. Having made a name for himself there on football fields, in debating competitions, and in classrooms, he graduated valedictorian and moved to New York City to study law, a career that he reluctantly abandoned in the face of pervading racism. He had gotten a taste of the stage at the turn of the 1920s by performing in a couple of plays and in an Off-Broadway production. The experience would lead him to star in Eugene O'Neill's *The Emperor Jones*, which was later made into a movie with Robeson himself on the screen. For a detailed chronicle of his life and a critical reading of his legacy, see Duberman, *Paul Robeson*; and Redmond, *Everything Man*.

58 Opened in 1912, Copley Plaza Hotel occupied a central place in the cultural and political life of Boston. The city's elite congregated there to network, socialize, celebrate milestones, and attend conventions. Its social scene was made up of prominent political figures, including past presidents as well as foreign dignitaries and royals, as well as renowned artists and athletes.

59 The chronology here is likely inaccurate. Martin B. Duberman, in his biography of Paul Robeson, notes that the Copley Plaza Hotel event, held in early

November 1924, was the singer's "first formal concert." "It went well," he writes, "the ballroom was packed, the applause generous." The performance was preceded by less formal concerts "in public halls and at private parties in wealthy white homes." Hooper then accompanied Robeson at Rutgers University and Highland Park Reformed Church (possibly the New Jersey Church referred to in the text) on 17 December 1924 and 9 January 1925, respectively. Duberman relied on Eslanda "Essie" Goode Robeson's diary as well as clippings and programs held at Rutgers University Archives. Duberman, *Paul Robeson*, 77, 594n32. See also Schomburg Center for Research in Black Culture, The Paul Robeson Collection, MG170 3/2, Ballantine Gymnasium Rutgers College Concert program, 17 December 1924, and MG170 3/2, Copley-Plaza concert program, 2 November 1924.

60 According to Duberman, Paul Robeson was eager to reconnect with Lawrence Brown, whom he had met in England a few years earlier. As a former accompanist of Roland Hayes, Brown was a recognized arranger of spirituals when he settled in New York in March of 1925. Robeson's professional partnership with Brown presumably sprang from their friendship and shared commitment to explore the rich repertoire of African American spiritual songs. Alternatively, it is possible that Robeson's partnership with Hooper ended when the singer decided to part ways with his musical adviser Harry T. Burleigh. Paul Robeson Jr argues that his father was unsatisfied with the "decidedly classical European concert style" that Burleigh favoured in the fall of 1924. Hooper, who was "apparently a friend of Burleigh's," might have lost his position as accompanist because of the changing dynamic between Robeson and his singing coach. Both are valid hypotheses and neither of them contradicts Hooper's account of his association with Robeson. See Duberman, *Paul Robeson*, 78; and Robeson Jr, *The Undiscovered Paul Robeson*, 83.

61 The first time that Hooper met with Paul Robeson in Montreal must have been on 13 October 1935. Hooper had recently moved to the city and was evidently thrilled to reminisce about his Harlem days. His description of the singer's concert at His Majesty's Theatre, which he sent to *The Free Lance*, deserves to be quoted in detail: "Despite the fact that I have known Mr Robeson personally for several years this was my first opportunity of hearing him, as a member of one of his audiences, though I enjoy the honour of being his accompanist during the first six months of his artistic career. To hear Paul Robeson sing any song is to experience perfection in vocal performance for at

no time is the listener at a loss to understand distinctly every word, each word being borne to the ear upon the steadiest and truest tone." Hooper continued: "Bringing to his art an unusually delightful personality which is evident the moment he appears; to say his performance was an enjoyable one seems hardly enough, as his response to numerous encores bore witness." The two probably met again in late 1945 (Robeson gave two concerts in Montreal on 23 and 25 October). Hooper had just returned from the war in Europe and had not yet settled back into civilian life. In a letter to the singer written in 1971, he wrote: "Doubtless you will be surprised in receiving this word from me, your friend – Hooper, Louis S., your first accompanist when you embarked upon what proved to be a world-renowned career of Concert work." "I last saw you at Plateau Hall, here in Montreal, when my friend and I were still in uniform," he then explained. Hooper had heard Robeson on the airwaves of the Canadian Broadcasting Corporation, and so he wanted to share with him how "enthralled" he was to once again hear "the sound of that richest-of-all singing voices." LAC, Hooper Fonds, Vol. 1, No. 2, Louis Hooper to *The Free Lance*, 14 March 1936; and LAC, Hooper Fonds, Vol. 1, No. 3, Louis Hooper to Paul Robeson, 19 April 1971.

62 Thomas Brothers, drawing on Garvin Bushell, writes that the Lafayette Theatre "was the only theatre in Harlem … where African Americans could sit downstairs and did not have to climb up to the balcony. It was here that musicians Louis Hooper and Benny Waters first heard [Louis] Armstrong play." Brothers, *Louis Armstrong*, 152. See also Hay, *African American Theatre*, 20.

63 Both Perry "Mule" Bradford and Clarence Williams were African American jazz pianists with prolific stage and studio careers. They also had an acute sense of business; the former as musical director of blues singer Mamie Smith and the latter as one of the two driving forces behind the Black-owned Piron and Williams Publishing Company. See Bradford's own *Born with the Blues*; and Lord, *Clarence Williams*.

64 "Race records" were produced and marketed largely by white-owned labels that featured African American artists performing blues, gospel, and jazz material for African American audiences. The practice of grouping 78 rpm phonograph records into separate catalogues seemingly began with New York's Okeh Records, whose roster included Shelton Brooks, with whom Hooper worked during an Ethel Waters session, Sara Martin, and Mamie Smith. A mirror of the segregation that pervaded the United States at the

time, the "race records" movement was, incidentally, a long-overdue recognition that African Americans were a formidable force in the cultural and economic – not to mention political – spheres. For artists like Hooper, seeing the music circulating in this way throughout the United States and beyond, was exhilarating. David Gilbert, who uses the term "ragging uplift," argues that the movement formed part of a broader effort to promote "new ways" of representing and experiencing "blackness through the burgeoning avenues of commercial culture," notably by offering "new sounds, professional channels, commercial strategies, and different kinds of black identities to internalize and publicly represent." Gilbert, *The Product of Our Souls*, 11.

65 Joseph M. Davis's Triangle Music Co. was one of many Manhattan-based publishers that contributed to – and capitalized on – the explosion of jazz music in the 1920s by hiring composers and lyricists to write or record original material to help boost the sale of sheet music. Tin Pan Alley originally referred to a section of West 28th Street where some of the city's early publishers of popular music set up operations. In the 1910s, West 45th Street became "the focal point of the small-to-medium publishers." The Broadway Central building that Hooper describes was located a few blocks north of that, at 1658 Broadway, on the corner of West 51st Street. See Jasen, *Tin Pan Alley*, xiii.

66 Born in Cuthbert, Georgia, the band-leading pianist James Fletcher Hamilton Henderson (1898–1952) moved to New York City in 1920 and quickly made a name for himself on stage and in recording studios alongside singers such as Ethel Waters and Bessie Smith. By the mid-1920s, his band's stellar reputation was cemented with the addition of cornetist Louis Armstrong. In an interview with Jim Kidd, Hooper described Henderson as "a good personal friend" who kindly helped him on Sunday nights during a summer in the early 1920s, when he had double duties as a pianist at the Roof Garden Theatre in Washington Heights and as organist at St Philip's Episcopal Church in the Bronx. "Fletcher used to substitute for me" at the theatre, he remembered fondly. Cited in Kidd, "Louis Hooper," 4.

67 Like Clarence Williams, whom Hooper esteemed, W.C. Handy "showed that a black man could extract himself from the clutches of white publishers and successfully own and publish his own music." Handy, Bessie Smith, and others often crossed paths in the offices of prominent bandleading-producers such as Paul Whiteman, and they also played in radio studios such as those of

wor, which began broadcasting in 1922 out of Newark, New Jersey (the station opened its Manhattan studio shortly after). Brooks, *Lost Sounds*, 3.

68 For a detailed list of key works and a survey of the role played by near-monopolistic music publishers in the making of Tin Pan Alley history, consult Jasen, *Tin Pan Alley*.

69 *Blackbirds* was the brainchild of Lew Leslie, a white writer and producer who championed Harlem talent and cast Black artists in Broadway revues. The 1926 edition, featuring Florence Mills, dazzled audiences in London. *Blackbirds of 1928* also travelled to Europe, and won critical acclaim at the Moulin Rouge in Paris. Williams, *Underneath a Harlem Moon*.

70 George M. Cohan (born 1878) and Eddie Cantor (born 1892) were respectively of Irish-Catholic and Jewish heritage. They rose to fame by making their way through the vaudeville circuit and to Broadway. Cohan had a head start by virtue of his age, which positioned him to become one of the key songwriters and producers of stage shows in the opening decades of the twentieth century. Cantor debuted on Broadway in 1917 as a member of *Ziegfeld Follies'* cast, which Hooper mentions below. Incidentally, both artists sought to further capitalize on their celebrity by writing autobiographies in the 1920s: Cohan, *Twenty Years on Broadway*; and Cantor, *My Life Is in Your Hands*.

71 One of the best-known female impersonators of the vaudeville era, and later a Hollywood celebrity, Julian Eltinge was at the height of his fame in the 1920s. As Kathleen B. Cassey explains, he "both relied on and modified interrelated understandings of race, sexuality, and class-based American gender norms, achieving mainstream acceptance at a time when female impersonation was an increasingly endangered endeavour." She adds: "As a beloved icon for over fifteen years, Eltinge reassured audiences that ... the elegant Victorian white lady was not yet dead." Casey, *The Prettiest Girl on Stage Is a Man*, 76.

72 Bert Williams and Eddie Cantor, whom Hooper mentioned above, performed in *Ziegfeld Follies*, a series of Broadway revues that ran with almost no interruption from 1907 to 1936. Williams was on the cast for Cantor's debut in 1917. In mentioning Will Marion Cook's "Exhortation," subtitled "A Negro Sermon" and written in 1912, William H. Tyers's 1908 Latin style "Maori," and James Tim Brymn's 1924 "Ghost of Blues," which contributed to the decade's blues craze, Hooper presents a cross-section of the era's soundscape as he experienced it.

73 Striver's Row refers to New York's St Nicholas Historic District, an area

consisting of townhouses built in the closing decade of the 1800s and originally intended primarily for whites, who "evaporated as the surrounding areas
were taking over by African Americans; and although the two blocks [138th
and 139th Streets] held out for some time against black tenants and owners,
they became home to a largely upper-class black coterie by the mid-1920s."
The new residents, many of whom were light-skinned and "slavishly imitating
the white upper classes," were strivers who adhered to the ideology of racial
uplift. Balshaw, "Sugar Hill and Strivers' Row," 478.

74 Hooper is referring here to architect Stanford White.

75 The trials of Harry Thaw for the murder of Stanford White partly inspired
E.L. Doctorow's 1975 novel *Ragtime* and the 1981 Miloš Forman film by the
same name. Both were preceded by *The Girl in the Red Velvet Swing* (Richard
Fleischer, 1955), a 20th Century–Fox film starring Joan Collins as Evelyn
Nesbit Thaw (Marilyn Monroe was apparently considered for the title role).

76 Lew Leslie was, of course, the writer who spearheaded the many editions of
the musical revue *Blackbirds*, among others. Florence Mills and her husband
Ulysses Thompson performed in several Broadway shows, including *Blackbirds of 1926*, which starred Mills. Her untimely death the following year cut
short a promising international career.

77 When Hooper arrived in Harlem, he was already well acquainted with W.E.B.
Du Bois's work, having cited *The Souls of Black Folk* in his Detroit Conservatory of Music thesis, "The Afro-American Folk-Song: Its Origin and Evolution." As David Levering Lewis explains, by the mid-1920s, Du Bois was "the
senior intellectual militant of his people, a symbol of brainy, complex, arro-
gant rectitude widely respected by the common people." Lewis, *When Harlem
Was in Vogue*, 6. Also see his two-volume *W.E.B. Du Bois*.

78 Hooper was likely referring to the exorbitant rental rates that white landlords
charged African American tenants, who often had to pay more than double
what white tenants paid for similar apartments. "Landlords Taking Last
Minute Gouge," 11.

79 Presented at His Majesty's Theatre, the last representation of *Blackbirds* in
Montreal was on 18 May 1929. "Blackbirds Revue Outstanding Show."

80 Possibly the country's first organized Black jazz band, the Canadian Ambassadors debuted at the Gatineau Country Club in Aylmer, Quebec, in December 1931. Its founder, the Niagara Falls–born saxophonist Myron Sutton, had

cut his chops playing on Buffalo's jazz circuit throughout the 1920s. Hooper was not the first to play piano for the group; John Walden, Brad Moxley, and Buster Harding (who was also from Buxton and would go on to have a successful career in swing-era New York) preceded him. Originally from Guelph, Ontario, the Canadian Ambassadors relocated to Montreal in the winter of 1933 where it made quite an impression at Connie's Inn, a booming nightclub formerly known as the Frolics. Plagued by high personnel turnover, Sutton's band now found stability, gaining recognition for its superb musicianship and interesting repertoire, with Hooper at the piano. Had immigration policies not barred foreign musicians from playing in the United States during the economic downturn of the 1930s, Sutton and his bandmates would have held their own alongside other jazz greats. "The fate of the Canadian Ambassadors was sealed," writes John Gilmore (*Swinging in Paradise*, 77), and "they would remain in Canada, enjoying local popularity, but never testing the limits of their ability and ambition in the more advanced and competitive American jazz market." After Connie's Inn, Hooper performed intermittently with the band until it broke up in 1939. Gilmore, *Swinging in Paradise*, chapter 3.

81 "Bringing Harlem to Montreal," read the promotional brochure that announced the official opening of Connie's Inn, formerly known as The Frolics, at 1417 Saint Lawrence Boulevard. A reproduction of the document appears in Gilmore, *Swinging in Paradise*, 61–3.

82 Born on 7 April 1915, Billie Holiday would have been eighteen or nineteen years old at the time of her performance at Connie's Inn, as Hooper himself notes in the following paragraph.

83 For a look at the role of Black dancers during the Jazz Age in Montreal, see Lam, *Show Girls*; Blais-Tremblay, "Jazz, Gender, Historiography."

84 Located in the area where Manhattan's Lincoln Center for the Performing Arts sits today, San Juan Hill was once a thriving place for jazz. "In 1910, San Juan Hill was still the largest black community in Manhattan," writes Robin Kelley in his autobiography of one of the neighborhood's most famous residents: Thelonious Monk. "The combination of anti-black violence … and deteriorating housing conditions spurred a mass exodus … into the next up-and-coming black neighborhood: Harlem." Kelley, *Thelonious Monk*, 17. See also Sacks, *Before Harlem*.

85 Marcus Garvey became a prominent figure in Harlem when he relocated

there from Jamaica in 1916. Two years earlier, he had founded the Universal
Negro Improvement Association, an organization dedicated to Black nation-
alism and economic self-sufficiency. Established in 1917, its New York branch
was incredibly popular: its weekly meetings and first International Convention of the Negro Peoples, held in 1920, drew thousands of people. Martin,
"Garvey, Marcus," 420–4. See also Garvey and Hill, *The Marcus Garvey and
United Negro Improvement Association Papers*.

86 Harlem experienced two riot-like episodes, one in July 1926 and the other in
July 1928. The events of July 1926 arose out of tensions between Puerto Ricans
moving into the neighbourhood and more established residents. The July 1928
confrontation was much more violent. The riot began when some residents
intervened when they witnessed four police officers assaulting an African
American man already under arrest. The riot was quelled an hour later when
backup police officers with machine guns arrived. "Trio Held as Police Block
Harlem Riot." See also King, *Whose Harlem Is This, Anyway?*, 177–83; and
Greenberg, *Or Does It Explode?*

87 In one of the many recorded conversations that Hooper had with James Kidd
in the 1960s, he explained: "I took my eleven years old daughter to New York
not long ago … I was anxious to show her Harlem. I almost cried … really I
did … Harlem had been people … people who were really people, churches at
the height of dignity, people of all professions, some fine night clubs … the
Nest, the Paradise. I can remember Boute's Drug Store … the doctor and his
wife were Creole … they spoke French so beautifully and the drug store was a
place to go … a lovely YWCA … the Renaissance Theatre … the dance hall
upstairs … a complete department store, the Renaissance block … St Phillips
Church … the Abysinia Church. I went back in 1962 … I purposely got off at
125th and Lennox, just to show my daughter what Harlem was. First of all, the
type of person whom I saw disturbed me … it was a hot day and we went into
a soda bar … I asked the lady if she could tell me if the Martin Smith Music
School was still in business … she looked at me as if I was someone from
Mars. I asked another place … There was a middle-aged man sitting with his
father … I asked them. He said it was not there anymore … everything was
gone … 'there's a different type of person here now … the people that were
here when you were here are now all gone' … I was heart-broken." Cited in
Kidd, "Louis Hooper," 4.

88 In the 15 November 1932 edition of *Variety*, which reported on the Toronto

performance of *In Abraham's Bosom* and listed Hooper as a member of the cast, the critic McStay wrote that "innovation here was the placing of a Negro chorus in the orchestra pit, their spirituals paralleling the dramatic progress of the play." McStay, "In Abraham's Bosom," 50.

89 Rouyn and Noranda were founded as mining communities in Quebec's Abitibi region in the 1920s. By 1931, the year before Hooper's visit, they had a population of 5,700. Linteau et al., *Quebec since 1930*, 39.

90 The Canadian National Exhibition (CNE) is an annual fair held in downtown Toronto during the final two weeks of summer. The displays of new technology, agriculture, and the arts attracted a cross-section of Toronto residents: men and women of all ages, social classes, and ethnicities. Live entertainment performances ("sideshows") were especially popular among the varied audiences of the late-summer event. Sideshows included daring bike stunts and parachute jumps, comedic skits, and music concerts. CNE organizers purposefully scheduled "clean" (non-vulgar, non-sexual, not dangerous) attractions like Hooper's piano concert to create a pleasant mood and prevent rowdiness while still entertaining fairgoers. See Walden, *Becoming Modern in Toronto*, 261–74.

91 A few years younger than Hooper, Canadians Myron Sutton (born in 1903) and Buster Harding (born in 1912) were accomplished musicians who left their mark on both sides of the Canada–US border. The former, an alto saxophonist, refined his chops in Cleveland before forming the Canadian Ambassadors and eventually retiring in his birthplace of Niagara Falls, Ontario. The latter also began his career in Cleveland, then played piano in Sutton's band before eventually giving up his place in the group to pursue other career opportunities, notably in New York where "he would be admired as a dynamic and innovative composer and arranger in the Swing idiom." Miller, *The Miller Companion to Jazz in Canada*, 91.

92 Hooper's reference to that area as "Black Bottom," a term used in reference to a Detroit neighbourhood, is surprising. As John Gilmore notes, none of the interviews for his book on Montreal jazz referred to that part of the city as "Black Bottom." It is possible that the term gained currency in the 1960s, when Hooper began work on his autobiography, with the opening of The Black Bottom, a seminal venue first established at 1350 St-Antoine West (it later moved to Old Montreal). Gilmore, *Swinging in Paradise*, 278n12.

93 The 1930s were, in fact, a period of labour conflict in Montreal, especially in

the textile industry. See Dumas, *The Bitter Thirties in Québec*; Lévesque, "Les midinettes de 1937"; and Pesotta, *Bread upon the Waters*.

94   Located at 92 Sainte-Catherine St East, the Hollywood Club introduced Montrealers to up-and-coming African American artists, many of whom hailed from New York. Emmett "Babe" Wallace and Ralph Brown, for example, both performed at New York's famed Cotton Club in the mid-1930s. Like Wallace, who appeared in *Stormy Weather* (Andrew L. Stone, 1943) and *Rhythm in a Riff* (Leonard Anderson, 1947), Brown occasionally danced for the cameras in *Harlem after Midnite* (Oscar Micheaux, 1934) and *Jivin' in Bebop* (Leonard Anderson and Spencer Williams, 1947).

95   Montreal's music scene had long been shaped by racial segregation, as many venues were off-limits to Black musicians. Other clubs welcomed Black musicians and entertainers, but barred Black patrons. Only the clubs in the Saint-Antoine district were truly welcoming to both Black entertainers and clients. This segregation began to come undone during the Second World War when non-white servicemen began to be admitted into clubs from which they had previously been excluded, and the local of the AFM began accepting Black members. Despite these openings, however, de facto segregation remained after the war, especially in places that were considered to be upscale. See Mills, "Democracy in Music," 357–60, and Gilmore, *Swinging in Paradise*, 52–7.

96   In January 1935, Hooper formed the Hooper Southern Singers of Canada to interpret African American spirituals. In June of that year, Hooper wrote to Dr York, his old teacher from the Detroit Conservatory of Music (who was now at the Institute of Musical Art in Detroit), asking for a copy of his thesis, as he planned to set out on a lecture tour about African American music and its origins accompanied by "a group of singers which I have organized here." The group quickly began to proceed with rehearsals and signed contracts with various venues in Montreal. As Hooper would state in 1936, "Rehearsals proceeded at regular intervals until a degree of proficiency was reached sufficient to warrant our first public appearance, this taking place at Union United Church – Delisle Street, five members making the appearance. Engagements followed rapidly including appearances at Emmanuel, Erskine and St James churches; The Forum, Windsor Hotel, three broadcasts over local stations and during which time we presented the first of a series of public concerts which are intended to be an annual event. Several benefit concerts have been among this group of appearances as well as concerts in several of the public schools

and High Schools of the suburbs, and MacDonald College at St Anne's." LAC, Hooper Fonds, Vol. 1, No. 13, Louis Hooper to Dr F.L. York, Institute of Musical Art, Detroit, 13 June 1935; "First Anniversary Meeting of the Hooper Southern Singers of Canada" reproduced in this book.

97 For more on Oscar Peterson's sister and the important roles she played as a piano instructor and mentor in her community, see Campbell, "Life Notations of Daisy Sweeney."

98 It is worth quoting at length the passage in Oscar Peterson's autobiography that describes his encounter with Hooper: "By the time he entered my life Professor Hooper was a distinguished figure in the Montreal music community, well known as a piano teacher and also actively engaged in jazz. It was this that made me particularly keen for our lessons to get under way. At last the day arrived; precisely at four o'clock on a Thursday afternoon, Lou Hooper arrived at my house for our first get-together.

"He was a fairly tall man, immaculately but not over-dressed for the occasion, handsome, with slightly greying hair and a warm smile. He said a very friendly 'Good afternoon, Oscar,' seated himself in the chair next to the piano while motioning me to the piano seat, and immediately got down to business. 'Let's see what we can learn about this marvelous instrument.' Almost before I knew what was taking place, we were flying through major and minor scales and arpeggios at an unbelievable rate.

"Then we came to the point in the lesson which dealt with actual pieces; it was here that I gained my first real insight about communicating with the instrument. Professor Hooper listened attentively to my performances, then politely asked me to allow him to sit to the piano. He replayed the pieces that I had just played (or so I thought!) and while effortlessly doing so offered comments such as, 'You know, Oscar, I have always felt that Chopin was looking at a lovely landscape at the time he composed this piece because everything about it is so lush and green-like' or 'Franz Liszt must have been feeling his own strength at this point because as we play it we can almost feel the transmission of power from his music to us.'

"These comments affected me deeply, causing me to take an entirely new look at what I had been playing. I have used this approach at various times with students whom I felt had lost that dimension in their playing, and it has proved gratifyingly successful. Thank you, Lou, wherever you are!

"Before I had fully taken in all that had happened at my first lesson,

Professor Hooper stood up, wrote out a receipt, shook my hand, smiled, and vanished from the building. Our lessons proceeded well, and once I had accepted the need to respond in full to his efforts by learning the assignments he left me, we enjoyed a great association. Eventually I plucked up the courage to ask him about his jazz playing; he gave that marvelous smile and said, 'I've been waiting for you to get around to that, young man.' He hesitated for a moment and then went on, 'I'll tell you what: I'll play one of the jazz pieces that I know if you play one of yours in return. Agreed?'

"Now uncontrollably curious, I of course said 'Yes.' He sat down and played one of the prettiest ballads I had ever heard, then got up: 'It's your turn.' I responded by playing a piece I felt comfortable with, and once into it gave it my all. At the end I turned and looked over my shoulder at Professor Hooper as he stood silent. He had his chin cupped in the palm of his right hand and was looking at me oddly. He simply said, 'Interesting, interesting.' Puzzled, I didn't pursue it further, but I felt he had made some kind of decision about me.

"That turned out to be true, for several weeks later, at the end of another lesson, he asked to speak to my Dad. He told him that he didn't think he could take me any further in the direction that I should and would go. Despite Dad's pleas, he stuck to his decision, adding that it would be better for me to have some more specialized help and tuition, for that would allow me to attain the heights he thought me capable of.

"This came as a shock to me. I had come to love this gentle, congenial statesman of the piano. He had brought into my life a newfound understanding of how best to interpret a musical selection; he had also made me much more aware of the delicacy and beauty of the instrument. Even today, when people are moved at my performance of a ballad, my thoughts go back to that debonair and subtle gentleman, for Professor Louis Hooper went out of my life, as the Ellington song has it, All Too Soon." Peterson, *Jazz Odyssey*, 12–14.

99   Norman Granz's Jazz at the Philharmonic performed at various Montreal venues over the years, including at the Auditorium de Verdun, Plateau Hall, and the Forum. Their performance at His Majesty's Theatre was on 30 September 1947. The Dizzie Gillespie concert at the Danceland Chez Maurice, which Hooper refers to above, likely took place the following year, on 20 or 21 April 1948. See "Dizzy Gillespie Due in Montreal Tuesday," 6; and "Récital de jazz, ce soir, au Majesty's," 8.

100 Hooper is referring here to the Advanced School of Contemporary Music,

which Peterson opened in 1960 on 21 Park Road, in Toronto. In addition to double-bassist Ray Brown and drummer Ed Thigpen, clarinetist Phil Nimmons, trombonist Butch Watanabe, and trumpeter Eric Traugott were also heavily involved in the school. DeMichael, "Oscar Peterson."

101   The concert took place on 2 April 1967. Place des Arts, Montreal's state-of-the-art venue, had opened just a few years earlier in anticipation of Canada's Centennial. For reviews of the concert, see Thériault, "Ella Fitzerald et chats 'jazzés'"; and Gingras, "Ella Fitzgerald et les autres."

102   Olga Spencer and Bernice Jordan (referenced in the following paragraph), feature in Lam, *Show Girls*. See also Blais-Tremblay's dissertation, which makes use of interviews conducted during the making of the film: Blais-Tremblay, "Jazz, Gender, Historiography."

103   Located on the "corner" (the corner of Saint-Antoine and Mountain Streets), the Monte Carlo was across the street from the famed Rockhead's Paradise. The Monte Carlo opened in 1934, and by 1936 Hooper had come to play a major role in the club. He received a payout from his time in the army during the First World War, and put his money into becoming part-owner at the Monte Carlo club. And in this role at the club, he brought up American shows and acted as the bandleader. The club had a difficult time competing with Rockhead's, and ultimately would not be around for very long. But the club eventually became the Café St Michel, famed club that would become the site of innovations in the Montreal jazz scene, such as the introduction of bebop. Marrelli, *Stepping Out*, 96; Miller, *Such Melodious Racket*, 152; Gilmore, *Swinging in Paradise*, 48; Gilmore, *Who's Who of Jazz in Montreal*, 127; Concordia University Special Collections, Gilmore Fonds, Lou Hooper, Interview with Lou Hooper Jr, 1 September 1982.

104   Born in Amherstburg, Ontario, in 1886, Shelton Brooks spent the greater part of his life in the United States. Growing up in Detroit, the aspiring Black artist entered the spotlight in the 1910s as the author of songs popularized by the likes of Sophie Tucker, Benny Goodman, and Mae West. He wrote "ragtime-influenced songs" that were "brash, sexually suggestive, and perfectly suited the changing social context of the early twentieth century." Fats Waller and His Rhythm, Ella Fitzgerald, and the Original Dixieland Jass Band are among the many groups who recorded his "Darktown Strutters' Ball." He was eventually inducted into the Canadian Songwriters Hall of Fame. Keillor, *Music in Canada*, 189.

105 Al Palmer was a newspaper columnist and well known throughout the city. In the 1930s, Hooper and Palmer inhabited the same world of the late-night Montreal music scene, and during the Second World War they met and socialized in London. Throughout his career, Palmer worked for a number of different publications. Al Palmer, "Ourtown: Our Tune."

106 For a history of Montreal's burlesque past, see Palmer, *Montreal Confidential*; Mansbridge, "In Search of a Different History"; Cuccioletta, "The Américanité of Quebec Urban Popular Culture as Seen through Burlesque Theater in Montreal, 1919–1939"; Hébert, *Le Burlesque au Québec*; and Blais-Tremblay, "Jazz, Gender, Historiography."

107 Hooper is likely referring here to the election of Union National premier Maurice Duplessis in 1936 and the economic hardship that would follow the closing of nightclubs.

108 Bernice "Bunny" Jordan Whims accompanied the band on tour. She shared a story about how Hooper stood up for her when they checked into their accommodations in the YMCA in Peterborough, Ontario. The YMCA accommodated the male band members but refused to allow her to have a room. Hooper insisted that the whole band sleep in the car. See Lam, *Show Girls*, 17 min. 42 sec.

109 At time of the declaration of war in September 1939, official and de facto discriminatory policies of racial exclusion limited recruitment across the various branches of the armed forces. While in the Air Force and the Navy, official policies restricted the recruitment of non-white personnel, militia units were "able to decide for themselves whether or not to accept visible minority volunteers, with many deciding not to do so." Joost, "Racism and Enlistment," 17.

110 Hooper likely spent the night at the police station, which was located downstairs in City Hall at the time, not the "Kingston Pen." The latter had opened its doors a little over 100 years earlier to house Canada's most notorious criminals, not "rubby-dub bums."

111 They would have been travelling toward Toronto if they picked up Hooper in Kingston after leaving Gaspé. In any case, they headed back east and took him to Montreal where he enlisted in the army. Born in Montreal in 1916, Hugh Sealey played clarinet and saxophone, joining other Black musicians at Rockhead's Paradise and Roseland Ballroom, among other venues. See Gilmore, *Who's Who of Jazz in Montreal*, 258–9.

112 Born in British Columbia, Gerry Wilmot worked for the CBC in Montreal, where he held celebrity status due to his work as a hockey announcer. He travelled to Great Britain to serve as master of ceremonies with the CBC Overseas Unit during the Second World War.

113 See the radio script reproduced in this book.

114 The Beaver Club was the Canadian Leave Centre for soldiers in central London. Vincent Massey (high commissioner to the United Kingdom) spearheaded the club's opening because he wanted to create a welcoming space for Canadian military personnel who were on leave. All Canadian soldiers were automatically Beaver Club members and could access the club's many services. The Beaver Club's services and facilities included: a library that carried Canadian newspapers, game and lounge rooms, a canteen that served Canadian-style meals, and an Information Bureau that helped soldiers on leave find accommodations, plan sightseeing activities, and access discounted show tickets. Stacey and Wilson, *The Half-Million*, 102–6.

115 Warrant Officer Class II.

116 Canadian Concert Parties, wartime entertainment units that had become popular during the First World War, officially began touring Canadian military bases in 1942 to improve morale and reduce exhaustion. Their variety shows included live music, dancers, and comedic skits, (sometimes) including drag performances. The female impersonators dressed up in costumes that exaggerated "feminine characteristics to the necessary point of caricature by cultivating huge hair, big eyes, massive breasts and incredibly high falsetto voice." Female characters that conformed to traditional gender roles were treated with respect and female characters that deviated from normative models were portrayed negatively. These drag performances comforted the soldiers, who felt uneasy about women stepping into traditionally male roles. Even though drag performances were well received, they lost their appeal and became less frequent once women enlisted and began performing in concert parties. Halladay, "A Lovely War," 25–6.

117 Inspired by the late nineteenth-century character Johnny Canuck, Canada's counterpart to Great Britain's John Bull and the United States' Uncle Sam, the show originated from *The Maple Leaf Matinee* and aired every Saturday night on the BBC and the Allied Expeditionary Forces networks. Stephens, *The Canadian Entertainers of World War II*, 47.

118 Mepacrine, which was used as an antimalarial drug.

119 Hooper's copy of *The Red Patch*, Canada's "Front Line Newspaper," is preserved in LAC, Hooper Fonds, Vol. 1, No. 14.

120 That is, mepacrine.

121 Eden, 1st Earl of Avon, served as Prime Minister of the United Kingdom from
1955 until 1957.

122 As Jason Wilson writes elsewhere in this collection, it was in Avellino, in
southern Italy, "where many of the so-called and uncharitably nicknamed
'D-Day Dodgers' were stationed and later served as reinforcements in the bid
to break the Gothic Line." The Gothic Line was a fortified defence line in
northern Italy. Dancocks, *The D-Day Dodgers*, 293–4, 351, 434.

123 These soldiers (many of whom were Australians, not just British) inherited
the nickname because of their role in the Western Desert campaign to push
the Axis Powers out of North Africa. 20th Century–Fox immortalized the
siege of Tobruk in the film *Desert Rats* (Robert Wise, 1953).

124 The Union Jack was commonly used in Canada until the official adoption of
the Maple Leaf Flag, Canadians' new national symbol, in 1965.

125 The Lee-Enfield Rifle No. 4 was the British Army's standard issue rifle. Made
in the United States, the Thompson M1 was a popular albeit expensive sub-
machine gun. The Sten sub-machine gun was the British-made alternative to
the Thompson gun. Hogg, *The Complete Illustrated Encyclopedia of the World's
Firearms*, 214, 288–9, 292–3.

126 This "war diary," the Bandoliers' daily report of performances, is preserved in
LAC, Hooper Fonds, Vol. 1, No. 14.

127 To consult the score of Hooper's "Victory Song" (for trumpet, trombone,
piano, and bass), see LAC, Hooper Fonds, Vol. 6, No. 8.

128 Among the jazz superstars who performed with local musicians in the
Netherlands before the war, one finds the Missouri-born saxophonist Coleman Hawkins. For a chronicle of his time there in the mid-1930s, see Chilton,
The Song of the Hawk, 110–24. For a discussion of the history and legacy of
other such encounters with Dutch musicians, see Bakriges, "Musical Transculturation."

129 "O Canada" became, albeit unofficially, Canadians' national anthem with the
visit of King George VI in 1939. It was officially adopted as the national anthem of Canada in 1980. See Bethune, "A Gift Fit for the King."

130   The Siegfried Line, also known as the Westwall, was a 630-kilometre fortified
      line that spanned Germany's western border. American, British, and Canadian
      soldiers crossed multiple points along the line during the Siegfried Line cam-
      paign from September 1944 to March 1945, at the cost of over 250,000 casual-
      ties. The battle was a far cry from the quick victory described in Jimmy
      Kennedy's upbeat "We're Going to Hang out the Washing on the Siegfried
      Line," released at the start of the war. Whiting, *West Wall*, vii, 6, 10, 16, 115; and
      listen on Various, *The World at War*.

131   London's music scene did not fully recover until the early 1950s. The immedi-
      ate postwar scene was somewhat bleak. The war halted much of London's
      nightlife: many nightclubs were heavily damaged during air raids, postwar
      austerity made it difficult for clubs to turn a profit, and many musicians (and
      former employees) had not yet been demobilized from the war front or essen-
      tial wartime industries. Rainbow Corner, the venue Hooper mentioned book-
      ing, was an exception because the club was primarily a recreation centre for
      American servicemen. The American Red Cross opened the club during the
      war to provide American and Allied servicemen a place to unwind, socialize,
      and enjoy the occasional live performance while stationed or on leave in Lon-
      don. Although live performances were mostly limited to a few music venues,
      jazz was more popular than ever thanks to BBC's *Radio Rhythm Club* show.
      The weekly jazz radio show entertained listeners at home and abroad, lifted
      the country's spirits, and brought jazz more into British mainstream culture.
      See Frith et al., *The History of Live Music in Britain*, 1–2; Baade, *Victory
      through Harmony*, 108; and Savage, "Pop at the Pictures."

132   After the war, Montreal experienced a severe housing shortage. Not only had
      the building of new housing been stalled by the depression of the 1930s, but
      the influx of workers during the war and then the return of veterans after the
      war created a demand that far outstripped supply. Hooper, as he notes above,
      had to contend not only with these conditions, but also with the city's long-
      standing patterns of racism in housing. Wade, "Wartime Housing Limited,"
      41–4; Fahrni, "The Second World War," 49. For a look at the long history of
      anti-Black racism, see Williams, *Road to Now*.

133   The school was established by Pat Marrazza in the mid-1930s. Of Italian her-
      itage, he had immigrated from Great Britain to Canada in 1911. He helped
      popularize the accordion in Quebec as a performer and as an educator. He

eventually broadened his school's portfolio of music lessons to include the ukulele and the piano, among other instruments. "L'école de musique de Pat Marrazza."

134 We have not located any references in the local press of Hooper performing in front of an audience with the young singer, whose name remains unknown. The planned series of concerts might have been intended to set the stage for the release of *Night and Day* (Michael Curtiz, 1946), a biopic of the composer Cole Porter.

135 Wooden Acres was a resort hotel in Sainte-Agathe-des-Monts that catered mostly to a Jewish clientele. The Alex Dworkin Canadian Jewish Archives in Montreal holds archival materials that tell a partial history of the site. See "Wooden Acres [Ad]" and consult the following article for details on the fire that Hooper mentions further below: "Fire Destroys Resort Building."

136 No recordings of these songs exist, but Hooper did keep acetates of sessions recorded in the 1940s, 1950s, and 1960s, including one during which he rehearsed different versions of "Montreal, Our Town." We have reprinted the lyrics of the song in this book.

137 Although Hooper does not identify the "young fellow," he was likely one of the four jazzophiles (Peter Johnson, Marv Ekers, Jack Sadler, or Hank Fleischman) who went on to form the Montreal Vintage Music Society with James Kidd, who was researching the history of Ajax Records at the time. The group would be instrumental in bringing Hooper back to the limelight in the 1960s, prompting him to begin work on *That Happy Road*. In 2016, Kidd reminisced in the pages of *Vintage Jazz Mart* about the encounter. "I was very impressed," he explained; Hooper "was tall, in great health, taught piano … played tennis regularly and was very active." He continued: "One of my colleagues in the Montreal Vintage Music Society … and a regular tennis partner with Lou, introduced me. My friend had assumed that Lou was white [and therefore had not considered the possibility that his tennis partner was the legendary pianist]! Once I had determined that was, indeed, the Lou Hooper of the Ajax sessions, I called Carl [Kendziora of the *Record Research* team] in New York to let him know of this wonderful discovery!" Kidd, "Listening with Louis," 17.

2
Documents

A "Over the Sea to My Soldier" (1918)

Over the sea to my soldier
My that's ever
Longingly roam over the sea
The sea with a greeting
That bears him a blessing from home
Over the sea with a message
Hope rendered deeper by prayer
That safely back home
God will bring him as well as bring victory
There that safely back home
God will bring him as well as bring victory

Louis Hooper
1918 (In France during the First World War)

Source: LAC, Hooper Fonds, Vol. 10, No. 2.

B Constitution of the Hooper Southern Singers
of Canada (1935)

Status
An institution comprising an unlimited membership of male and female
singers. It shall be artistic and educational; non-partisan and non-sectarian
and for the entertainment, edification, and self-expression of all the people.

Purpose
To foster music generally and to encourage and maintain a knowledge and
the tradition of American folk-music. To encourage and develop individual
talent in the direction of a higher standard of vocational activity. To assist aspiring musicians to artistic careers as specialists in their field of endeavor.

Representation
It shall have as its representative, primarily a singing group not to exceed eight
members, male. It shall develop and maintain also a mixed chorus of male
and female voices, and of unlimited membership. It shall include professional
groups of smaller number to supply the theatrical and purely professional
demand, etc.

Program
To present annually or semi-annually as decided, a representative musical
work or group of compositions by Negro composers. To conduct, at convenient intervals, programs of an educational and historic nature.

Governing Board
Its Governing Board shall consist of:

1 (Pres. & Dir.) This Office to be filled by one member or singly
  by two members
2 Vice-president
3 Secretary
4 Treasurer – Asst Treas

5 Bus. Manager
6 Librarian

A mixed chorus is now being formed, their first public demonstration to be a song festival. This chorus is made up of the membership of two parishes, primarily, but is open to any person possessing a voice and a desire to work. Its membership is purely voluntary. It is hoped such a chorus may remain a permanent unit.

Louis S. Hooper
Mus. Bac. Pres. & Dir. of
The Hooper Southern Singers of Canada

31 October 1935

Source: LAC, Hooper Fonds, Vol. 1, No. 13.

C Letter to the *Free Lance* (1935)

It is with a combined feeling of pleasure and privilege that I today congratulate the *Free Lance*, Canada's leading Negro weekly, upon the occasion of your first anniversary. This feeling is both personal and on behalf of The Hooper Southern Singers of Canada.

True our efforts please some and displease others, but if our purpose be right, we carry on finally to receive, with friendliness, the plaudits of those who would once be our enemies.

May your success be even more convincing with the coming years.

Louis S. Hooper
June 1935

Source: LAC, Hooper Fonds, Vol. 1, No. 13.

D   First Anniversary Meeting of the Hooper Southern Singers
of Canada (1936)

Read before the first anniversary observance meeting of The Hooper Southern Singers of Canada held at the residence of Mr John H. Madison, 1309 Tor-
rance Street, Montreal.

To the members and friends of The Hooper Southern Singers of Canada I
wish to extend good wishes on this, the eve of the anniversary of our organization and I wish to pass on to you this brief record of the activities of the
Hooper Southern Singers during the year of 1935.

On Wednesday, 16 January 1935, a group of eight gentlemen met and organized themselves into the group now bearing the name of The Hooper Southern Singers of Canada with the following members elected to the various
offices: Mr Hooper (Pres. & Dir.), Mr Harris (V. Pres.), Mr Phillips (Secretary),
Mr Trott (Treas.), Mr Madison (Bus.Man.), Mr Garneau (Librarian).

Rehearsals proceeded at regular intervals until a degree of proficiency was
reached sufficient to warrant our first public appearance, this taking place at
Union United Church – Delisle Street, five members making the appearance.
Engagements followed rapidly including appearances at Emmanuel, Erskine,
and St James churches; The Forum, Windsor Hotel, three broadcasts over
local stations and during which time we presented the first of a series of public concerts which are intended to be an annual event. Several benefit concerts
have been among this group of appearances as well as concerts in several of
the public schools and high schools of the suburbs, and MacDonald College
at St Anne's.

Many of these concerts came to our records after business contact had been
made with Mr Robin MacKay who now serves the group in the capacity of
business agent, operating in a thoroughly energetic manner.

Through many and varied phases of sacrifice and performance we come
down to this anniversary, having closed our most recent engagement on 10
January 1936 at St Lambert High School. We now stand upon the proverbial
doorstep of added success with the advent of the New Year and a new phase
of activity becoming to us, that of a possible road tour.

These brief remarks may and could only serve simply to give a vague idea
of the activities of The Hooper Southern Singers of Canada and are in no

way detailed. However in closing I wish to pay a tribute to the earnest endeavor and co-operation of the members individually and as a group; to express my appreciation to you for the honor which you have conferred upon me; that of serving you as your president and chief-representative by a unanimous vote of consent and have tried and shall continue to strive to serve you and the public which we do profess to edify, in the most intelligent and honest manner. And as I close may I ask you to turn with me to one whose prayers, good wishes, and earnest efforts have followed, encouraged, and helped us all along the way. I speak of Mrs John Madison, her daughter, and Miss Eileen Hogan. As I close and leave you my good wishes I ask for a rising vote of respect, appreciation and best wishes for them, from The Hooper Southern Singers in a body. I thank you.

Louis Hooper
15 January 1936

Source: LAC, Hooper Fonds, Vol. 1, No. 13.

E *The Canadians Entertain* (1941)

On red light …

ORCHESTRA: Fanfare

GERRY: The No. 1 ARTILLERY HOLDING UNIT IS ON THE AIR!

ORCHESTRA: "Hello Buddies"

GERRY: Yes, it's time again for the Canadians to entertain you – time to send our regular Monday afternoon greetings to all of you, our friends here in the British Isles. As your Christmas week hosts, we're welcoming back your old friends from the No. 1 Canadian Artillery Holding Unit of the Canadian Army Overseas – a group of Canadian soldiers who've been with us on many pleasant previous programs, and who've something extra special for you in the way of songs and music, today. Sergeant Lou Hooper is at the helm, as always

– he's at the piano, as well, and he's all set this moment to give the downbeat to the orchestra for our No. 1 tune today. It's a tasty little morsel especially for you who like a little lick of swing in your music – so step right up, won't you, and help yourself to a portion of our special SOUTHERN FRIED!

ORCHESTRA: "Southern Fried"

GERRY: You who remember the previous broadcasts that these lads of the CAHU have brought you – and I'm sure you ALL do – will remember that they're among the most versatile of our Canadian soldier-performers. For as well as the orchestra you've just heard – there's another one coming up a little later – there are some songs and solos – and there's also a grand Glee Club that you're going to hear from right now. We're going to look a little beyond Christmas for THEIR contribution – look ahead just ten days, in fact, to New Year's Eve, when all of you up there in Scotland will be doing the bulk of your celebrating. And to you, especially, the lads in the Glee Club would like to dedicate their first song – a fine medley of some of your most celebrated airs and melodies. The Glee Club – and their SCOTTISH MEDLEY!

GLEE CLUB: "Scottish Medley"

GERRY: From looking up north to Scotland, we're going to look a long way out west now – out to our own Dominion of Canada. We've got one of those grand old-time songs that you usually expect from us Canadians – and to bring it to you, we've got the Rhythm Ranch Boys, whose music is one of the highlights of the CAHU concert party. This song you're going to hear is a real railroad song – a young fellow called Carl Aspluni is going to sing it – and it's going to give you a little insight into the things that go on – DOWN BY THE RAILROAD TRACK!

RANCH BOYS: "Down by the Railroad Track"

GERRY: Well – we've paid a musical visit north, and west – and now, we're going to head south. This time, the three lads in our trio are going to lead the way – Lou Hooper, Eldon Richie, and George Lalonde – aided and abetted

by the boys in the orchestra – and there's some pleasant South Sea Island at-
mosphere coming right your way. Specifically, it's the trio's own Hawaiian
Medley – including two of your favorite tunes – BLUE HAWAII and ALOHA
OE!

TRIO: "Hawaiian Medley"

GERRY: Now Lou Hooper's really going to rise and shine on his own. On our
previous programs, you've heard Lou in the roles of songster, maestro, harmony singer, choir conductor – just about all there is, in fact – but today, for
the first time, we're going to present him as the fine solo pianist he is. In answer to a number of requests, Lou is going to play one of the most famous of
all classic compositions – the lovely 1ST MOVEMENT FROM BEETHOVEN'S
MOONLIGHT SONATA!

LOU: "Moonlight Sonata"

GERRY: We're going to call for an encore from the Rhythm Ranch Boys next
– and for their second contribution, they're going to break out into some of
those good old fashioned hoedowns that you all like so well and which they
make such a grand job of playing. Here's the place to roll back the rug, and
really have yourself a time – to the tune of SOLDIERS JOY ... and THE
CHICKEN REEL!

RANCH BOYS: "Hoedown Medley"

GERRY: Well, all too soon, that brings us to the place for our goodbye song
from your Canadian hosts of the CAHU – but we've got a finale for you that
I'm sure will leave you with very pleasant memories for a long time to come.
The choir and the orchestra are going to combine to bring you a medley of
familiar and beautiful Christmas music – in an original, special arrangement
that Lou has made – and while we send it with our very best wishes to all of
you, we would especially like to send a greeting to the members of the male
chorus of the Workmens' Club in York, who we hope are listening. Au revoir
to you then – with our CHRISTMAS MEDLEY!

<u>CHOIR & ORCHESTRA</u>: "Xmas Medley"

GERRY: So – friends in the British Isles – we've come to the end of this special Christmas week edition of the *Canadians Entertain*, presented by your old friends of the CAHU … lads from every province of our Dominion. If you have enjoyed their half hour as much as the boys have enjoyed bringing it to you, they'll be amply repaid – and for my part, I promise you we'll have them back with us soon. Now, till next Monday – when we'll have more Canadians and more songs and music to bring you – we'll say "au revoir" as always – with a good luck to you – and we'll add to that – a very, very Merry Christmas from us all!

<u>WHEN YOU'RE SMILING</u>

The Canadians Entertain
No. 1. CAHU
Program for the Forces
Monday, 21 December 1941

Source: LAC, Hooper Fonds, Vol. 1, No. 14.

F "The RCA Band" (1942)

The RCA have a band of eight,
The music they play is really great.
They broadcast and play in London too,
Their leader's a man who is known as "Lou."

The piano he plays with the greatest skill,
And inspires the rest to play with a will.
A verse or two he sometimes sings,
Of "Blues in the Night" and other things.

One saxophone is played by "Cobb,"
He really makes the best of his job.

You'll always see a gleam in his eye,
When pretty girls are passing by.

The clarinet by Jimmy's played,
A place for himself in the band he's made.
A lot of girls he seems to have met,
But his music comes first, so don't forget.

Norman Vail, he slaps the bass,
In the rhythm section he has a place.
He sometimes has to leave his stand,
To go and sing in front of the band.

Wilkie always plays the drum,
He's very fond of a drop of rum.
His drums he treats just like a child,
To tamper with them would make him wild.

"Mac" a trumpet always blows,
Good music from it lightly flows.
As "Little Gate," he's known to most,
He tries his best to fill the post.

Lou's son the other trumpet plays,
He has some very taking ways.
He really likes to jitterbug,
And cuts a very fancy rug.

"Max" can play a fine trombone,
He has a very pleasing tone.
He's one of the hardest to understand,
But he'd always give a helping hand.

Source: Buxton National Historic Site and Museum, Hooper Collection.

G "Montreal, Our Town" (1966)

Most people like to talk about their hometown,
"A very loyal past-time," I might say,
For me to put you in the know about this town of mine,
I feel that I can do it best this way.

It's —
Montreal, our town, we're going to sing about you,
Everywhere we go,
Every Jacques and Jill together showing how we grow and grow.

Concert nights at Place des Arts,
Teens at Paul Sauvé,
And les grands Canadiens — on Hockey Night,
Boy! What a sight!

In —
Montreal, our town; we see your gleaming towers,
Reaching to the blue,
Boulevards aglow with daring nite-life,
Love, and lovers too,
So take a tip from all who know,
It's EN AVANT! Let's Go! EXPO!

In Montreal, our town that everyone loves so.

— MUSICAL INTERLUDE —

In Montreal, our town, above your gleaming towers,
Proud Mount-Royal too,
Ships and men who sail your mighty seaway,
Dear old Main Street true.

So –
All join hands, obey cause we know,
It's EN AVANT! Let's go!! EXPO!!!

In –
Montreal, our town – that everyone loves so.

Words and Music by Louis and Barbara Hooper

Source: LAC, Hooper Fonds, Vol. 4, No. 13.

H *Music through the Years* (1973)

"Music through the Years": A Concert of Original Compositions by Lou Hooper from 1918 to 1970.
Westmount High School Auditorium, 25 May 1973 – 8:00 P.M.

<u>The St Lambert Choral Society:</u>
The St Lambert Choral Society was formed in 1920 "to promote the study, performance, and appreciation of vocal music." The original name of the group was the St Lambert Amateur Operatic Society, and it was renamed in 1971 to reflect the evolution to the performance of major choral works by Handel, Bach, Mozart, Haydn, etc. with the repertoire currently expanded to include Canadian composers such as Gould, Willan, and others.

Mr Denis Whyte is the musical director and members of the Chorus include: Sopranos – Ruth Barker, Veronica Beros, Donna Caruth, Vesta Crooks, Michelle Duquette, Madeline Dyer, Doris Flynn, Nancy Gamble, Jennifer Hooper, Suzanne Jones, Mary Karout, Carmen King, Nickie Lamarre, Audrey Lecours, Helen MacLean, Beth McKnight, Phyllis Newell, Pamela Poulin, Margaret Richards, Cynthia Seath, Iris Terry, and Frances Youngman; Altos – Doreen Beaman, Rene Bedford, Myfanwy Burbidge, Norma Carruthers, Shirley Cohen, Kay Duncan, Marie Hooper, Suzanne Hooper, June McKechnie, Terry Pallant, Jeannine Powers, Diana Thiriar, and Margola Whyte; Tenors – Eber Carruthers, Pierre Duquette, Dick Faller, Fred Glasspole, Harry McGee, and Grant Noakes; Basses – Harold Brazier, Nicholas Burbidge, James

Desmond, Bob Gander, Douglas Hinton, Frank Thorp, and Denis Whyte; Stage Managers – Bob Church and Jack Orchard.

<u>Special thanks and acknowledgments to members of the 1st / 5th Medium Artillery Association:</u>

Brigadier E.R. Suttie	Colonel G.W.F. Johnston
Major L. Withers	Major G.A. Wright
Major A. McLeod	R.S.M. W.F. Glover
R. Almond	D.H. Bennett
J. Filiatreault	J.W. Forrest
B. Goodson	A. Holmes
B. Lidstone	T. Lidstone
J. Madden	E. Mais
A. Nicoll	A.W. Rump

<u>Best wishes, Lou, from your fellow members</u>:
Jim Baldwin, Ches Beachell, Dick Bourcier, Pierre Brosseau, Paul Carroll, Ted Comben, Harry Currie, Mush Davis, Howard Donald, Marv Ekers, Coralie Farlee, Hank Fleischman, Roy Fleischman, Gordy Fleming, Jean Paul Frerault, Bob Fuller, Johnny Holmes, George Humble, Peter Johnston, Jim Kidd, Jerry Lefebvre, Jack Litchfield, Mike Litvack, Courtland MacNeil, Gardner Moore, George Pendleton, Warren Reid, Jacques Richard, Jack Sadler, Gerry Schlaer, Bob Shea, Keith Stowell, Ron Sweetman Olaf Syman, Serge Trepanier, and Jerry Valburn.

<u>LOUIS STANLEY HOOPER (May 18th, 1894)</u>:
Born on a farm in Raleigh Township (now called North Buxton), Ontario, Canada; one of 11 children. Family moved to Ypsilanti, Michigan and Lou began musical career at age 3 singing in a programme of Christmas music at the 1st Baptist Church. At age 17 he enrolled at Detroit Conservatory of Music, graduating in pianoforte in 1916. His studies were interrupted by World War I and after a year in France with the U.S. Army, he returned home to graduate in 1920 with a Bachelor of Music degree.

In 1921, Lou left for New York City and entered the jazz scene with Elmer Snowden and his Band; when Duke Ellington took his place with Elmer, Lou branched out making recordings by the dozens with various groups and artists such as Bubber Miley, Louis Metcalf, Elmer, Bob Fuller, Johnny Dunn, Ethel Waters, Ma Rainey, and played dozens of stage shows with the likes of the immortal Bessie Smith, among others.

Louis returned to Toronto, Canada, in 1932 and by 1933 he had made his permanent home in Montreal where he now resides. Enlisting in the Royal Canadian Artillery in 1939, the next 6 years saw Lou in charge of Canadian concert parties, seeing action in the U.K., Italy, and the other European theatres of World War II.

As of today, Lou is a life-member of Local #406 American Federation of Musicians (U.S. & Canadian), still active professionally, and a member of the Montreal Vintage Music Society.

Throughout his career, Lou has written and conducted many of his own compositions for voices, piano, and orchestras; he has taught music and piano specifically, even teaching classics on the faculty of the Martin-Smith Music School in New York's Harlem, where he met and accompanied the great American singer, Paul Robeson.

Jazz historians throughout the world were overjoyed when Lou was "rediscovered" living in Montreal back in 1962; he has been interviewed and recorded many times since then and Lou's amazing memory for detail has proven invaluable to the historians/collectors of his fellow-members of the Montreal Vintage Music Society. On August 17th 1973, the International Association of Jazz Record Collectors' annual convention will be held at the Berkeley Hotel in Montreal, and both Lou and Elmer will be honoured guests of the 700-member world-wide organization, reminiscing and re-creating some of their recorded tunes of the '20s.

On May 25th (tonight), one week after Lou's 79th birthday, the Benny Farm Tenants' Association together with Lou's buddies of the 1st /5th Medium Artillery Association are sponsoring the concert of Lou's compositions from 1918 to 1970, called "Music through the Years," and conducted by Lou, himself. The net proceeds of the performance are for the Quebec Division of the Canadian Paraplegic Association.

<u>Patrons:</u>

The Honourable and Mrs Warren Allmand   Mr James Bellin
Mr and Mrs Nathan A. Cayne   Mr and Mrs K.W. Clark
Mr and Mrs H. Fleischman   Mr and Mrs L. Hooper, Jr
Mr and Mrs P. Hooper   Mr and Mrs P.K. Johnston
Colonel and Mrs G.W.F. Johnston   Mr and Mrs James Kidd
Mr Guy Lacoste   Mr John P. Parker
The Honorable and Mrs William Tetley   Mr and Mrs J.P. Sadler

<u>PROGRAMME:</u>
O CANADA!
 1 PROLOGUE (Recitative & Aria) "He That Hath My Commandments"
   (1918)
   Roger Doucet, Tenor
 2 INTRODUCTION "Grace Be to You" (1920)
   St Lambert Choral Society with Solo for Tenor
 3 ORATORIO "RUTH" (1920)
   For Chorus and Soloists
   Narrator – Edgar Charlebois, Baritone
   Naomi – Thelma Battey, Soprano
   Ruth – Hasmig Injijikian, Mezzo-Soprano
   Boaz – Roger Doucet, Tenor
   Orpah – Helen MacLean, Soprano
   Musical Director – Louis S. Hooper, Mus. Bac.
   Choral Director – Denis Whyte
INTERMISSION
 4 WANDERLUST (For Woodwinds & Strings) Dance Interpretation
   (1921)
   With Paula Layne and Ricky Keens-Douglas
 5 THREE SONGS FOR SOPRANO
   With Margo MacKinnon
 i) "Over the Sea to My Soldier" (1919)
 ii) "Ballad for a Grand-Daughter" (1969)
 iii) "Address to the Ocean" – Text by Barry Cromwell (1970)

  6 THE CONGO - Poem by Vachel Lindsay (1947)
    Reader: Oscar Paris
    With Orchestral Accompaniment
  i) Their Basic Savagery
 ii) Their Irrepressible High Spirits
iii) The Hope of Their Religion
  7 A BIT OF NOSTALGIA (1918–1960)
    Lou & Small Group
  8 "GOIN' TO SEE MY BABY TO-NITE" (1960)
    Ricky Keen-Douglas
    Song with Jazz-Group Accompaniment
  9 FINALE – "Say Hello" (1959)
    The Daughters Four (Barbara, Jennifer, Marie, and Suzanne) with
    Jazz-Group, Orchestra, and the Entire Ensemble

Master of Ceremonies – Jim Kidd
Production under the direction of Louis S. Hooper

<u>THE STORY OF RUTH:</u>
In the days when the Judges ruled in Bethlehem-Judah, when a great famine had fallen upon the land, a certain man named Elime-lech with his wife Naomi and their two sons, left Judah. Journeying to the country of Moab they remained there, where Elime-lech later died; their two sons had married, the names of their wives being Orpah and Ruth. During their ten-year so-journ in the land of Moab the two sons died; then it was that Naomi and her two daughters-in-law left the country to return to Judah. And Naomi urged them to return each to her mother's house; but Ruth refused, saying "Entreat me not to leave thee – thy people shall be my people and thy God my God." Orpah left them and Ruth and Naomi went on their way to Bethlehem and it was the time of harvest.

Here Ruth learned about a kinsman of Naomi's husband, named Boaz, a wealthy agriculturist and with whom she found favour. As was the custom in Israel, Boaz bought the land previously owned by Elime-lech and the deceased husbands of Ruth and Orpah; and the people and Elders were witnesses and they said, "The Lord make this woman – like Rachel and like Leah; and make you famous in Bethlehem." So Boaz took Ruth for his wife and in God's time she conceived and bore a son who was named Obed, the father of Jesse; the father of David; and Naomi was left not without a blood kinsman.

Source: LAC, Hooper Fonds, Vol. 1, Nos. 4–5.

I Concert Programs

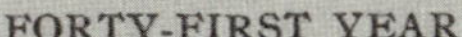

Program 1 *Opposite*

Masters of the Vaudeville Stage program, "under the careful manage-
ment of the Hooper Brothers," at the Good Samaritan Hall in
Ypsilanti, Michigan (1907). Buxton National Historic Site and
Museum, Hooper Collection.

Program 2 *Above*

Program for the Detroit Conservatory of Music's weekly concert series
in Detroit, Michigan (1915). LAC, Hooper Fonds, Vol. 1, Nos. 4–5.

Program 3
Copley Plaza Hotel concert program with Paul Robeson (1924).
Schomburg Center for Research in Black Culture, The Paul Robeson
Collection, MG170 3/2.

Program 4
Standard program for the Hooper Southern Singers of Canada's performances in Montreal, Quebec (1935–36). LAC, Hooper Fonds, Vol. 1, Nos. 4–5.

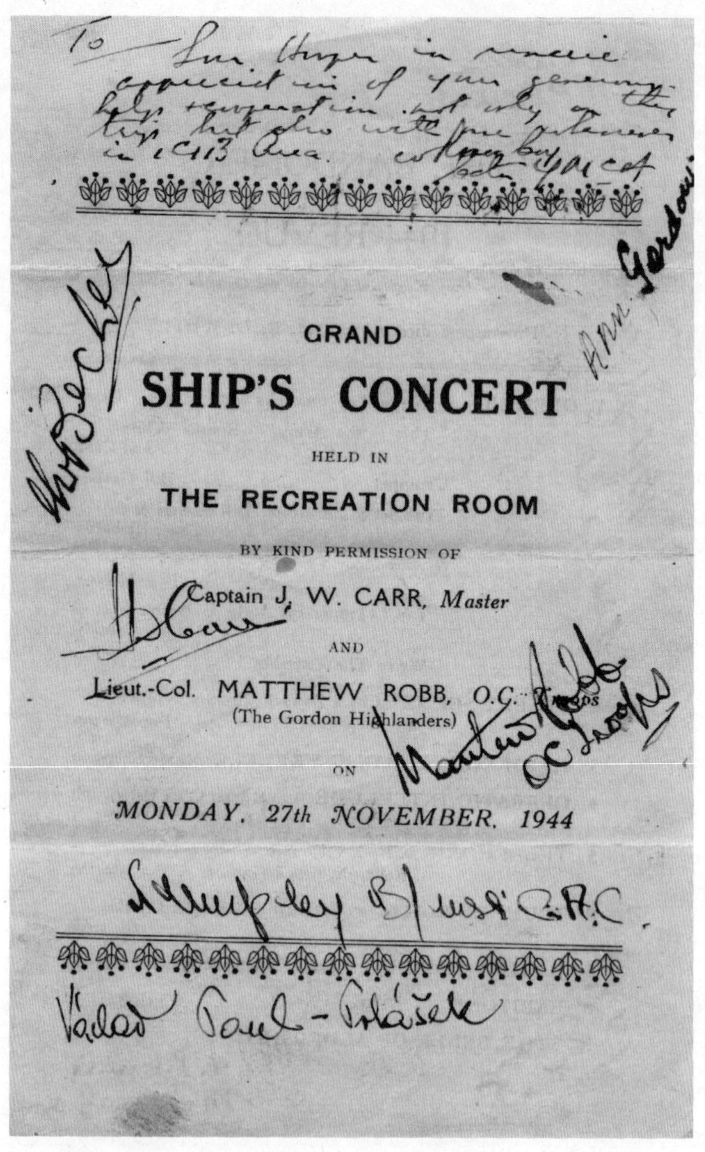

Program 5
Signed and annotated program for the Grand Ship's concert
at sea (1944). Buxton National Historic Site and Museum,
Hooper Collection.

The

Negro Theatre Guild

presents

"EMPEROR JONES"

by EUGENE O'NEILL

CURTAIN RISES 8.40 P.M.

AT M.R.T. - 1550 GUY STREET

APRIL 9 to 17 - excluding Sunday

Program 6

Program for *Emperor Jones* by the Negro Theatre Guild with Lou Hooper in Montreal, Quebec (1948). LAC, Hooper Fonds, Vol. 1, Nos. 4–5.

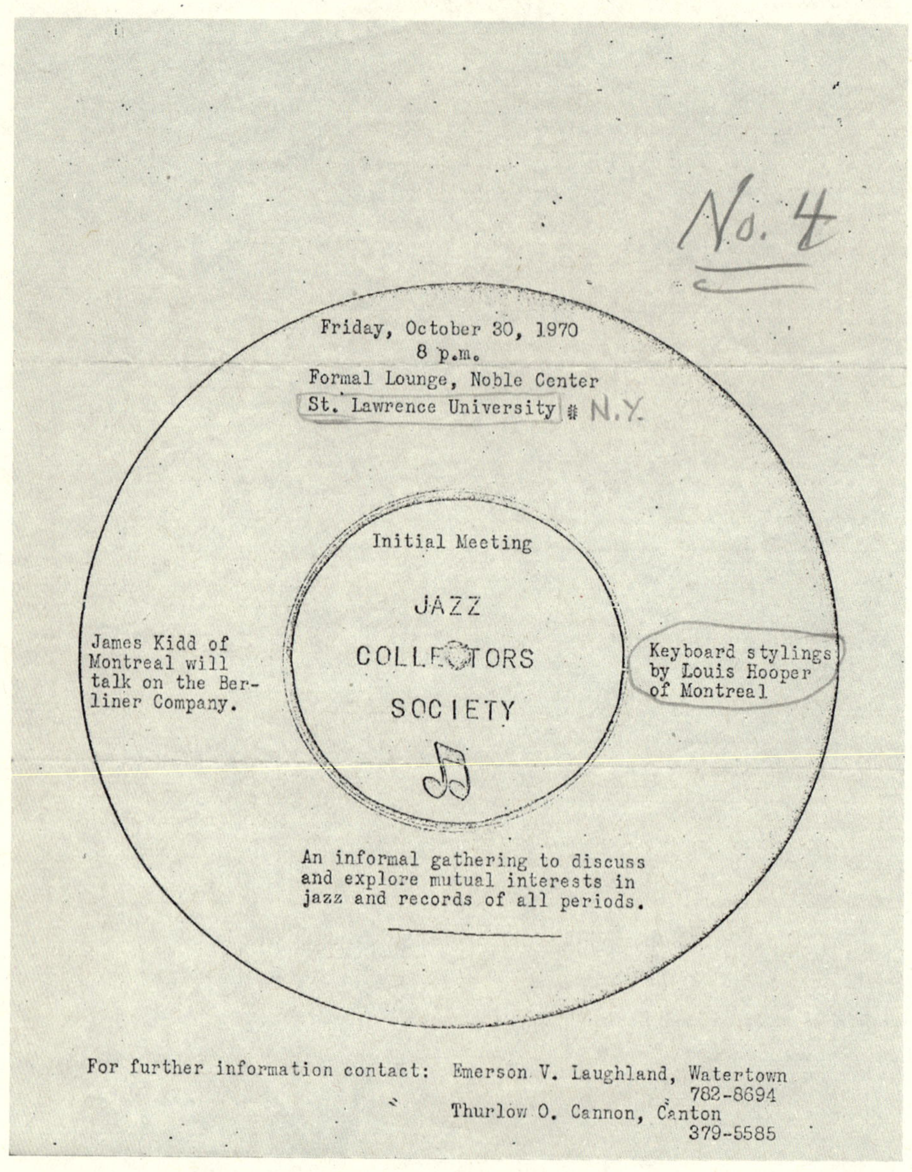

Program 7

Initial Meeting of the Jazz Collectors Society at St Lawrence University in New York City (1970). LAC, Hooper Fonds, Vol. 1, Nos. 4–5.

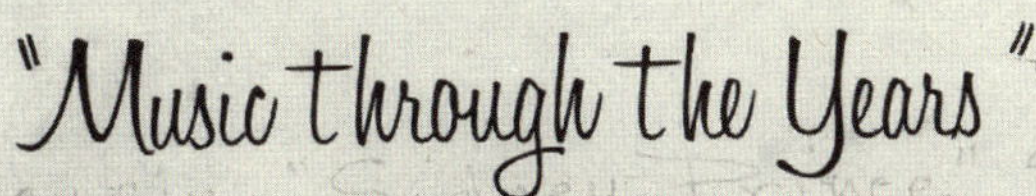

Program 8
Program for *Music through the Years* presented in Montreal, Quebec
(1973). Buxton National Historic Site and Museum, Hooper Collection.

Program 9

Program for a performance of *The Congo* in Charlottetown, Prince Edward Island (1976). Buxton National Historic Site and Museum, Hooper Collection.

Co-Editors' Note

Lou Hooper clearly intended to continue the chronicle of his life beyond 1953. For reasons that we may never know, he unfortunately did not get the chance to – or simply could not – bring *That Happy Road* to completion; hence the autobiography's abrupt ending. However unfortunate it is to not have Hooper guide us through the remaining stages of his career, the closing paragraphs of his autobiography open possibilities for us to continue the conversation, adding our own words to his story and inviting reflections on his life, music, teachings, and movements across spaces. It also allows us to explore his participation in the multiple communities of which he was a part.

Hooper's archives and autobiography lend themselves to be examined from a rich variety of perspectives, as evidenced by the contributions in the next section. The five authors – Sunita Nigam, Jason Wilson, Arshad Suliman Desai, Kristen Young, and Julie Richard – come from diverse disciplinary backgrounds: from history to archiving, literature, music, and community education. The topics they write about reflect the multiple perspectives that can be used to examine the textual, iconographic, and sonic records that Hooper left behind. Their chapters deal with questions (and the politics) of narration, archiving, curation, activism, community making, and musicking. This diversity of voices, or rather fingerprints (to borrow from Eric Ketelaar), suggests ways of engaging with Hooper's story and his cherished legacy.

The broader "Hooper Archive," from which the autobiography as well as the various documents and photographs reproduced in this book come, consists of different repositories and institutions, each with varied mandates and publics. Like us, our contributors are based in Canada, and they write primarily from a Canadian perspective, using as a starting point the particular moment and place that saw Hooper enter the limelight again and put pen to paper to tell his story, in his own words. That said, we also call attention to the importance of cross-border and transnational movements in Hooper's life and hope that the following chapters will inspire others to engage with Hooper's archival materials from – and through – different geographical or thematic lenses. Like *That Happy Road*, the "Hooper Archive" remains open-ended, extending into the world and towards the future.

Figure 19
Lou Hooper listening to one of the Historical Records reissues of his work, possibly the label's volume 14, *Rare and Hot! 1923–1926: Female Vocals with Accompaniment.* Courtesy of Adam Barken.

3

Reading Lou Hooper's Autobiography as an Ecobiography

SUNITA NIGAM

With the publication of Lou Hooper's autobiography, *That Happy Road*, for the first time in this edited collection, questions arise about how it should be read, and what some of its meanings might be for audiences today. As a piece of Black life writing that recounts the life and career of a prodigious jazz musician of mixed African American, Cree, and European ancestry who lived and worked on either side of the Canada–US border, *That Happy Road* expands the archive of Black self-representation in the Americas. Hooper's autobiography also includes first-hand accounts of serving in both World Wars, of living in New York at the height of the Harlem Renaissance in the 1920s, and of moving to Montreal at the peak of its prohibition-era nightlife scene in the 1930s. As such, Hooper's manuscript contributes to archives of urban scenes in the early twentieth century and of Black war writing.

While *That Happy Road* can be illuminated using a range of interpretive strategies, this chapter reads Hooper's manuscript through the lens of the ecobiography. Ecobiographies chronicle the lives of human subjects as they interact and develop with their environments, detailing how a subject's environmental surroundings shape her sense of self. Ecobiographies ask, "Where does a myth of self attach to geographic location?"[1] As Peter Perreten writes, autobiography is less a genre than "a class of landscape/life writing where the two elements work together to form a richly textured, nuanced text."[2] In *That Happy Road*, Hooper presents his life as a series of linear episodes shaped by the places in which he lived during different periods in his life. In this chapter,

I examine Hooper's life, as it is presented in his autobiography and reflected in his thesis for his bachelor of music at the Detroit Conservatory of Music, as a series of personal processes that were influenced by his environments. Acknowledging the importance of the war in Hooper's autobiography, but leaving out an analysis of these sections because of how little they focus on the relationship between geography and self, this chapter has six parts: (I) Understanding: Ypsilanti; (II) Critiquing: Detroit; (III) Awakening: Harlem; (IV) Flourishing: Montreal; (V) Restoring: Chambly; and (VI) Settling: Montreal and Sainte-Agathe-des-Monts.

I. Understanding: Ypsilanti

In the opening scene of *That Happy Road*, the reader is presented with an image of an extremely bright, sensitive, and mischievous young Lou of prodigious musical talent, who is nevertheless most concerned with more ordinary childhood things like Christmas gifts and cherished toys. Hooper recounts a scene from when he was three years old, and a friend broke his Christmas gift of a small air pistol with a rubber-tipped ramrod. As Hooper relates, he was very angry and began screaming at his friend. "That black n***** broke my gun," was one of the things the young Lou screamed. Here, Hooper explains how the n-word was used differently by Black and white people at the time and how he meant to convey the scorn of the word as it was used by white people.

While Hooper portrays a largely happy upbringing in which he was surrounded by the simple pleasures of nature, the church, and family, he also describes a world in which danger was never far off. In the opening section of *That Happy Road*, Hooper lingers over scenes of getting stung by wasps, falling through a frozen river, and his sister Sade nearly plummeting to her death over the ledge of a cliff overlooking the Huron River on a trip to gather wild phlox. In another passage, Hooper recounts how at twelve he went out to dine with the family of a white friend, but ended up having to eat in the restaurant's kitchen. With these descriptions of his early life in Ypsilanti, Hooper does something interesting with the pastoral mode of writing, or a mode of writing that is concerned with the countryside, and which idealizes the natural world as a place of innocence and harmony. Instead of a world of perfect innocence and harmony, Hooper portrays a world that is much more complex. While his childhood may have been largely happy and full of music, it also contained frequent revelations about the dangers of the world, both natural and social. Even in the most bucolic, relatively integrated setting of Ypsilanti, the many forms of racist violence were not lost on Hooper. The natural world he describes may be a place of simple pleasures, but it is also full of danger.

This opening section, full of emotion in itself, but expunged calmly by the stoic narrative voice of Hooper, sets the tone of *That Happy Road* as a whole. As an autobiographer, Hooper takes a nostalgic posture towards his past. But the happy, often bucolic scenes from his childhood in Ypsilanti are markedly tinged with stings of violence and loss. And indeed, at the onset of *That Happy Road*, the reader is given descriptions of idyllic church picnics, possum dinners, choir practices, camping trips, mischievous moonlit fruit-thieving, fishing, and flowering excursions, all of which Hooper enjoyed with his siblings. He describes his childhood as "happy and full of music," and portrays a family life enriched by close relationships with his older siblings and his mother. He remembers Ypsilanti at that time as a relatively racially integrated community in which he was able to enjoy social interactions across racial lines. Notably, the social and artistic world of his predominantly white choir, where he excelled as a soloist, allowed him to experience a sense of belonging and accomplishment. But this sense of belonging was never total or perfect. While Hooper reflects that he "spent an integrated life, at school and socially to a great degree" growing up in Ypsilanti, he also notes that he grew up "knowing and feeling the ever-present discrimination."[3] The reader will note that the happiness of Hooper's childhood as described in his autobiography is regularly qualified by incidents and exceptions.

In *That Happy Road*, Ypsilanti figures as an environment in which Hooper is able to develop a sense of belonging in nature, music, and family. At the same time, he gains an understanding of some of the pain and danger of life. In his narrative, the Ypsilanti of his youth emerges less as a place of childhood innocence, than as a place of childhood understanding.

II. Critiquing: Detroit

If Hooper's upbringing in Ypsilanti fostered an understanding of the racial discrimination that qualified Black life in the United States, his time in Detroit, during which he studied at the Detroit Conservatory of Music and played in Black orchestras (including in the Hooper Brothers' Orchestra with two of his brothers), served as an incubator for the development of his racial critique.[4] Examples of Black urbanism, or writing that reflects on and exposes how race works in given locales, Hooper's sections on Detroit, Harlem, and Montreal read as reflections on the relationships between race and the city. Detroit, in particular, figures in Hooper's autobiography as a place that allowed him to develop his critical spirit and, specifically, what Hooper refers to as "colour consciousness," or a critical consciousness about race and racism. In this section, the mode of writing shifts from the pastoral to the increasingly sociological.

Between his experiences of discrimination in the city at the time, his participation in the popular music and dance scene, and his training in classical music at the conservatory, Hooper reflected increasingly on the relationships between music, race, and urban and national belonging. Hooper describes one incident in the nearby town of Mount Clemens in which his band had to seek out the city's lone Black hotel in the middle of the night after they were kicked out of the hotel in which they were registered when the staff saw them in person.[5] Hooper writes that in Detroit he "noted more colour consciousness: here [he] had learned and played St Louis and Memphis Blues; heard Negro Spirituals etc."[6] Hooper's own developing "colour consciousness," as he calls it, is reflected in his bachelor of music thesis, which he titled "The Afro-American Folk-Song: Its Origin and Evolution," and was subsequently published in three parts by *The Negro Musician* magazine in 1920. This remarkable piece of musical criticism (and an exciting specimen of critical race theory) was in conversation with other vital works dealing with race and music at the time. Hooper uses his thesis to focus on the nature and value of African American folk music which, he notes, has for too long remained in the background of serious musical discussions. In particular, Hooper critiques the argument of a Dr Richard Wallaschek that Black folk music was a primitive form of music that was merely aping European compositions. With his thesis, he rebukes arguments that would question the "Americanness" of Black music, staking a place for the African American song in the very heart of the American musical canon. Most strongly, he argues that the slave song is the "purest and most original example of American folk-music."[7] In his autoethnography, *The Souls of Black Folk*, W.E.B. Du Bois (an eventual acquaintance of Hooper) describes the doubleness of the experience of being a Black man in post-slavery America:

> One ever feels his two-ness, – an American, a Negro; two souls, two thoughts, two unreconciled strivings; two warring ideals in one dark body, whose dogged strength alone keeps it from being torn asunder.
>
> The history of the American Negro is the history of this strife – this longing to attain self-conscious manhood, to merge his double self into a better and truer self. In this merging he wishes neither of the older selves to be lost.[8]

In Hooper's thesis, the reader witnesses a negotiation of this "two-ness," of Americanness and Blackness, that Du Bois describes. Interestingly though, Hooper's analysis presents this "two-ness," not as warring forces confined within the same body. Instead, he arrives at a different critical resolution that positions Blackness in the centre of Americanness. Hooper proposes a path towards a form of reconciliation through the acknowledgment of the centrality of Blackness to Americanness. The thesis is central to the development of Hooper's critical racial imagination during his time living, thinking, and playing in Detroit. It was in Detroit that he first articulated a framework that allowed him to reconcile his Blackness and his Americanness as he connected the musical theory he was reading in school with his lived experiences as a Black musician in Detroit.

Notably, in 1928 when he was back in Detroit, Hooper was widowed when he lost his wife one winter to a serious case of pneumonia. In keeping with the stoic tone that he employs throughout his writing, Hooper mentions the incident only briefly. To be sure, the reader of his autobiography will note that, the greater the incident of loss, pain, or violence, the smaller mention it tends to receive in the narrative. Other incidents include the death of Hooper's father before he was born, the death of his brother Fred during the Second World War, the enslavement of his grandmothers, and the loss of friends. These incidents exist more as haunting absences, passing mentions, or narrative interruptions, than as tangible scenes in the narrative. They are nevertheless there, quietly undercutting the title *That Happy Road* and reminding the reader that there is much that the narrative leaves out. To say much more about the effect of the passing of Cecilia on Hooper would be speculation.

III. Awakening: Harlem

If Ypsilanti was the place in which Hooper first developed an understanding of the pervasiveness of racial discrimination, and Detroit was the place in which he first synthesized a critical racial critique, it was in New York that he experienced a new kind of racial awakening.[9] His time there coincided with the height of the Harlem Renaissance, that era of Black intellectual and cultural revival and political activism that energized the city throughout the 1920s and 1930s. This period in Hooper's life would be profoundly affected by the cultural awakening happening in Harlem at the time. While Detroit had been more "colour conscious" than Ypsilanti, Harlem, Hooper writes, "displayed far greater awareness – a 'doing something about it' attitude," which we might take to mean an attitude of hopeful and energetic participation in enacting socio-political transformation.[10] Hooper's section on Harlem occurs in a writerly mode that I would like to call "renaissance writing." By renaissance writing, I intend a nostalgic mode of writing about a period of cultural renaissance that embodies something of the exuberance and excitement of the period itself. Less sociological than celebratory, renaissance writing might be understood as an energetic mode of writing that citationally and affectively revives the energy of the period it describes. In this way, renaissance writing itself enacts a kind of affective revival. In this section of *That Happy Road*, the revival of the energy of the Harlem Renaissance occurs, for example, through the proliferation of exclamation points and highly descriptive if not hyperbolic adjectives.

Following his move to New York, Hooper recounts that he "gradually absorbed the Harlem of the twenties," which was "all so beautifully 99 per cent Negro."[11] As the Harlem of the twenties impressed upon Hooper, he fed his investigative spirit by researching the sources of Black cultural productions. He describes his time there as a new beginning in which he became increasingly attuned to Black history and culture that was made by and for Black folks. Hooper offers here a window into the effervescent intellectual, political, and creative energy that characterized Black Harlem in the early twentieth century. During his time there, Hooper moved in the same circles as Black intellectuals and artists like W.E.B. Du Bois and Claude McKay, played with music legends such as Paul Robeson and Louis Metcalf, toured American and Canadian cities as a musician, and taught piano to young Black pupils. Echoing other writers and thinkers, Hooper describes Harlem in terms of a racial "awakening," in which Black people were becoming increasingly alive to their situation in the United States and to their capacity to "do something about it." The Harlem Renaissance was a precursor to the "Black Is Beautiful" movement of the 1960s. Part of the cultural awakening that enlivened Harlem was a new appreciation of the beauty and richness of Black culture and life.

In his recollections about New York, Hooper mentions, if only briefly, two so-called race riots that occurred during his time there as well as a parade led by Marcus Garvey for his United Negro Improvement Association (UNIA). Hooper relates that he and many of his friends "laughed at" Garvey's efforts but he now wonders, in retrospect, if the "'vision' for blacks" championed by the founder of the UNIA "was not without some merit."[12] To be sure, Hooper enjoyed a more comfortable life than many of his Black counterparts in New York in the 1920s. As he notes, unlike the poorer Black people and South Americans who were concentrated in San Juan Hill, he and his family were protected from the harsher realities of being Black in the city. As Hooper had come from the relatively integrated town of Ypsilanti and had received a formal education at the Detroit Conservatory of Music, his perspective on Black experiences would have diverged from those of many of his urban Black counterparts.

Nevertheless, Hooper's description of the cultural awakening he experienced during his years in Harlem is a transitional moment in *That Happy Road*. It provides insight into the cultural movements that shaped his own relationships to Black culture, history, and activism as a young adult and performer. With his description of what he calls "the fantastic, flamboyant, beautiful, artistic Harlem," Hooper revives on the page for his reader some of the enthusiasm and energy of the Harlem Renaissance itself, giving the reader a sense of what this period might have felt like.

IV. Flourishing: Montreal

In 1933, Hooper moved with his son to the bilingual Canadian metropolis of Montreal. This was the peak of the city's prohibition-era nightlife scene, animated by jazz, burlesque, variety shows, and a popular red light district. At this point in the city's history, Montreal was part of the Eastern touring circuit of performers, including musicians, burlesquers, minstrels, and variety act performers, which included New York, Philadelphia, Detroit, Chicago, Baltimore, Pittsburgh, Boston, and Toronto.[13] From the 1920s to the 1950s, top musicians from New York and Chicago regularly flowed into Montreal's jazz scene. It featured many Black performers and audiences, with cabarets on Sainte-Catherine West being patronized by white audiences and featuring white performers, and the clubs in the Saint-Antoine neighbourhood, located to the south below the railway tracks, being primarily Black, but with increasingly mixed audiences. "By the 1940s," Joanna Mansbridge explains, these "clubs were racially integrated, with ... Café St Michel leading the way with a fully integrated jazz band directed by Louis Metcalf."[14] While Montreal during the interwar period still had a number of all-white clubs, and while the AFM remained segregated until the Second World War, Montreal's nightlife scene was, to a large degree, a space of racial and linguistic mixing organized around entertainment and the pursuit of social pleasures. This moment of cultural flourishing coincided with a flourishing in Hooper's own career. Reading like a curriculum vitae of one of the most lively and accomplished episodes in his life, this section on Montreal offers the reader a portrait of what the work life of a Black jazz musician in Quebec's metropolis during the 1930s might have looked like. Perhaps even more remarkable is the way in which Hooper's autobiography as a whole offers a portrait of a Black jazz musician on the Eastern touring circuit more broadly, as it offers an account of his time and career in Detroit, New York, Montreal, and (briefly) Toronto.

Hooper describes Montreal at this time as a wide-open city with buzzing nightlife, a flourishing red-light district, daily burlesque and neo-burlesque shows, company stage plays and comedies, and booze unlimited. During this era, Hooper played regularly, as part of Myron Sutton's Canadian Ambassadors (possibly the first organized Black jazz band in Canada) at venues like Connie's Inn and the Hollywood Club. He also played gigs at The Standard Club (a beloved after-hours spot later renamed the Terminal Club in the Saint-Antoine and de la Montagne Street area, where most of the Black clubs were concentrated), The Paramount Grill, and the Cabarets Chez Maurice and El Morocco (a white-only joint). Other performers with whom Hooper played included Billie Holiday, Buster Hardin, the baritone George Dewey, Marcia Marquez, Myra Johnson, Ralph Brow, and Babe Wallace, who later had a leading role in the film *Stormy Weather* with Bojangles and Lena Horne.

As in Harlem, Detroit, and Ypsilanti, Hooper found himself at the centre of the social and musical life of the city. Notably, during this period, he began giving piano lessons to a young Oscar Peterson, who would go on to become one of the great jazz legends. The Montreal section of *That Happy Road* presents a lively, joyous, and exciting time in Hooper's life and career in which he and Montreal's nightlife scene symbiotically energized one another.

V. Restoring: Chambly

In the summer of 1937, Mario Cummano, a classically trained Cuban musician, invited Hooper to join his five-man band for a summer contract at the Chambly Hotel, located in Chambly, a small town connected to the five Great Lakes and the Atlantic Ocean via the St Lawrence River. Hooper describes the Chambly Hotel as "a rather attractive building, spacious and sprawling over a fairly wide area; its inviting verandahs ran nearly all the way around it at two separate levels and were ideal for reading in the late afternoon or even for letter writing."[15] Cummano's band included his friend, the trombonist Frank Johnson, a vocalist named Eddie, and a nineteen-year-old sax player named Leo Alarie, a francophone who spoke little English at the time. That summer, the five men stayed at the Chambly Hotel and, when they were not playing to crowds of dancers, joined locals in tennis matches, baseball games, swimming practices, and canoeing. Hooper recounts that there were many excellent swimmers in Chambly, some of whom had even qualified for the Canadian National Exhibition swim. Hooper and his bandmates made friends with these young athletes, who invited them as guests to their local tennis club and baseball team. In *That Happy Road*, the summer in Chambly figures as a period of healthful restoration.

Hooper was able to retreat from the rhythms of everyday urban life and to fall into sync with the slower time of summer in a close relationship with his natural surroundings. He describes a season of contemplation and physical wellness. Beyond playing to summering crowds, Hooper's stay in Chambly was marked by reading and letter writing and sports and leisure. As he relates, "I used to swim early in the morning with my 'trainer' rowing and coaching me until I swam nearly the mile across – not exactly an Olympic feat but it did contribute to my general fitness."[16] While Hooper's time in Montreal had been full of late nights and busy schedules, his summer in Chambly was marked by early mornings and lots of time for rest and relaxation.

Hooper found himself immersed in a largely francophone culture, in which the townspeople were very friendly and where he could interest himself in observing the local customs. This was a period of immersion and inclusion in the summer activities and social life of Chambly. In the lifelong friendship that Hooper began building with Alarie, he describes a breaking down of racial prejudice through which his young bandmate came to reverse his views about racial difference. The Chambly of *That Happy Road* is a liminal, even miraculous time-space in which normal social rhythms and norms were reversed, new relationships could be forged, and new spiritual states could be brought about. Perhaps one of the most remarkable images of this section is that of Hooper and his new friends "swimming together in [the Chambly Basin] that spacious body of water," which presents his summer there as an environmental tonic in which he could be reinvigorated through his immersion in the social and natural world of Chambly.[17] With this section we see a return to a pastoral mode of writing that is less complicated by violence and loss than his engagement of this mode at the opening of the autobiography.

VI. Settling: Montreal and Sainte-Agathe-des-Monts

Following the Second World War, during which he met his second wife, Hooper returned to settle in Montreal with his growing family. Finding a home proved to be a feat due to a combination of factors, including the postwar housing shortage and racial discrimination. After a few stays in uncomfortable living quarters, Hooper was able to rent a house and to enrol his children in the Royal Arthur School. During this time, Hooper's musical activities were divided between teaching piano at the Marrazza School of Music and carrying out a radio broadcast at the school. He also played in a quintet, accompanied soloists, and made appearances in dance bands. This final section of the unfinished autobiography marks the beginning of a period of settling into Montreal and family life for Hooper, his wife, and their three children. During this period, Hooper continued to leave the city in the summertime for contracts in rural Quebec. In 1947, he began the first of four summers playing at Wooden Acres, a resort that catered to Montreal's Jewish communities and was located in Sainte-Agathe-des-Monts in the Laurentians region, just north of Montreal. As with Chambly, Hooper describes a summertime life surrounded by natural beauty and full of sport, socializing, and lots of swimming. After Wooden Acres was damaged by a fire in 1950, Hooper began playing with his band at the Hotel Vermont in the same region. It is at this point that his autobiography stops. While Hopper notes that his time at the Hotel Vermont "forms a vital link in [his] story," promising to elaborate upon it in later chapters, he never does.[18] By 1953, he had moved his family permanently to Sainte-Agathe, where they spent the next fifteen years. There, he writes, they had "many experiences, good and otherwise, among kind and unkind people." Their children, he adds, "grew up in an atmosphere of natural beauty, with birds, lovely trees, lakes and mountains, while to [his] wife and [himself], it was indeed, God's country."[19]

It is interesting that Hooper's autobiography ends, as it started, in a pastoral place and mode. By his descriptions, the natural world of Sainte-Agathe must have reminded him of the "God's country" of his childhood in Ypsilanti. And yet, it is clear that the social world of Sainte-Agathe was different from the Ypsilanti in which Hooper grew up. While racial discrimination had not disappeared, and antisemitism and white supremacy were part of the dominant culture of Quebec at the time, Hooper does not describe incidents of racial segregation and experiences of anti-Black racism in this section.[20] Sainte-Agathe was also a primarily francophone place, which meant that the linguistic and cultural fabric of the environment in which Hooper and his wife raised their children was very different from the environment of his youth. While the pastoral descriptions with which Hooper begins his autobiography are punctuated by scenes of danger, violence, and pain, his descriptions of Sainte-Agathe belong to the world of the traditionally pastoral. While *That Happy Road* takes the reader through a winding road and a variety of worlds, it ends in a place of natural simplicity and harmony, in God's country.

The experience of reading Hooper's autobiography is likely to leave the reader with questions, even skepticism about its title. While the road traced throughout the text includes moments of joy and warmth, it is also punctuated by incidents of deep loss and violence. What is the reader, then, to make of Hooper's decision to use *That Happy Road* for the title? This and many other questions remain to be explored as the autobiography is taken up by the new readers it is sure to find following its publication.

NOTES

1   Smith and Watson, *Reading Autobiography*, 249.

2   Perreten, "Eco-Autobiography," 21.

3   Hooper, *That Happy Road*, 59.

4   Soon after his eighteenth birthday, Hooper moved to Detroit to pursue a bachelor's degree at the Detroit Conservatory of Music. Between the ages of fourteen and eighteen, Hooper had moved between Detroit (where he stayed with his older sister Sarah) and Ypsilanti, working odd jobs and practising piano. By sixteen, he had joined the musician's union and began playing in Black orchestras (there was no integration in orchestras at the time). But by eighteen, Hooper decided to resume his studies and move to Detroit full time. During this period, he lived with two of his still unmarried brothers and the three of them played together in their four-man band, the Hooper Brothers' Orchestra. Hooper describes the popularity of dancing schools in Detroit at the time, a scene he knew well as he and his brothers performed there regularly.

5   During his time in Detroit, Hooper married a woman from Ontario named Cecilia Johnson after courting her for two years. He also left the city to serve in France during the First World War from August 1918 to July 1919. Upon returning to Detroit, he enjoyed great popularity with the Hooper Brothers' Orchestra at the Koppin Theatre (where legends like Ma Rainey and Ethel Waters also played) while writing his thesis for his bachelor of music.

6   Hooper, *That Happy Road*, 59.

7   LAC, Hooper Fonds, Vol. 1, No. 6, Hooper, "The Afro-American Folk Song: Its Origin and Evolution," honors thesis, Detroit Conservatory of Music, 1920, 1.

8   Du Bois, *The Souls of Black Folk*, 5.

9   In 1921, Hooper moved with his wife and son, Louis Jr, to Harlem, where they stayed for eight years.

10 Hooper, *That Happy Road*, 59.

11 Ibid., 57.

12 Ibid., 65.

13 For more information about touring circuits (or "wheels"), see Allen, *Horrible Prettiness*.

14 For histories of the burlesque and jazz scenes in Montreal, see Mansbridge, "In Search of a Different History," 7–12.

15 Hooper, *That Happy Road*, 75.

16 Ibid., 77.

17 Ibid.

18 Ibid., 117.

19 Ibid.

20 As noted above, Hooper does mention that his family lived "through many experiences, good and otherwise, among kind and unkind people," but he neither elaborates on nor emphasizes the negative, choosing instead to recall the "atmosphere of natural beauty, with birds, lovely trees, lakes and mountains." Ibid.

4

Brave Sergeant Hooper and His Bandoliers

JASON WILSON

One can sense the mixture of gratitude and pride with which Lou Hooper wrote about his service during the Second World War. With such an impressive pre-war résumé – particularly his education in music that gave him the ability to read, write, and arrange for orchestras large and small – Hooper was able to escape the terror and drudgery of combat and spent much of the war entertaining troops from the relative safety of the stage. Certainly, Hooper and other entertainers within the ranks of Canada's military services were never far from danger, often performing on open-air makeshift stages along the frontlines. There were, however, other far more comfortable venues well behind the lines and also back in England where Hooper and his music-making comrades could ply their trade. Such comfort was not afforded to those men and women who were less musically inclined. Hooper, and others like him, knew this and could be racked with guilt in the knowledge that the battalions they had trained with had suffered tremendous losses in the fight against the Nazis. While he may have at times struggled to reconcile these feelings, Hooper was also filled with pride about his time in Europe: not only had his musicality offered the privilege of avoiding actual combat, it gave him an opportunity of rising to the officer ranks during a time when systemic racism in the army and Canadian society at large afforded few opportunities for men like him. While a return to the pre-war bigotry and xenophobia the pianist had at times experienced was waiting for him back in Quebec, Hooper often found himself as "the man in charge" during the Second World War. It was not, of course, without its trials, but we must nevertheless take our cue from the words of the soldier-entertainer himself. Given the star-studded collaborations and his propinquity to the evolution of jazz itself, he might have been forgiven for brushing past his six years in the Canadian military when his professional career was put on hold. Instead, Hooper devotes over a quarter of his autobiography to this special chapter in his life. In this sense, Hooper clearly saw his wartime experience as something of a triumph. And it was.

There had been various entertainment units operating in the Canadian military right from the outset of the war (including ten staff army bands that were formed in 1940). Yet, a more comprehensive scheme of official touring concert parties was undertaken in 1943 by the entertainment program of the Department of National Defence. Given the significant losses Canada had suffered to this point, and the fact that war's end remained very much in the distant future, the Royal Canadian Air Force Show, the Royal Canadian Navy Show, and the Canadian Army Show (CAS) were called upon to raise the morale of servicemen and women, which they would do from their inception right through to war's end in 1945. These various "concert parties" would carry with them the tradition of Canada's famous Dumbells from that earlier twentieth-century conflagration, honouring the same mandate of keeping the troops smiling.[1]

The entertainers for this new generation of concert parties were taken from within the personnel of Canada's troops already stationed overseas. Importantly, many of these talented Canadians were able to make the jump to the professional ranks following the war. There were, however, some soldiers who had been in the entertainment game long before the war, and Lou "Pops" Hooper was one such entertainer. Hooper had no doubt earned the "Pops" moniker on the strength of his long and impressive pre-war resumé: this Canadian-born musician of African, Cree, and Irish descent, who had worked with Paul Robeson, Ma Rainey, Bessie Smith, Ethel Waters, Rosa Henderson, and Billie Holiday, who had been in the pit bands for Broadway shows such as *Blackbirds of 1928*, and who had taught an eleven-year-old Oscar Peterson, was now poised to write an entirely different sort of chapter in his immensely interesting life.[2]

Early in the war, the morale of Canada's fighting forces on land, in the air, and on the seas was in need of repair. In December 1941, Canadian forces — namely the Royal Rifles of Canada from Quebec City and the Winnipeg

Grenadiers – suffered greatly during the fall of Hong Kong. Three hundred Canadians were killed and an additional 493 were wounded. Many others were placed in prisoner-of-war camps, where they endured starvation, torture, and enforced labour at the hands of the Japanese. As a result, another 272 Canadians would perish.[3] A few months later, the colossal and heartbreaking disaster of Dieppe occurred on 19 August 1942. Of 4,963 Canadians involved in the failed attack, 916 died and another 1,946 were taken prisoner by the Germans.[4] For its part, the Canadian Navy was also dealing with the constant threat of German U-Boats on the Atlantic and, indeed, sometimes in Canadian waters as well! Though the Battle of Britain had largely been decided and the German invasion of England was forever postponed, the war's outcome was still uncertain and there was great urgency within Canadian military circles for morale-raising entertainment.

Hooper had had a dalliance with concert parties in the First World War while serving in General John J. Pershing's American Expeditionary Force. Lou enlisted in the summer of 1918 and received his training first at Camp Custer, Michigan, before moving on to Alexandria, Virginia, and eventually the battlefields of Europe. As a member of an American Engineer Battalion in France, Hooper soon identified several other musicians in his midst.[5] What, in Hooper's mind, had begun as "some vocal-harmonizing" among fellow soldiers quickly morphed into something resembling an official concert party, giving performances in the small French village in which Lou's battalion was stationed and at the YMCA (much like the ones Captain Mert Plunkett had, since 1916, been organizing for soldiers in the Canadian YMCA huts where The Dumbells were born).[6] Yet Hooper would enjoy much more than a dalliance with entertaining soldiers in the next war as a soldier in the Canadian Army.

Not long after the Second World War began, Gunner L.S. Hooper became Battery Trumpeter, enlisting with the 7th Medium Battery in Montreal. Hooper was among those troops that crossed the Atlantic in January 1940 on the RMS *Aquitania*. Perhaps unsurprisingly, Lou, alongside other musicians who were also aboard, played their way across the ocean. The ship arrived in Greenock, Scotland, on 10 February.

Hooper eventually made his way down to the unit's base in Hampshire in the south of England. Thanks to an eye infection that Hooper believed had been caused by the "sun-glare" off of the Atlantic and exacerbated by the "blacked-out, smoke-filled, barrack rooms," he had been held back when his regiment had moved out. When he was released from the hospital, Hooper was sent to the Canadian Artillery Holding Unit (CAHU) in Bordon. This was the first of several fortuitous moves for the musician. Constrained as he had been from joining his regiment in the field, Hooper, with bad eye and good chops, was able to join the CAHU concert party, which had, by this time, already established itself as a premier entertainment party in the Canadian military.

The CAHU concert party was, in Hooper's mind, a "complete show" by theatrical standards. Its host was Gerry Wilmot, a popular war correspondent for the Overseas Unit of the Canadian Broadcasting Corporation (CBC).[7] Lou performed throughout the United Kingdom with the CAHU. This included a special performance for the Canadian Military's top brass at London's Cambridge Theatre. There were also several appearances on the airwaves of the British Broadcasting Corporation (BBC). Several of these short-wave broadcasts were piped back to Canada, including a special Mass on Christmas Eve and a Mother's Day broadcast from the Beaver Club on Sunday, 11 May 1941.

Despite these choices and comfortable gigs, Hooper and his entertaining comrades never needed reminding of how close they were to the actual war. Several entertainers would, for example, return to active duty when needs required. In many cases, these soldiers would serve as stretcher bearers or in other first-aid capacities. Many were killed in action.[8]

There was also the threat from above. Even before his Bandoliers found themselves in the thick of it on the European mainland, the terror of German bombing served as a constant and unpleasant companion. Stationed less than an hour's drive from London, members of the CAHU were well within the Luftwaffe's reach. The Canadian units were victims of at least one particular frightful and, for some, fatal dive-bombing attack.[9]

It was much the same on the seas. The Tin Hats, the first established CAS concert party formed in 1941, knew too well the closeness of the war.[10] Early on 27 July 1944, the SS *Empire Beatrice* was torpedoed by a German E-boat just off the coast of Dover. The ship was carrying the Tin Hats, who were on their way to France to follow those Canadians who had landed in Normandy on D-Day on 6 June. Four members of the concert party were killed and several others were injured but managed to survive in a lifeboat after the ship had been hit.[11] Following this incident, all concert party personnel were trained and equipped with arms and ammunition including the .303 Lee En-field rifle and the Thompson submachine gun.[12]

Meanwhile, the Department of National Defence was ramping up the organization of soldier entertainment. The CAS had, by 1943, absorbed all of the official Canadian concert parties and their personnel.[13] There were five principal Canadian concert parties during the Second World War: the afore-mentioned Tin Hats, the Kit Bags, the Forage Caps, the Haversacks, and the Bandoliers, all of which were composed entirely of active-combatant personnel.[14] While these five parties may represent the CAS's *best remembered* concert parties, there would, by war's end, be over forty CAS concert parties entertaining Canadian troops in various theatres of war.[15] This was a necessary expansion. Prior to the Allied invasion of Sicily, the concert parties could scarcely keep up. Given the over 250,000 Canadian troops in the UK in the months leading up to the operation in Italy, something more muscular in terms of planning and organization was required, and the CAS answered this need comprehensively.[16]

By now, Hooper's particular concert party had been taken over by the Artillery Base Band. Lou would become that concert party's (later known as the Bandoliers) permanent musical director, which included the eight-piece band that Hooper had already been leading. The CAS, however, would be sure that Lou followed a circuitous route before he permanently settled in with the Bandoliers. This meant leaving Bordon and his band of brothers in the Artillery Base Band for the Canadian Army Show headquarters in Aldershot. The move left the pianist feeling melancholic. Adding to this malaise was the fact that Hooper was also moving farther away from his future war bride, Sergeant-Major Alice Margaret Hadwell of the Auxiliary Territorial Service, whom he had met during his time in Bordon.[17]

For now, though, the CAS used the multi-talented Hooper in a variety of ways. Sometimes, Lou would be sent out as a pianist with one concert party, then as a drummer with another, and then again as a vocalist in a "singing-group." During this time, Lou also served for a time as director of the Kit Bags concert party replete with a sixteen-piece band and female impersonators. As director, Hooper conducted the band on-stage and in rehearsal, and also wrote for and sang with six others as part of the show.

With the Kit Bags, Hooper had taken part in the BBC's weekly radio production *Johnny Canuck's Revue*. The show was produced by the CBC's London Office and was popular among Canadians stationed overseas.[18] Hooper had mixed feelings about his short stint with the Kit Bags. While he enjoyed the weekly BBC appearances and the large company of performers he was working with, Lou believed that his leadership was being questioned by forces outside of the show itself. Indeed, Hooper was so agitated by the amusical tensions (quite possibly racially charged, though not concretely stated in the musician's autobiography) that he was prepared to resign his position and take a military demotion. Before this occurred, however, Lou was once again reassigned to the Bandoliers, who were in London preparing to set out for a tour in Italy. Back with the people he "liked even more," Battery Sergeant Major Hooper was – perhaps unknowingly – about to spend the rest of the war with his Bandoliers, chasing the Canadians' march to victory in Europe.

The Allied invasion of Sicily in 1943 went fairly well and as a result the "Long March" had commenced in earnest for the Canadians. While the trek north would, in the end, be successful, the Italian campaign was dreadfully slow moving and Canadians paid a terrific price: over 5,000 were killed and nearly 20,000 wounded. Another thousand Canadians had been captured.[19] At the same time, German V-1s (flying winged bombs powered by a jet engine) began to wreak havoc across London just as the Bandoliers were preparing to embark for Italy. The group's own tenor Harold Taylor suffered facial lacerations from flying glass after a bomb exploded near his London home.[20] With V-1s, among other things, on his mind, the ship Lou was on sailed in strict blackout conditions. This made the lights of "far distant Algiers" pop majestically as they passed. The ship also made a stop in Gibraltar, and later Hooper caught a glimpse of a mildly erupting Vesuvius off the coast of the Isle of Capri. When they finally arrived at Naples, the troupe was met by the officer commanding the Forage Caps, the concert party that the Bandoliers would replace.[21]

The troupe was temporarily based in Avellino in the south of Italy, where many of the so-called and uncharitably nicknamed "D-Day Dodgers" were stationed and later served as reinforcements in the bid to break the Gothic Line.[22] From there, the concert party performed in various venues including hospitals and detention camps as they began the long upward journey to

Rome. When the Bandoliers passed Monte Cassino, Lou was acutely aware that his own artillery battery had, in the spring of 1944, helped the Allies take the mountaintop monastery in a seventy-two-hour non-stop barrage.

Hooper was transported back to his school days when the travelling entertainers came upon the Tiber. Lou was "deeply thrilled" as they crossed the river, having "once read a fine poem which uncovered the politics and intrigue which finally made necessary that defence of the proud city – Rome."[23] The poem was almost certainly *Horatius at the Bridge* by the nineteenth-century British politician-historian and author of the epic *History of England*, Thomas Babington Macaulay. The memorable ending was no doubt foremost in Hooper's memory as he crossed the Tiber:

With weeping and with laughter
Still is the story told,
How well Horatius kept the bridge
In the brave days of old.[24]

Brave Hooper and his troubadours continued to give performances at soldier clubs, hospitals, and even in the field for units stationed in and around Rome, as well as farther-flung places such as Pesaro, Fano, Perugia, and Jesi.

There was a modest nature to the concert party's shows during the Italian campaign. The concert party lived almost entirely "under canvas," with a small tent, a net canopy, and a daily Mepacrine tablet to ward off malaria. The Bandoliers slept and ate out in the open like this for approximately six months.[25] The performances themselves were also largely out in the open, and the concert party usually performed within a twenty-five-mile radius from the unit's base following any given show, allowing the entertainers to return after each performance.

In his autobiography, Lou shares very little in terms of what music the Bandoliers actually performed. Hooper does, however, discuss Benny Goodman, Glenn Miller, and the Big Band sound in his autobiography.[26] It is on this strength and the instrumental make-up of the Bandoliers' band itself that we might hazard a guess. We might also take direction from one of Hooper's contemporaries (and acquaintances), William Raymond Stephens, tubist/bassist for the Canadian Infantry Division Band and later the Royal Canadian Artillery Band. In the visceral account of his own musical wartime service, *The Harps of War*, Stephens described the standard fare offered by his band:

> We played escape music. Music to take one-the-hell-and-gone-from-the-front-line. I Cover the Waterfront. It's Only a Paper Moon. It's the Talk of the Town. Have You Ever Been Lonely? What a Difference a Day Makes. It's a Sin to Tell a Lie. Stompin' at the Savoy. You Go to My Head. If I Didn't Care. Stairway to the Stars. Sunrise Serenade … All or Nothing At All. Dance with a Dolly with a Hole in Her Stocking. Fools Rush in Where Angels Fear to Tread. Chattanooga Choo Choo. Pennsylvania 65000, Flamingo … Holiday for String. This is a Lovely Way to Spend an Evening … I Couldn't Sleep a Wink Last Night … Moonlight Becomes You. No Love No Nothing. Shoo Shoo Baby. So Tired. You'll Never Know. Don't Fence Me In. I'll Walk Alone. Sentimental Journey. Long Ago and Far Away … No messages to the world. No revolutions against society. No ripoffs. We had all those things for real. What we wanted were dreams.[27]

It was slightly different for the Tin Hats, who performed a liberal blend of old and new. The troupe, for example, included First World War chestnuts such as "Under the Yum Yum Tree," "Give My Regards to Broadway," and the patriotic American number "Over There," alongside contemporary pieces such as Al Jolson's hit "Little Pal," the Kern-Harbach song "Smoke Gets in Your Eyes," and the Second World War anthem made popular by Vera Lynn, "The White Cliffs of Dover."[28]

To get a sense of what the Bandoliers might have played, however, we must also consider Hooper's own formidable canon. Previously, Lou had penned "Over the Sea to My Soldier" while serving with the American Army during the First World War. We also know that Hooper wrote and arranged several songs for the Kit Bags *and* the Bandoliers, including his 1945 "Victory Song," which he penned in Arnhem, the Netherlands.[29] To what extent Hooper's own material featured in the Bandoliers' repertoire is uncertain, but surely the troupe performed some of the numbers, as mentioned above, which made the respective set lists of other Canadian soldier-entertainer groups during their tenure overseas.

Concert party humour too offered the audience an escape. In some ways, the comedic nature of CAS shows was an extension of what Canadian soldier-entertainers had pioneered during the First World War: lightly irreverent, sometimes sentimental, usually absurd, often satirical, and mostly mocking of all aspects of military life. Yet, while the Bandoliers and other CAS parties may have grasped the torch from their First World War predecessors, its flame was an altogether different shade.

Some soldier-entertainers from that earlier war had lent their hand to the morale-raising efforts for Canadian troops in Europe. This was not always favourably viewed by the younger entertainers. Drummer Les Abrum, who worked with Hooper in the Royal Canadian Artillery concert party, for example, had directed *Chip Up*, a show that included some of the Dumbells including Al Plunkett, Red Newman, Jack Ayre, and Ross Hamilton. The review lasted only one week at the Royal Alex in Toronto. As Abrum observed, "nobody wanted that World War I stuff … and it was rough watching those old guys trying to buy a little more time down memory lane."[30] Hollywood and the advent of radio had redefined popular culture, musical tastes, and what constituted "funny" for the generation fighting this new war.

Fast forward to the late summer of 1944 when the Bandoliers were watching – from a safe distance – Allied plane strikes on the city of Rimini on the Adriatic coast. This was part of Operation Olive, the main Allied offensive on the German's Gothic Line. Rimini, which would soon serve as the concert party's home base, was largely destroyed during the battle. The Bandoliers also spent some time in the badly flooded area of San Lorenzo in the south (where, incidentally, Hooper and some of his bandmates met the future British prime minister Anthony Eden), before heading back to their base in Avellino.

On their way back, the concert party performed at Canadian military hospitals in Caserta, Perugia, and Arezzo. It was here among the wounded in the autumn of 1944 that Hooper recognized the true value in what his and the other Canadian concert parties had provided during the Second World War. The gratitude that the wounded men and the doctors and nurses expressed towards the entertainers was humbling for the Bandoliers as Lou confessed, "despite the numerous and varied disabilities from which these men were suffering, they repeatedly thanked us for bringing these excerpts from our show to them in the privacy of their own ward … the question we asked of ourselves was, 'Who should be thanking whom?'"[31] Indeed, from a variety of accounts, the audience was particularly receptive to what the concert party had on offer. From the No. 3 Canadian concert party's (the Bandoliers) official *War Diary*, for example, we find that after a thirty-minute Bandoliers show, patients in the No. 14 Canadian General Hospital delivered a reception, "the best yet received in hospitals."[32] This goodwill was followed by good fortune and by early December the concert party was on a ship returning to England. The Bandoliers' war, however, was far from over.

Hooper was particularly fortunate to have spent Christmas 1944 at home in Petersfield, Hampshire, with his new wife, his sons Lou Jr and Paul, and baby daughter Barbara.[33] Leading the Bandoliers through the pivotal Italian campaign as he had done, Lou was now a Senior Non-Commissioned Officer. With this, Hooper returned to his unit's base in Guildford, Surrey, to ready his troupe for a tour of the Netherlands, Belgium, and eventually Germany. On Robert Burns's birthday, 25 January 1945, Hooper again crossed the English Channel.

The Bandoliers kicked off the next leg of their tour – officially called "Bronco" – in Ghent, Belgium.[34] On 30 January, Lou began his own "War Diary" into which he would make entries until the end of the war. Ghent proved to be something of a home away from home for many Canadian soldiers, including the Bandoliers. The troupe's first show was given successfully on 5 February in front of approximately 450 Canadian soldiers and local citizens.[35]

The Bandoliers would, as they had in Italy, make short sojourns out to various spots in Belgium and the Netherlands, often returning to their base in Ghent immediately following a performance. At this time, Lou was in charge of a sizable party: one driver, two attendants, two sergeants, two corporals, six musicians, and two female impersonators.[36] The concert party played throughout the north of Belgium to audiences ranging in number between 300 and 1,300. On 12 February, the troupe's base was moved to Turnhout, Belgium, where they performed in a YMCA theatre for Headquarters, No.1 Canadian Army. From here, the Bandoliers would again follow the pattern of driving out to other towns – sometimes in dangerous conditions, as the area had not yet been fully liberated from the Nazis – before returning back to their billets in Turnhout.

By the spring, and with Allied successes mounting, the Bandoliers began performing in the Netherlands. The Dutch were, as the Belgians had been, incredibly friendly and welcoming to the Canadian troops.[37] Over the course of twelve days, the concert party performed day and night in front of nearly 10,000 people including civilians, as well as Dutch and Polish troops. With each liberated town and village, millions could now, with greater conviction, imagine an end to the darkness.

The Bandoliers, though, had one remaining leg to tour which would start in Germany's Reichwald Forest. Running through the Reichwald was the German's infamous and, for much of the war, highly effective chain of fortifications dubbed the "Siegfried Line." Between September 1944 and March 1945, fighting along the line resulted in over 700,000 casualties (300,000 Allied and 400,000 German). The line was namechecked in Jimmy Kennedy and Michael Carr's morale-boosting hit of 1939 "(We're Gonna Hang Out) the Washing on the Siegfried Line":

> We're going to hang out the washing on the Siegfried Line.
> Have you any dirty washing, mother dear?
> We're gonna hang out the washing on the Siegfried Line.
> 'Cause the washing day is here.[38]

The song was recorded several times by different artists in the first couple of years of the war.[39] Yet, as the war dragged on and "washing day" had not yet arrived, the song lost some of its pep among the troops and was even parodied in much the same way "It's a Long Way to Tipperary" had been in the First World War.[40] Nevertheless, "The Washing on the Siegfried Line" retained some currency with members of the Bandoliers, who were well aware of the cost of life involved. The troupe, as an eerie example, came across a young dead German sniper whom they buried, later forwarding his personal effects to the Commission for Enemy Dead.[41]

Hooper and company then crossed the Rhine, which brought them impossibly close to the actual fighting. The Bandoliers performed in the open air, sometimes with Allied air cover, sometimes without, but at no time did the concert party cancel a show.[42] There were, however, many occasions when there was very good reason to cancel. On 12 March 1945, for instance, the Bandoliers were packing up when enemy aircraft flying overhead fired down upon them. The next day, the troupe dug "slit trenches" in anticipation of another attack. There was also the constant threat of snipers hiding in the foliage nearby. A wire alarm system was set up around the entertainers' camp, which set off flares whenever the wire was tripped, and no one in the unit was spared from their fair share of guard duty.[43]

With VE Day now on the horizon, the troupe performed in various cities, including but not limited to Nijmegen and Almelo in the Netherlands, and in the German towns of Kleve, Goch, and Emmerich. The Bandoliers often provided the soundtrack to the newly liberated. On one occasion, Hooper and company performed for collaborators who had – only twenty-four hours earlier – been liberated from an enemy labour camp. Although the mood was positive, the war was very much still on. The concert party, tired after back-to-back shows and driving in the requisite blackout conditions, lost their way on the road home. But for the intervention of a young Canadian officer who stopped the touring entertainers, Hooper and his Bandoliers may have met an untimely end, headed as they were directly for enemy lines at Duisburg, Germany. They didn't, of course, and the concert party was eventually recalled to Ghent. From here, the Bandoliers joyfully headed back to the safety of CAS headquarters in Guildford, England. On 7 May 1945, the Germans surrendered. While this in itself did not end the war, Hooper was able to celebrate VJ Day while on leave in Britain. With the Japanese surrender on 2 September 1945, the war really was over.

Although his new family was in England, Hooper was still in the Canadian Army and had to return to Canada before his discharge. Lou played his way across the Atlantic on the HMT *Cameronia*, where he provided the entertainment for many battle-weary veterans, civilians, and nurses of the war who were returning home. By Christmas 1945, Hooper was discharged and returned to his family in Britain. While a return to professional music was waiting for him in Montreal, Hooper now had time to exhale and reflect on the massive ordeal in which the world had been engaged for six years. In particular, Lou thought of the courageous Dutch, seeing "new hope lighting their faces" after their liberation.[44] Over one million Canadians saw full-time service during the Second World War. Over 42,000 of these men and women died.[45]

The First World War had given Canada its Dumbells. Few soldier-entertainers outside of this famous concert party, however, were able to convert their wartime performances into a postwar profession. The Second World War was different in this regard. A number of Canadian entertainers who honed their craft during the war, returned to a country experiencing something of a cultural awakening. The nation was hungry for Canadian-made entertainment, and war veterans such as the composer/arranger Robert Farnon, comedians Johnny Wayne and Frank Shuster, actress Lois Maxwell (later James Bond's Miss Moneypenny), and, of course, Louis Hooper were among those who were able to build on the momentum of what they had done for Canadian troops. And it wasn't just the "stars" who benefited, as Canadian historian Laurel Halladay explained: "Other veterans became key creative staff of CBC radio and television and the National Film Board, while many of their comrades took their talents back to small communities across Canada, providing instruction to hundreds of students and organizing local performances of all kinds."[46] Perhaps, as Halladay has contested, the formation of an armed forces–wide entertainment to combat a variety of issues served a dual purpose for the Canadian government. On one level, the soldier-entertainers clearly helped to assuage the waning morale especially in the miserable middle of the war. On another level, the process offered an opportunity for the Canadian government: Canada was able to support a number of talented entertainers as they developed their trade during the war. In no accidental way, and with an eye to peacetime, the CAS nurtured Canadian arts and culture.[47] "Pops" had more than done his duty in entertaining the troops and would return to the country of his birth when he and his family left Blighty for their new home in Canada.

Home presented new challenges. The Hoopers – a mixed-couple living in Montreal – experienced various episodes of racism in the immediate years that followed the war. And while Oscar Peterson, a Black Canadian pianist was making a name for himself in New York City and elsewhere, Hooper may have been limited, professionally and otherwise, by the sheer fact that he lived and worked in a country where there were fewer than 25,000 Blacks. Change for non-white Canadians was still very much in the future: the Toronto-based Negro Citizenship Council, led by the Bajan-born Don Moore would effect some positive change, but not until the mid-1950s; the Royal Commission on Bilingualism and Biculturalism which would, for the first time, officially recognize Canadians who were of neither French nor British heritage wasn't established until 1963; and by the time the White Paper on Immigration (1966) and the Points System (1967) came about, Hooper had already been back in Canada for over two decades.[48] Ideally, we would have been able to compare Hooper's material lived experience with other extant sources on these sorts of questions. But we can't. After an engaging, sometimes detailed, sometimes muddled overview of his time in the Canadian Army, Lou leaves us with a meagre ten pages after his wartime story resolves. Perhaps that's what he wanted: a foregrounding of Sergeant Hooper the musical director of the Bandoliers of the Canadian Army Show, "the man in charge."

Anecdotally, when Hooper was doing his duty with the Bandoliers during the war, Allan Lund and his future wife Blanche Harris were doing the same as members of *Meet the Navy* show. Long afterwards, and to honour Canada's famous First World War concert party, Lund wrote *The Legend of the Dumbells*, which premiered in Charlottetown, Prince Edward Island, on 27 June 1977. The musical ran until 3 September. Two weeks later, on 17 September, Lou Hooper, one of Canada's most important, if largely unheralded soldier-entertainers of the Second World War, passed away in that same city of Charlottetown.[49]

NOTES

1 The long-standing tradition of the "concert party" had featured in the military forces of many nations for centuries. And while they might not have invented the concert party, it might be argued that Canadian soldier-entertainers of the First World War perfected it. For further discussion on The Dumbells see Wilson, *Soldiers of Song*.

2 See Lanken, "Lou Hooper"; Batten, "Harlem Cakewalk."

3 McRae, "A Cauldron of Hell."

4 Zuehlke and Daniel, *The Canadian Military Atlas*, 150–3; Canada, "The Dieppe Raid."

5 Hooper, *That Happy Road*, 48.

6 See Wilson, *Soldiers of Song*.

7 Drawbell, "This Is London Calling," 9, 24.

8 Stephens, *The Canadian Entertainers of World War II*, 13.

9 One young officer was cut in half by a German bomb that exploded nearby his machine gun post. Hooper, *That Happy Road*, 88.

10 The Tin Hats first performed in Canada in the autumn of 1941 before eventually heading over to England, as was the protocol for the early CAS shows. Stanley, *A Different Type of Bombshell*, 24–5.

11 The four dead included musicians Sergeant Charles More and Gunner Bert Witherall, and support member Gunner Joseph D. Renney and the troupe's driver Bliss Macdonald. Stanley, *A Different Type of Bombshell*, 172–7, 235.

12 Hooper, *That Happy Road*, 100.

13 Overseeing the entirety of Canada's concert parties were Captain Frank Andrew and Sergeant Stan Sheddon.

14 Hooper, *That Happy Road*, 91; Terrence Spencer quoted in Stephens, *The Canadian Entertainers of World War II*, 31.

15 A perhaps incomplete list of forty-one concert parties from the Canadian Army during the Second World War includes: Tin Hats, Kit Bags, Bandoliers, Forage Caps, The Army Show, Swing Patrol, Haversacks, Invasion Revue, About Faces of 1944, Pass in Revue, Combined Ops, Après la guerre, Play Parade, Ward Healers, About Turns, Rapid Fire, Fun Fatigues, Stag Party, Hillbilly Blues, In the Mood, 5 Hits and a Miss, Musical Maneuvers, Commando Performance, What's Cooking, Gloom Busters, Mixed Fun, Repat Rhythm, Comedy Convoy, You've Had It, Melody Round-Up, In the Mood, Funborne Follies, Showboat, Downbeat, Free and Easy, Khaki Kollegians, One Meat Ball, Pardon My Glove, Varieties of '46, Black/White Bombers, and Rhythm Rodeo. See Halladay, "Ladies and Gentlemen, Soldiers and Artists," 147.

16 Halladay, "It Made Them Forget about the War for a Minute," 25–6.

17 Hooper, *That Happy Road*, 90.

18 Gerry Wilmot served as host, Sgt Sheddon supplied much of the music for the show, and the broadcast often featured the popular tenor Bill Smith. See "Johnny Canuck's Revue," 7.

19 Zuehlke and Daniel, *The Canadian Military Atlas*, 163; Dancocks, *The D-Day Dodgers*, 293–4, 351, 434.

20 See Halladay, "Ladies and Gentlemen, Soldiers and Artists," 102.

21 Ibid., 55.

22 Allied servicemen fighting in the Italian campaign believed that their efforts and sacrifices were being obscured by those soldiers involved in the perhaps more glamorous – at least in terms of international media coverage – invasion of Normandy. For further discussion see Dancocks, *The D-Day Dodgers*.

23 Ibid.

24 Macaulay, *Lays of Ancient Rome*, 98.

25 Hooper, *That Happy Road*, 94.

26 Ibid., 68.

27 Stephens, *The Harps of War*, 110–11.

28 Stanley, *A Different Type of Bombshell*, 224–31.

29 Hooper, *That Happy Road*, 102.

30 Les Abrum quoted in Stephens, *The Canadian Entertainers of World War II*, 36.

31 Hooper, *That Happy Road*, 96.

32 Quoted in Halladay, "Ladies and Gentlemen, Soldiers and Artists," 133n154.

33 Hooper, *That Happy Road*, 99.

34 Ibid., 100.

35 Ibid., 101.

36 Bandoliers trombonist Terrence Spencer remembered that the concert party even included, at least at one time or another, a fire eater! Certainly, The Bandoliers had several members, some who were with the troupe for a brief spell and others, such as Hooper, who enjoyed a long tenure with the concert party. Members included (but were perhaps not limited to): Harold Jackson, drums; Albert King, bass; Bill Graham, trumpet; Griffin, sax; Vic Turland, trumpet; G. Red Nicol, trumpet; John Somers, stage manager; Bill Caswell, lights; Pee Wee Beaudain, fire eater; Lou "Pops" Hooper, musical director; A.S. Gorguin, electrician; A. Scott, vocals; Harold Taylor, vocals; S. Ginsberg, piano; Terrence Spencer, trombone; Garfield White, female impersonator; Ronne White, master of ceremonies; Chick Gardner, singer; Billy Thompson, dancer; Chick Zamick, monologist; and Steve Stevenson and Paul Cassidy. Compiled in Hooper, *That Happy Road*; Stephens, *The Canadian Entertainers of World War II*, 32, 34.

37 Hooper, *The Happy Road*, 105.

38 Ambrose and His Orchestra, "The Washing on The Siegfried Line" b/w "I'm Sending You the Siegfried Line to Hang Your Washing On."

39 See Flanagan and Allen, "Run, Rabbit, Run" b/w "The Washing on the Siegfried Line"; Ambrose and His Orchestra, "The Washing on the Siegfried Line"; Joe Loss and His Band, "And That Started It" b/w "The Washing on the Siegfried Line."

40 Civilians most likely sang these sorts of patriotic tunes long after soldiers had tired of them. "It's a Long Way to Tipperary" serves as such an example from the First World War. The song was a "soldier's song" for only a short while. It was sung by British soldiers marching to Mons during those first months of the war, but later troops who knew well the horrors of the war had little time for the song. As John Brophy and Eric Partridge observed: "To sing, to hum,

or to whistle 'It's a Long Way to Tipperary' was the patriotic and cheerful thing to do … although civilians retained their affection for it, the New Armies were nauseated. Attempts to start it were often howled and whistled down." Brophy and Partridge, *The Long Trail*, 213. For further discussion on "The Washing on The Siegfried Line," see Whiting, *West Wall*; and listen to Various, *The World at War*.

41 Hooper, *That Happy Road*, 106.
42 Ibid.
43 No. 3 Canadian Concert Party (Overseas), "The Bandoliers" quoted in Halladay, "Ladies and Gentlemen, Soldiers and Artists," 105, 140.
44 Hooper, *That Happy Road*, 108.
45 Zuehlke and Daniel, *The Canadian Military Atlas*, 173.
46 Halladay, "It Made Them Forget about the War for a Minute," 21.
47 Ibid., 34.
48 For further discussion on race and Black migration to Canada in the postwar years see Wilson, *King Alpha's Song in a Strange Land*, 60–70.
49 "Golden Jazz Age Pianist Dies"; "Services Held for Veteran Jazz Pianist."

5

To Be "Un/silenced": The Interplay of Archives, Blackness, and Canadian History in That Happy Road

ARSHAD SULIMAN DESAI

In summer 2019, I visited four archives in Lisbon, Portugal, for an undergraduate research project.[1] It was my first experience in an archive, and, reflecting on it now, I learned more about the politics of archives than about the history I went to research. I came up against an overwhelming amount of "red tape": I had to register my research project with the archive; I was not allowed to digitize in certain archives; and I had to provide my passport information along with my institution's approval. Yet, I was most unsettled by my repeated engagement with the brutality and violence enacted against enslaved Africans in the archival materials.[2] As a research assistant, my role was to analyze a registry of enslaved people, which identified, among other attributes, the "markings" or brands that enslaved people had on their bodies – which denoted the enslavers. The experience reinforced that these Africans, who could have been my ancestors, were viewed not as people but as commodities.

After returning from Portugal, I had a conversation with my father regarding how unsettled I felt about presenting a paper that further accounted for African people as objects and a means to colonial wealth. In response, he informed me that his great-grandfather had brandings on his body when he was buried. My father then went on to share more about my great-great-grandfather's life: he was a pious man who had converted to Islam after meeting a Malay woman. Only recently have I realized that our conversation progressed beyond the violence and brutality against my great-great-grandfather to focus on the rest of his life story as a Southern African Muslim man.

As a Coloured South African/Black Canadian, I can attest that the quotidian experiences of Blackness in Canada are more than the salacious violence that appear in popular media and that historians extract from the archives. Black life is more than the records of enslavement that I discovered in Portugal. After studying the Hooper fonds, I am beginning to realize that some clues to the vastness of Black life might be found in the archives themselves, and we are not necessarily served well by talking only about archival silences as a form of absence. The Hooper fonds reveals the quotidian experiences of Black life. By looking at these experiences, the silenced multiplicity of Blackness comes into greater focus. To cite the Black feminist historian Tina Campt, "the quotidian must be understood as a practice rather than an act/ion. It is a practice honed by the dispossessed in the struggle to create possibility within the constraints of everyday life."[3] These everyday practices of *Black being* – of *the veil* that we wear, especially in white-dominated spaces – are silenced when we search the archives for particular stories of oppression or resistance.[4]

Hooper's autobiography surprised me. It awoke me. It invigorated my thinking. It pressed me to understand why I was so annoyed by the "current moment" of popular interest in violence on Black bodies. More importantly, it inspired me to think about Black multiplicity. Hooper's autobiography is about the quotidian experiences of a Black man who lives with a *veil*, as most of us do. Yes, he was a talented pianist and Oscar Peterson's tutor; he worked with Rosa Henderson, Art Gillam, Monette Moore, Maggie Jones, and Ella Fitzgerald; and he lived next to Dr W.E.B. Du Bois in Harlem and remembered the mocking of Marcus Garvey's United Negro Improvement Association parade.[5] In spite of Hooper's encounters with racism, *That Happy Road* illustrates his assertions of dignity. He seeks not only to be remembered for more than what was enacted upon him but to demonstrate all that he did.

That Happy Road represents different histories of Black Canadians, whether it be living in rooming houses with railway porters, playing shinny on a frozen pond, participating in baseball on an integrated recreational team, or confronting segregation in housing, the military, and entertainment establishments.[6] Reading these moments in Hooper's autobiography was a significant moment for me as a budding Black Canadian historian because it combined the histories of Black Canadians in one primary source, which I have yet to encounter. *That Happy Road* demonstrates the synchronicity of Black Canadian history – not as separate, easily definable events but as overlapping, simultaneous life stories that influence and permeate one another.

This "critical edition" of Louis "Lou" Hooper's autobiography presents not a record of the prejudice and suffering faced by Hooper but a focus on his life as a Black Canadian jazz pianist, composer, and teacher. Hooper's manuscript – sitting in a folder at Library and Archives Canada – allows us to see Black Canadian history in a new light. The image of the manuscript as an almost forgotten and disregarded history stuck with me.[7] Undoubtedly, many other histories of Black Canadians collect dust on shelves in state archives – individuals whose lives we will never know because the existence of those archival sources and the categories that can better illuminate their stories are unknown. The records of other Black Canadians who, unlike Hooper, did not keep meticulously curated records are far less accessible to the public and less likely to be discovered without being "stumbled upon."

In the Lou Hooper fonds, Hooper focuses not on the violence and discrimination he experienced as a Black man in North America but on his day-to-day life as a jazz musician in Canada and the United States. When I began reading over his archival documents, I was immediately brought back to interviews that I conducted with Black elders while working on my master of arts at York University, written amid the public awakening to Black Lives Matter. Day after day, news stories and social media displayed images of violence on Black bodies. Scholars spoke about how to acknowledge and write the history of anti-Black racism. Yet all these discussions appeared to have the same PowerPoint slides strewn with images of brutalized Black bodies from across history: the standard images of a burned lynched body, the scars of the whipped back of an enslaved person, and the videos of Black death – in different forms but always centred around Black death. It was infuriating.

The archive can be a place of trauma for both the researcher and the researched. The often-violent legacies of the past live in both what is present and what is missing. As scholars of the Black Atlantic have noted, "the archive often records blackness only as an absence of human subjecthood, as when the enslaved enter the historical record as a number, a mark, or a notice of death."[8] As a collection of historical documents, the archive often includes written and visual depictions of violence on Black bodies as well as court testimonies against such violence. The archive is home to "the routinized violence of slavery and its aftermath through invocations of the shocking and the terrible."[9] For those who study the African diaspora, "the archive [i]s a site of irrevocable silence that reproduces the racial hierarchies intrinsic to its construction."[10] Reflecting on the problems she encountered while searching for Black Canadian history in the archives, Cheryl Thompson notes archivists either did not know the Black Canadian documents or did not have designated Black Canadian collections.[11] Thompson asserts that archives contribute to the "erasures, invisibilities, and blind spots" related to marginalized histories and that researchers need to constantly question whom the archive serves and "how … histories are written and remade."[12] The absence of particular individuals and events in the archives – the *silences* and *silencing* in the creation of the archive – is not an "innocent" process.[13] These silences "frame what is consigned in the archive as a unified whole and repress what is left outside the archive, denying its existence and consigning it to oblivion."[14]

State and institutional archives reproduce narratives supportive of state goals and legacies – and in the nation-state of Canada, these narratives centre around white supremacy. As such, these archives are limited in their ability to chart the complexity of Black life. Returning to the Portuguese repositories I visited, I recognized that they rendered enslaved Black and colonized peoples only in terms of their commodification because they assembled the colonizer's priorities, values, and knowledge. I quickly understood that the records held in these "traditional" archives were written and compiled by Portuguese colonizers and could only reflect their colonial categories, narratives, and discretion. Through my archival work, I came to learn that "the boundaries of what enters the archive are usually determined by those in power, and the power to record is also the power to leave unsaid, to classify, or to keep secrets."[15]

In this sense, "the archive" most often serves to recreate violence against Black bodies. It normalizes violence on Black bodies and the historical numbness that results from commodifying Black history.[16] As Katherine McKittrick poignantly puts it, "[i]f our analytic *source* of blackness is death and violence, the citation of blackness – the scholarly stories we tell – calls for the repetition of death and violence."[17] As an emerging historian of Black Canadian history, I must now confront the question (or fact) of my complicity in the reproduction of Black death. While the stories of anti-Black police brutality (still) need to be told, it was the interviews with the Black elders that pushed me to engage another dimension of Black life. In contrast to the prevailing images and narratives, they insisted on sharing and documenting personal and collective histories beyond police violence. These accounts encouraged me as an emerging historian to reflect on, interrogate, and appreciate the fullness of Black life both in Toronto and Canada more broadly. Their interviews taught me about the diversity of Black experiences – from the different ways individuals engaged in "activism" to the multiple yet intersecting community projects they designed. I have come to acknowledge that the relegation of Black existence to the binary of suffering and resistance leaves no space for the "in-between," for the kind of hopeful agency that spurs community development projects and investments in educational and social programs.

Having worked in and outside of the archives, I expected to learn that Lou Hooper was a Black jazz musician whose life was filled with struggle and constant battles against discrimination, that he was angry but somehow had overcome it all. I began by reading his autobiography, *That Happy Road*. In Part 1, Hooper recalls being called the N-word at choir practice and his reaction to it: "I was mad and hurt and I told Claude if John ever used that 'word' in speaking to, or about me there would be a real fight."[18] I immediately thought, "Here we go again. Another story of the exceptional Black Canadian filled with resilience and triumph."

However, I was struck by the last sentence of the recollection: "Nothing further occurred except to say that John and I never became friends."[19] Hooper did not allow the incident to define him or his story. Despite the attempts made by many Black Canadians to bear the burden of everyday indignities and incidents of anti-Black racism, these incidents have long-standing implications for how one lives and moves in the world. Hooper's later reflection on the moment when he was forced to eat in the kitchen not only indicates the ways in which experiences of racism and discrimination were part of his everyday life but also articulates an interrogation of who bears the responsibility and burden of shame for practices of anti-Black racism. Hooper writes, "I have thought of that incident often in the course of my life, and have wondered who felt worse or who felt the greater shame, Mr Len Beatle, the father of the boy, or twelve-year-old Louis Hooper."[20] On his return home to Montreal from the Second World War, Hooper describes the discrimination he experienced while searching for an apartment: "The days following my return were given over largely to house-hunting where, I must admit, I experienced some discrimination, especially where apartment buildings were visited, although their sign-boards displayed a vacancy in large letters. Already, Canada was not extending the same welcome to all her returning sons, and my search continued for a few weeks, even after my family had arrived."[21] Hooper was "Canadian enough" to join the Royal Canadian Artillery and rise to the rank of W.O.II (Sgt Major), but upon his return home he was not "Canadian enough" to find accommodation. Hooper was aware that he lived a *two-ness* as Black and Canadian.

After some contemplation, I realized that Hooper's reflections on these incidents reminded me of W.E.B. Du Bois's conceptualization of "double consciousness" in his iconic *The Souls of Black Folk*:

> [T]he Negro is a sort of seventh son, born with a veil, and gifted with second-sight in this American world, – a world which yields him no true self-consciousness, but only lets him see himself through the revelation of the other world. It is a peculiar sensation, this double-consciousness, this sense of always looking at one's self through the eyes of others, of measuring one's soul by the tape of a world that looks on in amused contempt and pity. One ever feels his two-ness, – an American, a Negro; two souls, two thoughts, two unreconciled strivings; two warring ideals in one dark body, whose dogged strength alone keeps it from being torn asunder.[22]

Hooper did not forget his experiences of anti-Black violence and discrimination; as his reflections indicate, he perceives these moments as a way to both understand his place in Canadian society and articulate his experience of the unsettling nature of Blackness within the Canadian national imaginary.

Hooper's double-consciousness extends to the photographs he included in his archive, many of which are included in this book. I read these photos as "vernacular photography," defined as "a genre of everyday image-making most often created by amateur photographers and intended as documents of personal history."[23] These images contextualize his memoir, such as pictures of him as a choir boy and with his recreational baseball team. Within his archive, these images disrupt the reproduction of violence on and through his Black male body. I frequently revisited these images while writing this reflection, perhaps because of my training as a historian or because I was subconsciously searching for signs of struggle and resistance. My visits with the images became more personal each time I viewed them. I often returned to the image of Hooper's baseball team, which records his time in Montreal playing for an integrated recreational team. I attempted to find out more about this baseball team, but my searches yielded no results.[24] I was frustrated because this photograph showed him playing integrated baseball pre–Jackie Robinson, yet I could not find any information – another indication of the legacies of silence within the archive.

As I ruminated on this image, I began to reflect on the notion of "the exceptional unexceptional" – individuals who are often not remembered or celebrated because of the perceived ordinariness of their actions and lives. The photo of Hooper's baseball team, along with the other eighteen photographs reproduced in *Statesman of the Piano*, reveals the "ordinariness" of his everyday life – moments marked by leisure and joy. These documents of Black joy and leisure remind us that Black life in the Americas consists not simply of stories of struggle and resistance but also of happiness, resolve, and fulfillment, despite broader social and political mechanisms that sought to limit persons of African descent from engaging in these experiences. Hooper's archive asks us to see what other archival spaces do not. It presents a lens by which to view Black people in their fullness, taking into consideration the coloniality of the archive itself but prioritizing the ways in which persons of African descent sought to define their own humanity.

Black life in Canada has never been a monolithic experience. By documenting the lived experiences of musician Lou Hooper, *That Happy Road* draws attention to the multiplicity of the Black Canadian experience and reminds us of our obligations as historians to ensure that this multiplicity manifests in the field of Black Canadian history. Without negating the prejudice Hooper encountered as a Black man in early twentieth-century North America, *That Happy Road* centres on Hooper's life as a jazz pianist and teacher. The memoir does not recount – and therefore escapes the reproduction of – Black death and violence. Instead, its publication reminds us that Black joy and everyday living as a practice of Black futurity and refusal of death are equal parts of Canadian Blackness.

Bringing *That Happy Road* to public audiences has given me space to ask in what ways can my archival work be both political and restorative? I use "political" not just in the sense of approaching archiving practice as socially transformative or ensuring the archive is reflective of society's diversity but also in the sense of an intervention in the traditional archive to bring diverse and otherwise marginalized histories to the forefront.[25] Many Canadian archives hold the fonds of Black and other marginalized peoples that are very often ignored and overlooked. A commitment to spending time with these fonds is ethical and political. In response to the "bundle of silences" in these archives, scholars of Black Canadian history have used our "own" archives (oral histories, photos, communal engagement, etc.) to document our past.[26] However, the use of "alternative" archives often requires us to provide an enhanced justification in our methodology, to prove that these archival sources and repositories are as legitimate as those that are considered more traditional. Additionally, this methodological justification can result in an avoidance of the state archive because we assume it does not contain or care about Black Canadian history. This approach can lead to methodological conundrums in two ways: questioning the legitimacy of our alternative archival sources, and refraining from engaging with state archives because of our belief in the inherent absence of Blackness. What needs to occur is an accessible archive that decentres the salaciousness of Black history and recentres the quotidian histories of Black Canadians.[27]

The "Hooper Archive" demonstrates the importance of having designated collections for Black Canadians, such as the Lou Hooper fonds, making it easier to locate his records. However, even in the case of Hooper, Mills faced difficulties locating all of the artist's sources and travelled to institutional and private archives in both Canada and the United States.[28] Such experiences remind us of the challenges and complications in finding Black histories, requiring "that researchers become forensic investigators with clairvoyant tendencies."[29] Despite and in response to these difficulties, Mills, Fillion, and Rochat have produced a judicious contribution to Black Canadian history and a necessary reflection on what the Black Canadian archive must entail.

～

Hooper's autobiography compelled me to reconfigure my idea of the "exceptional" Black Canadian. Too often, Black histories tell a tale of Black exceptionality – of resilience and overcoming. Yet, Black life is more than Black struggle, and as historians, we must begin to narrate the multiplicity of Black living. The "Hooper Archive" has forced me to address my own reading and understanding of Black Canadian history. The "fabric" that made up Hooper's life in the early to mid-twentieth century moved far beyond racism and inequality – there was baseball, the military, music, family, and community. All of these elements contribute to the richness of Black life today.

Coming to this realization was not easy. I met with two Black Canadian historians, Drs Funké Aladejebi and Barrington Walker, to ask them about their own journeys. I discussed how working within the "Hooper Archive" has encouraged my thinking beyond Black struggle and recreating Black violence. Their responses were simultaneously profound and straightforward: why does it have to be one or the other? We do not live one Black reality, so why would history be written and presented that way? As someone at the beginning of what I hope to be a long career of studying the history of Black Canada, my encounter with the "Hooper Archive" has compelled me to challenge myself and how I write Black Canadian history. It reminds me that *unsilencing* the archives is an invitation to dig through dusty folders in basements, garages, and, yes, even in archives.

NOTES

1 These archives include Arquivo Histórico Ultramarino, Arquivo Histórico da Marinha, Arquivo Histórico Militar, Sociedade de Geografia de Lisboa, and Biblioteca Nacional de Portugal.

2 This project culminated in the joint publication of Curto and Desai, "The Early Demography of Moçamedes," 11–32.

3 Campt, *Listening to Images*, 4.

4 For more on "the veil," see Du Bois, *The Souls of Black Folk*.

5 Hooper, *That Happy Road*, 65; Du Bois, *The Souls of Black Folk*, 4.

6 For more on the history of railway porters in Canada, see Mathieu, *North of the Color Line*.

7 See the introduction to this volume by Mills, Fillion, and Rochat.

8 Helton et al., "The Question of Recovery," 5.

9 Hartman, *Scenes of Subjection*, 4.

10 Helton et al., "The Question of Recovery," 2.

11 Thompson, "Searching for Black Voices in Canada's Archives."

12 Ibid., 94.

13 Hamilton et al., eds, *Refiguring the Archive*.

14 Ibid., 9.

15 Helton et al., "The Question of Recovery," 8.

16 McKittrick, *Dear Science and Other Stories*, 105; Downs, "When Black Death Goes Viral."

17 Emphasis in original. McKittrick in Hudson, "The Geographies of Blackness and Anti-Blackness," 240.

18 See Hooper's *That Happy Road*, 29.

19 Ibid.

20 Ibid., 30.

21 Ibid., 111.

22 Du Bois, *The Souls of Black Folk*, 5.

23 Campt, *Listening to Images*, 7–8.

24 The baseball team was an amateur team composed of people who worked or performed at a Montreal nightclub. As such, it was unlikely to find its way to an institutional archive until someone decided to research the history of jazz/nightlife in Montreal. The history of Black Canadian baseball can be found at the Chatham Black History Society's baseball collection.

25 Flinn, "Archival Activism."

26 Trouillot, *Silencing the Past*.

27 Various projects have sought to make alternative archives available, such as Natasha Henry's work with the Ontario Black History Society (https://black historysociety.ca/about-the-founder/), Cheryl Thompson's new research on Black archives in Ontario ("Mapping Ontario's Black Archive: Building an Inventory through Storytelling"), and Rachel Lobo's work on Black photography. See also Stanger-Ross and Sugiman, *Witness to Loss*.

28 See the preface to this volume.

29 Thompson, "Searching for Black Voices in Canada's Archives," 93.

6

Black Community Archives in Practice

KRISTEN YOUNG

My foray into archives began with the recognition that, as a Jamaican immigrant to Canada and a third-culture kid, I needed to understand not just the history of the country my family left behind, but the history of the country we now live in. Further, I wanted to learn how others who look like me and share my background lived and worked in this country we now call home. What better place to learn about that than archives? However, when I began to work as a professional archivist, I realized that this community history I was looking for was not adequately documented in mainstream institutional archives. If community history was documented, it was generally in spaces outside the mainstream archives, within the cultural and diasporic groups creating the history as part of their work or as part of their cultural practice.

While diasporic communities within Canada offered me the history I was looking for as a kid, their community archival practices and collections remained mainly absent from the training I received as an archivist as well as from larger mainstream archives. Historically, the various modes and methods of self-representation and heritage preservation that minoritized communities have developed to safeguard their collective history have not been of interest for traditional approaches to archiving.[1] In recent years, however, their collections have increasingly been recognized as places where memory and history are kept for generations to come, and their practices are now gaining the respect they deserve. Unfortunately, in my experience, there often continues to be a tension between those who are academically trained in archival practice and those who are trained in community archives spaces. Hence my commitment to developing a community archiving practice, which involves working with individuals and groups to give them the tools they need to ensure they – and their history – are adequately represented in spaces outside of their own.

Lou Hooper's *That Happy Road* and his fonds at LAC are of particular interest to me, because they are compelling examples of the self-representation of Black Canadians that is so desperately needed. Hooper's autobiography and the documents that are preserved in Ottawa open an extraordinary window onto the history of Black Canadians from the perspective of a person who has lived and experienced it. The stories they tell are in Hooper's own words. They are not told through records created by others. The distinction is important. By examining this material, placing it in its larger context, and encouraging people to engage with it from multiple angles, we can encourage a deeper reflection on the intersections of history, community preservation, and memory, and the archives of Black communities in Canada. More importantly, we can help bridge the gap between traditional archiving approaches and methods of community archiving that seek not just to document and provide access, but also to ensure broader participation in the documenting of history and in the activation of archives. This is crucial, timely work.

Growing up, I experienced the lack of representation of minority communities in portrayals of Canadian history. This history was presented as one dominated by white conquest, militarism, European migration, and industrialization. Often, when my community's history was represented it tended to be tokenized or presented as a side note to the broader narrative. The need to see and understand that the history of my community was central to Canadian history (and not adjacent to it) drove my interest in cultural work, and specifically my passion for archives.

Like many Black folks in memory work, as I came into my archiving practice, I started to draw connections between the limited representations of Black communities that I witnessed growing up and the limited instances of self-representation of Black communities within many archival repositories.

In addition, many of the traces and records about Indigenous, Black, and other marginalized communities held in institutional and government archives were produced through interactions with the state – encounters characterized by colonial violence and asymmetrical power relationships.[2] The policing and surveillance of Black Canadians, for instance, has produced documents that tell us more about state-embedded systemic racism than they do about these communities.[3] As repositories of these records, institutional archives can thereby reproduce this misrepresentation, perpetuating the oppression and harm caused in the first place, within the context of creating the records. In such a case, self-representation and self-narration through community archiving become especially critical. What, for me, started out as an endeavour to understand community history, has now turned into a practice that allows me to learn the history of the people and groups I work with while at the same time helping them acquire archiving and records-management skills. Community archiving has given me the tools to uncover and make audible those voices that have been silenced or misrepresented in government and more traditional records and repositories. It has led me to ask: What methods – other than those taught in institutions that uphold archival hierarchies – can be used to counter invisibility and misrepresentation?

At its core, my practice is about inviting people to consider archiving as an active, ongoing process rather than a distinct, episodic activity that one thinks about or engages in only after a particular record has been created and used. Community archiving is about the everyday. It starts with small, daily efforts to document the events and stories that shape social and cultural life. It consists of developing awareness of the ways in which we capture these everyday moments, embedding multiple views in the records thus produced to ensure they convey the broader contexts and interactions from which they originate. It is a collaborative effort, and it ties in with the work accomplished by those who advocate for and provide all kinds of support for their communities in the face of persistent challenges. This practice, rooted as it is in the present, not only deepens our understanding of history, but also brings people together through discussions about memory and the future.[4] The awareness gained in community archiving can be transformative. It can foster community and spark social change.

In my practice, I work with individuals and groups to teach them how to archive their history in ways that complement the knowledge and the resources they already have. I encourage them to be conscious of the ways in which their actions, activities, and events are documented, preserved, and described. I also encourage them to understand and document the various connections that tie this material to ongoing community life to show that archives are not stagnant or separate from their communities and contexts of creation. Though the groups I work with have fewer resources than larger institutions, they are still able to record themselves and to document their history to effectively challenge archival misrepresentations and silences.

My longest-running project is with the Montreal-based Head & Hands Inc. (H&H). Since 1970, this social services organization has offered health and social services to youth aged twelve to twenty-five in the Notre-Dame-de-Grâce borough of Montreal. With such a long history, H&H's staff and community already had a good understanding of its collective history. As well, having survived a fire and many moves, there were some within the organization who understood what it meant to sift through documentary heritage with an eye for records that speak to what ties a community together. My work with H&H has been to add standards and archival practice to a community archival practice that was already alive and thriving, even if those who were doing the work did not necessarily use that vocabulary. We work together to standardize cataloguing procedures, create guidelines that will outlive employee turnover, and embed records-management practices into the everyday workflows of the various programs. This is in addition to the continuation of the sharing and storytelling that takes place at H&H's many programs and events. By documenting these activities and properly organizing documents, it will be easier to recall them in the future, allowing the organization's history to be reinterpreted by future generations of community members. In this way, community and collective memory can continue to live on, and those who are creating history in the everyday are given the tools to produce their own archival representations of that history.

Through my collaboration with community groups, I bring the traditional archival practices I was taught, and they bring their current practices and understandings. Together we bridge the gap by adapting both practices and shaping them to ensure that what we leave behind is a more accurate and comprehensive representation of their communities. Centred as they are on casual conversations and informal learning opportunities, our collaborations allow us to pass on that history and to make accessible their resources and practices to others. It is always my hope that the materials preserved through community archiving can provide thoughtful and holistic glimpses of the past, and that they can inspire community organizations to make this practice integral to their own records-making process.

Going back to the topic of traditional archives and the silences surrounding the experiences of Black Canadians, I find it refreshing to be able to point to Lou Hooper's fonds at LAC, especially since the common perception is still that Black archives do not exist in this country's memory institutions. The fact that the pianist's personal papers and documents are held in the national archive is even more remarkable. Donated to LAC three years after Hooper's passing, the fonds consists of his unpublished autobiography, letters, photographs, sheet music, and much more. It gives us a real glimpse into the road travelled by the Buxton-born artist: his youth, the formative events of his life, and the different stages of his musical career. No less important, it sheds a much-needed light on the history of Black Canadians in mid-twentieth-century Canada, showcasing what was unique about that history and what it shared with the broader diaspora. Hooper, in other words, took self-representation to heart by writing a chronicle of his life and collecting mementoes that spoke of his experiences and those of the various communities of which he was a part. Significantly, he – or rather his family – took the added step of donating this material to the largest archival institution in Canada, thereby ensuring that his act of self-representation through archival curation and of self-narration through autobiographical writing would live (and hopefully find resonance) outside of his communities.

That Happy Road is perhaps the most revealing item in the Hooper fonds. The autobiography is a potent example of how one goes about documenting the everyday. It takes us through the story of Hooper's life, detailing the places he lived in or visited as well as the people who surrounded and accompanied him throughout his career. Through his first-person narrative, we learn what it was like to be a young Black artist in different spaces and contexts, at a time when race relations were constantly being renegotiated. For instance, the passage where he describes his collaboration with a young francophone tenor sax player from Quebec struck me as particularly illuminating. I learned that the two played together during the summer of 1937, the elder pianist having a profound influence on the aspiring jazzman, Leo Alarie: musically, but also in terms of a greater awareness of race and racism. Not only does Hooper paint a vivid picture of his bandmate, revealing something about his personality and commenting on his musicianship, he also weaves this intimate episode into a broader story about race and music.[5] Through the narration of his own life, Hooper also gives us a frank view of the various communities he was a part of over time, writing them into history as well. When he writes about his years as part of the Boy's and Men's Choir at St Luke's Episcopal Church, we learn how he and those around him both responded to or perpetuated racism. When he takes us on the road for musical adventures in Canada and the US, we learn about the ways that music fostered collaboration, growth, and community. When he writes about his experience in the military, we learn that songs were a means to maintain a connection to home and to forge camaraderie. I could, of course, go on and say much more about the mentorship he provided and what his words teach us about family and friends, bandmates, and compatriots. In doing so, he tells us about himself and his communities in relation to the different places where he lived, whether in Detroit or Harlem, or in the various Canadian cities where he played music, or through Europe during the Second World War. The fact that these stories live at LAC, in the nation's capital, is significant.

Although it may not be apparent, the Hooper fonds conveys something about the potential and vital need for approaches informed by community archiving. Within Black communities, storytelling is understood as a way to collectively preserve and share culture, pass on traditions, and heal together.[6] Through Hooper's collection, we engage with and gain understanding of the importance of storytelling in relation to individual and community archives as well as cultural preservation. At first glance, the fonds is typical of the traditional archiving practice in which I expected to work when I first entered the profession: it focuses on a prominent individual who kept records of the things in his life that he considered of importance. On his passing, his family donated all those records to an archival institution that assumed responsibility for processing and describing this material. This method of preservation is very individualistic, limiting descriptions to standard categories established by the processing archivists who learn about the records from the records, their own research, and potentially a donor interview. Researchers then help fill in some of the blanks in the course of pursuing their own projects, adding meaning and depth to the records, which they likely first discovered through finding aids and biographical sketches. Through the finding aid and biography/administrative history of the Hooper fonds at LAC, we gain an understanding of the artist as an individual.[7] Yet Hooper did more than document himself and the exceptional episodes of his life; he captured and reflected on the moments in between that shaped who he was and how he existed in the world, not to mention the friends, colleagues, and family members who joined him on his journey. Through his autobiographical writing, Hooper exemplifies how storytelling also participates in cultural and community preservation.[8] It is through sharing with each other that we build collective memory that can then be documented in historical records.[9] In doing so, Hooper arguably embodied a form of community archiving practice, bringing his communities with him into the archives, giving their history visibility and longevity. Yet these communities (their contours and wealth of history) are missing from both the finding aid and the biography/ administrative sketch. Traditional archiving methods of description are unfortunately not robust enough to provide nuanced descriptions for a fonds like Hooper's. We need to approach archival description and memory work differently to appropriately foreground this material and allow for a better representation – and self-representation – of minoritized voices.

In addition, for these community histories to be kept alive and passed on, we also need to create conditions for community engagement with archival collections. There is a real gap between how traditionally trained archivists and the general public understand the accessibility and usefulness of records. As Tom Nesmith argues, "much greater effort [must be made] to discover new uses of archives."[10] Making a fonds like Hooper's available for consultation in Ottawa does not guarantee that individuals and groups will know it exists or be able to use it. Institutional archives have at times been – and often continue to be – places where minoritized voices are silenced or feel unwelcomed.[11] Moreover, holdovers of institutional practices, such as requiring visitors to register before consulting materials, can replicate the history of surveillance embedded in state records, thereby reinforcing unbalanced power dynamics.[12] In such circumstances, it is easy to imagine that those in Black communities, who could greatly benefit from consulting fonds about their own history, are unlikely to make the trek to Ottawa. This unfortunately results in fonds like Hooper's "hiding in plain sight," publicly available but rarely consulted. The collection itself is accessible and available to all but it is most likely that only those within more formal memory professions know that it exists and even a smaller number will be able to make the trip to actually see the collection in person. It is unfortunately unlikely that those within different communities, such as young musicians, Black youth, community educators, and music teachers – all of whom would benefit from the exploration of a community archival collections like Hooper's – would be able to access it in its current location or would think to make the trip given the barriers (as well as the assumption of barriers) that they would encounter. This is reflective of a larger issue. Despite the best efforts of archivists and historians, for those outside of more formal memory professions and those within minority communities, there often continues to be a lack (both perceived and real) of accessibility and outreach, and a lack of understanding of their specific needs. *Statesman of the Piano*, therefore, becomes even more significant because it shows how collaborative work can help bridge the gap and open the lines of communication between different communities and institutional archives to make the latter more accessible.

Community archiving projects have shown that community members must be able to collectively browse, see, and talk about the records of their own history in order to engage with questions of memory and self-representation.[13] Through dialogue with each other and with the records, members are able to build a shared history, memory, culture, understanding, and more. Through sharing space, community can be created, collective healing can take place, and new futures can be envisioned.[14] These topics are of particular interest for Black[15] and Indigenous[16] communities in Canada as they fill the gaps in the mainstream historical record. Without a community able to access historical records in traditional archives, how do we facilitate dialogue and activate archives in meaningful ways? How do we foster collaboration with members of the heritage professions and fill the unintentional, but sometimes avoidable, silences? By bringing community members to the archives (and vice versa), we reactivate documented history and assert that archives can no longer solely be a place for those in power or those with the resources to conduct time-consuming, in-depth scholarly research. Through exhibitions and outreach events community members can be brought to the archive and made aware of what records are present in the archives. They can see themselves, their families, and their histories represented in the materials and engage with those who are responsible for preserving and describing that history. Through workshops and naming events, the archives can be brought to community members for the purpose of facilitating discussion, memory making, and healing together.[17] Naming events also gives the opportunity to gather and create a richer description for records and learn about the terminology that community members prefer to use in referring to themselves.[18] Further, by encouraging community members to freely explore their archives we create opportunities to serendipitously learn about a history that they might sometimes not already know about.

Though limited in number, as Hooper's fonds demonstrates, archival fonds that speak about Black history from the perspective of Black Canadians do exist in state-funded memory institutions. We have seen in recent years greater collaboration between government/university archives and Black historical societies and community organizations. This effort reflects a desire to bridge the gap between traditional archival methods and the community archiving approaches discussed above. It has led to outreach initiatives that cater more specifically to Black communities to highlight certain collections. For example, both Archives of Ontario and LAC have created pages on their websites detailing which collections in their holdings relate to Black history. Using such platforms, the two institutions have made available digitized copies of key documents to improve accessibility and bring awareness to them.[19] The material thus made available is intended to help amplify Black voices in archives – it constitutes an effort to deal with silences through a re-reading of the history held in different fonds at LAC and Archives of Ontario. However, these efforts and collaborations only partly address the desperate need for self-representation, which is crucial in countering (or rather subverting) the misrepresentations of Black Canadians that remain in many of the records created by settler colonial institutions and organizations. These initiatives do not fundamentally shift the asymmetrical power dynamics that allowed for silences and misrepresentations in the first place. For that to happen, we need to rethink traditional archiving by working more closely with communities and creating opportunities for their participation, contributions, and self-representation.

Statesman of the Piano enacts part of the ideals of community archiving. Together, the three co-editors and their collaborators, with the support of

Hooper's family, are bringing records held at LAC and in other institutions to a broader community so that its members can help activate this material and embed their own voices (or maybe their fingerprints) in it. This project shows how by thinking creatively about methodologies and participation we can bring people together to think more deeply about archiving and the importance of collaborative work to document and activate the multitude of voices that shaped our past and guide our future. Not only does this work offer a means to correct or remove silences from archives as they exist now, but it can help fill gaps in ways that are bound to help foster change, community making, and an understanding of history. I would like to conclude by thanking Lou Hooper's family for agreeing to the publication of *That Happy Road* and the other documents found in this book. This initiative offers one template among others to which individuals, families, and communities can turn for inspiration as they seek ways to preserve their archive or make them accessible on their own terms. The making of this well-curated publication has already started to spark conversations about Black archives, community, and legacy in ways that will continue in the years to come.

NOTES

1 For more on the lack of Black representation in Canadian archives see Thompson, "Black Canada and Why the Archival Logic of Memory Needs Reform." For the United States context, see Drake, "Liberatory Archives."

2 In their work, Ann Laura Stoler, Tom Nesmith, Jeannette Bastian, Andrew Flinn, Michelle Caswell, and Cheryl Thompson, among others, delve deeper into the structures that created colonial archives and, inevitably, continue to sustain them: Nesmith, "The Concept of Societal Provenance and Records of Nineteenth-Century Aboriginal-European Relations in Western Canada"; Bastian, "Reading Colonial Records through an Archival Lens"; Flinn, Stevens, and Shepherd, "Whose Memories, Whose Archives?"; and Stoler, "Colonial Archives and the Arts of Governance."

3 For more information on policing and surveillance in relation to archives see Austin, *Fear of a Black Nation*; Todd, "Power, Identity, Integrity, Authenticity, and the Archives"; and Brown, *Dark Matters*.

4 For examples of community-based digital archives projects, see the South Asian American Digital Archive, "Browse the Archive"; and Mukurtu, "The Mukurtu Community." For additional readings, see Mills, Rochat, and High, "Telling Stories from Montreal's Negro Community Centre Fonds"; as well as Caswell, Migoni, Geraci, and Cifor, "To Be Able to Imagine Otherwise."

5 Hooper, *That Happy Road*, 75–9.

6 Collier and Sutherland, "Witnessing, Testimony, and Transformation as Genres of Black Archival Practice."

7 See LAC, "Lou Hooper Fonds [Textual Record, Graphic Material]."

8 Drake, "Diversity's Discontents."

9 Bastian, "Taking Custody, Giving Access."

10 Nesmith, "Re-exploring the Continuum, Rediscovering Archives."

11 Tansey, "Institutional Silences and the Digital Dark Age."

12 Carter, "Of Things Said and Unsaid"; McKemmish, Faulkhead, and Russell, "Distrust in the Archive."

13 Douglas and Alisauskas, "It Feels Like a Life's Work."

14 Godoy, "Community-Driven Archives."

15 Lobo, "Archive as Prefigurative Space."

16 Ghaddar, "The Spectre in the Archive."

17 McCracken and Hogan, 'That's My Auntie."

18 For more on participatory description see Shilton and Srinivasan, "Participatory Appraisal and Arrangement for Multicultural Archival Collections." On rethinking archival description and terminology practices in relation to Black communities see: Sutherland and Purcell, "A Weapon and a Tool"; and Antracoli and Rawdon, "What's in a Name?"

19 See Archives of Ontario, "Resources Relating to Black History at the Archives of Ontario"; and LAC, "Black History in Canada."

7

The Path of Resiliency

❧

JULIE RICHARD

I live immersed in a world of music. Classically trained, I am well versed in vocal interpretation as well as jazz, pop, experimental, African, Roma, Jewish, and Creole sounds. I have toured across North America and performed in Eastern Europe, France, and Colombia. Alongside my musical practice, I am pursuing an interdisciplinary career in arts management, intervention psychology, cultural research, animation, and programming, notably at the Lux Magna and the Suoni Per Il Popolo festivals. My twenty-year commitment to Montreal artistic and musical scenes has allowed me to make important contributions as a musician, composer, and cultural worker. It has offered me abundant opportunities to think more deeply about the connection between our musical pasts and futures.

As I matured as a musician, I began to hear an echo of my heritage as a French Canadian Haitian woman in classical music. This led me to form two groups: the Black Ark Orchestra and Les Angles Mortes. Both are inspired by a desire to work with forgotten fragments of compositions by Black musicians who were predominantly active in the US in the 1920s. My aim with these two projects is to revitalize these marginalized works and to reintroduce them into contemporary culture. I seek to find, update, and recognize the value of what remains of these works and the stories that accompany them so that they do not remain forgotten. No less important, I want them to prompt new conversations on the histories of contemporary music. My goal is less to reconstruct the contours of these compositions accurately than to actualize non-linear, healing, transformative, and creative gestures. Although I have had success uncovering finished works through independent archival research, the majority of the scores left behind by artists are incomplete at best. Yet the fragments that subsist speak of the commitment and resistance of their authors. My years of research have made clear the importance of the act of archiving and preserving. They have made me a believer in the power of sharing lost histories to make the concertgoing public aware of racialized communities and to offer models for personal growth, healing, and even artistic development.[1] This experience now provides me with a unique vantage point from which to reflect on the meanings of Lou Hooper's life and work.

In my work as a researcher and creator, I have rarely encountered an archival fonds as comprehensive, detailed, and well preserved as that of Hooper. Its rich mixture of articles, correspondence, clippings, and scores reveals the artist's potential, desires, aspirations, and capabilities, but also the prevailing conditions that determined the opportunities offered (or not) to him as well as the subsequent courses of action taken. Although I had my preconceptions, the clues that I discovered in the broader "Hooper Archive" painted a complex picture that defied my expectations, allowing me to understand that we cannot grasp the full scope of an artist's endeavour by strictly examining their discography. Analyzing one's personal papers and archival materials enables us to observe the wide range of influences that shape their musical works. The desire and need to create are often informed by the choices one must make to survive and to achieve a certain quality of life. By immersing myself in Hooper's music, I was able to sense and visualize what he made available to me. Through listening, I became aware of the whole story, receptive to its poignancy in the present moment. I did so with a heightened sense of space and an expanded sense of perception. I sought to be grounded and submerged, better able to understand, hoping to approach the composer in the most unbiased way possible.

Hooper contributed to numerous musical endeavours via different artistic guises. Reading *That Happy Road*, I discern the gentility, generosity, genius, diplomacy, and professionalism that characterized all his artistic endeavours. From Mozart's sonatas to spirituals and ragtime, Hooper shifted from one style to another with ease. His versatility and uniqueness are apparent in many of his compositions. Take, for example, "Grand Opera Blues."[2] We hear references to *The Tales of Hoffmann*'s "La Barcarolle," a French opera by Jacques Offenbach, in the opening bars. Hooper likely drew these references from his time as a member of an entertainment unit with the US Army in Europe. His extensive knowledge of vocal and operatic art is evident if we pay attention to the clarinet parts, for example, which work just as well with a soprano voice. The transition brings us different energy, and for eight bars, we are swept away by a klezmer feel, and from there, it builds. As a composer, Hooper often offered a panoply of nuances and approaches, a journey to some of the places he had been. Although knowledgeable and capable on many fronts (as an expert in musicology, a community educator, or a valuable military officer), he cut a path that allowed him to create and navigate a viable outlet for his talent. If we approach his music with a trained ear and an astute mind, it is nearly impossible to miss the numerous classical references in his well-defined blues and ragtime compositions. This observation can also be inferred by piecing together the travel log entries he kept, which provide valuable context for assessing his creative endeavours.

When approaching Hooper's repertoire, it is necessary to study all the ins and outs. "Cakewalk" offers an enjoyable experience as the piece takes on a whole new meaning in our present-day context.[3] It calls up images that reinforce the rhythm and engage the heart on a deeper level. To grasp the full breadth of Hooper's singularity, I recommend listening to this composition alongside Robert Nathaniel Dett's own "After the Cakewalk."[4] The two composers followed a similar trajectory, and they are both skilled ragtimers.[5] There is a lightness and a sense of swing in Hooper's piece that is hard to match. He captures the wild essence of the cakewalk, which is often mistaken for ragtime. The beauty is that it always sounds impeccably cohesive and natural; the piece may seem more straightforward than it is, as is often the case with Hooper's compositions, but that is – in my opinion – because his playing is effortless. After much digging, I realized that his "Cakewalk," or a variation of it, had found its way into *The Congo*, a ballet for orchestra for which Hooper handled the narration and music.[6]

I was profoundly moved to learn that Hooper had written an oratorio in 1920 while studying at the Detroit Conservatory of Music. Had it not been for *Ruth* (based on the *Book of Ruth*), a biblical oratorio for soloists, mixed chorus, and orchestra, I would have concluded that Hooper was only a jazz, blues, and ragtime composer. But *That Happy Road* and the score for *Ruth* reveal that Hooper was also a capable purist and a true master of European-influenced classical music. It is essential to note that when Hooper composed his masterpiece, there were two primary currents at play among African American classical composers. One embraced the purist style (the music of racial uplift).[7] The other tried to forge a new style by merging vernacular, folk, and other popular forms of music with the classical form. Hooper took the least obvious route. Although able to operate in both realms, he took a path of his own. From my reading of the score, his oratorio seems to have a great deal of affinity with the French composers of the nineteenth century. With its very colourful but delicate arrangement, *Ruth* is nonetheless often intense without being dramatic.[8] Within Hooper's clearly defined blues and ragtime compositions, a trained ear and astute mind will uncover many references to classical music.

In his autobiography, Hooper describes the community of art and friendship that surrounded him during different periods of his life. He is always modest when expressing an opinion or judgment that might seem too harsh. He does not seem to hold a grudge or bitterness about the injustices he faced. He describes his involvement in the early careers of unquestionably famous artists with a humility reserved for giants. One that comes to mind is Oscar Peterson, one of his pupils. We know that Hooper's advice to the young pianist's father would push the prodigy to the next level.[9] We also find Hooper in Harlem, years earlier, acting as a pianist alongside Paul Robeson, who had yet to become the acclaimed and politically motivated artist we now know. Hooper declined the opportunity to tour with Robeson to stay closer to his family. Given how the singer-activist's career eventually developed, we can imagine the turn that Hooper's life might have taken had the two continued to work together.[10]

Probing Hooper's archives, I can't help but take note of his committed character. For example, it would be easy to see the Hooper Southern Singers of Canada, established in Montreal in 1935, as merely the creation of an additional vocal ensemble at a time when Quebec counted a large number of parish choirs, school establishments, workers' associations, and churches. The list of experienced singing ensembles that existed at the time is long; we could continue counting, reaching a list of ever exceeding lengths.[11] Hooper's desire to assist aspiring musicians in their development and education while providing performance space for the repertoire of Black composers was a singular act of generosity and community action. The Hooper Southern Singers of Canada were exemplary in advocating for musical education and music appreciation. It was an initiative that rested on a deep knowledge of art songs and Negro spirituals.[12]

It is easy to be enthralled by Hooper's extensive contributions and success as a Black jazz and blues musician in North America. However, it is also noteworthy that the pianist was drawn to these genres because he was denied the opportunity to pursue his genuine aspiration and talent in classical music. This rejection inevitably created a tension in his work. We must be mindful of it when examining his archival fonds and reflecting on his significant accomplishments in the realm of blues and jazz. In fact, the type of dismissal experienced by Hooper is hardly unique to his era.

While racial prejudice and social discrimination in classical music are less blatant today, the path forward is not always clear of obstacles for Black musicians in this field. I remember hearing Yannick Nézet-Séguin, conductor of Montreal's Orchestre Métropolitain, on the airwaves of Radio-Canada, announcing the program for the 2021 season, which included for the first time a work by the great composer Florence Price. Her "Symphony No. 1," which borrows the mould of the classical symphony while mixing genres by highlighting spirituals, hymns, and Afro-American dances, rarely appears in the repertoire of major orchestras.[13] At the same time, I saw the 2021 program from the New York Metropolitan Opera (commonly known as the Met). I was surprised to see that the second opera by six-time Grammy Award–winning trumpeter and composer Terence Blanchard, *Fire Shut Up in My Bones*, had just made history by becoming the first opera by a Black composer to be performed by the Met (conducted incidentally by none other than Nézet-Séguin).[14] In addition, Camille A. Brown, the opera's choreographer and co-director was to become the first Black director to create a mainstage Met production. As if these programs were not surprising enough, they aligned with the arrival of what is believed to be the first Black musician to hold the role of interim bass within the Montreal Symphony Orchestra, Mr Brandyn Lewis, who is also the co-founder and artistic director of the Obiora Ensemble, a group of some thirty musicians, primarily of colour, that promotes diversity and cultural representation in the world of classical music in Canada. Their inaugural concert at Salle Pierre-Mercure, on 28 August 2021, featured Jeff Scott, Samuel Coleridge-Taylor, and Joseph Boulogne (also known as Chevalier de Saint-Georges), three names that do not often appear on stage with Quebec ensembles.[15]

We might mistakenly believe that these efforts to promote Black artistic content do not have precedents. However, a review of Hooper's archival fonds and those of many other artists who have done similar work proves that this is not the case. If we pay close attention, it becomes clear that the structures put in place to allow for the retention of memories, inclusion, and recognition of the work of minority individuals have been sabotaged. Take, for instance, the Montreal Women's Symphony Orchestra (MWSO), founded in 1940 by Madge Bowen and Ethel Stark.[16] The openness and inclusivity of this orchestra were explicitly avant-garde, and its performances were of exceptional quality, going as far as to surpass the Montreal Symphony Orchestra in terms of representation beyond Canada's borders. The MWSO was a vehicle for leading artists of colour, including the clarinetist Violet Grant States who, in 1947, was the first Black Canadian to perform at Carnegie Hall amid pervasive segregation in the US.[17] These accomplishments did not sway the Montreal establishment, which decided to direct its resources and energies toward the Montreal Symphony Orchestra after years of relative neglect. In 1957, conductor and composer Igor Markevitch was brought in, and special grants were provided to employ more accomplished musicians. The revamped orchestra was to be the city's new pride, and the mere existence of the MWSO constituted a threat.[18] If Stark had not been cut off from financial and public support, she undoubtedly would have continued to promote non-traditional repertoires, creating a space for performers and creators of colour in the process.

This history gives us some idea of the efforts made throughout the years in Quebec to create ensembles that championed racialized and otherwise diverse performers. It also reminds us that their survival was not a priority for our funding agencies. It is not uncommon for Black artists trained in classical music to make a definitive leap toward other genres, not because they are following their heart, but merely to survive. Blind auditions, designed to discourage discrimination in the classical field today, are helpful only if racialized musicians have the support, financial and otherwise, to get that far. Nevertheless, despite all the pain, the positive side of this continued gatekeeping is that perhaps it will spark and nourish different musical forms and scenes where those excluded from the classical field will find a place.

～

Archiving classical music by Black composers in Canada should be a priority, but the challenges are apparent. For example, when searching for Black Canadian classical composers on the *Canadian Encyclopedia* website, the only name that appears is Robert Nathaniel Dett.[19] However, this discussion around Hooper offers much hope. Perhaps we should think differently about the framework within which we consider the achievements of our best-known jazz musicians. Hooper has, after all, always been depicted almost exclusively as a jazz pianist and composer. While no one can doubt that fact, does the oratorio *Ruth* (which he revisited in the 1970s), not indicate that he was also a classical composer? Unlike many of his contemporaries, he possessed a chameleon-like versatility and showed much ease with various styles. This allowed him to maintain an active, decades-long musical life. There are many others who are deserving of our attention, but they were never recognized because their archives were lost or destroyed.[20] The work of researching and creating must go on.

NOTES

1 For example, see Perry, *Stabat Mater*, performed by Les Angles Mortes. This performance, one of my latest finds, was presented as an online North American premiere by SuoniTV and Innovations en concert.

2 Hooper co-wrote this song with clarinetist Bob Fuller. See The Three Jolly Miners, "House Party Stomp" b/w "Grand Opera Blues."

3 Hooper, *Lou Hooper, piano*.

4 See track sixteen on Erickson, *My Cup Runneth Over*.

5 Incidentally, Hooper found himself performing "In the bottoms," a suite for piano composed by Robert Nathaniel Dett, while accompanying Paul Robeson in 1924. Schomburg Center for Research in Black Culture, The Paul Robeson Collection, MG170 3/2, Ballantine Gymnasium Rutgers College

Concert program, 17 December 1924, and MG170 3/2, Copley-Plaza concert program, 2 November 1924.

6 Buxton National Historic Site and Museum, Hooper Collection, Vol. 2, *The Congo*, program.

7 For more on the ideology of racial uplift as a factor in the African American elite's embrace of classical music and Robert Nathaniel Dett's role in this story, see Schenbeck, *Racial Uplift and American Music*, 108–38.

8 The score is available in LAC, Hooper Fonds, Vol. 10, No. 3, *Ruth*.

9 Peterson, *Jazz Odyssey*, 14.

10 Paul Robeson reflects on his tumultuous creative life in Robeson, *Here I Stand*.

11 For a survey of musical life in Quebec and Canada, consult Keillor, *Music in Canada*.

12 LAC, Hooper Fonds, Vol. 1, No 13, "Constitution of The Hooper Southern Singers of Canada," 31 October 1935.

13 See Orchestre Métropolitan, "Hélène Grimaud and Yannick Nézet-Séguin."

14 Metropolitan Opera, "*Fire Shut Up in My Bones*."

15 Ensemble Obiora, "Concert Inaugural."

16 Slatin and Noriega, "Montreal Women's Symphony Orchestra/Symphonie féminine de Montréal."

17 Keillor, *Music in Canada*, 209. See also Rachwal, *From Kitchen to Carnegie Hall*.

18 For an early history of the orchestra, see Pelletier, *Une symphonie inachevée*.

19 Kallmann, "Nathaniel Dett."

20 Dr Robert S. Pritchard II and Cy McLean, among others.

Bibliography

Archival Sources

Buxton National Historic Site and Museum, Buxton
  – Louis Hooper Collection
Concordia University Special Collections, Montreal
  – John Gilmore Fonds
LAC, Ottawa
  – Lou Hooper Fonds
Library of Congress, Washington, DC
  – Sanborn Maps
National Museum of American History – Archives Center, Washington, DC
  – Smithsonian Jazz Oral History Program Collection
Schomburg Center for Research in Black Culture, New York
  – The Paul Robeson Collection
USNARA, College Park
  – Ancestry NARA Microfilms
  – US Censuses (1900–1910)

Audiovisual Documents, Films, and Sound Recordings

Ambrose, Bert, and His Orchestra. "The Washing on The Siegfried Line" b/w "I'm Sending You the Siegfried Line to Hang Your Washing On." Decca F.7245, 1939, 78 rpm 10-inch.

Anderson, Leonard, dir. *Rhythm in a Riff*. Associated Producers of Negro Motion Pictures, 1947.

Anderson, Leonard, and Spencer Williams, dirs. *Jivin' in Bebop*. Alexander Productions, 1947.

Curtiz, Michael, dir. *Night and Day*. Warner Bros. Pictures, 1946.

Erickson, Clipper. *My Cup Runneth Over: The Complete Piano Works of R. Nathaniel Dett*. Navona Records NV6013, 2015, CD.

Flanagan, Bud, and Chesney Allen. "Run, Rabbit, Run" b/w "The Washing on the Siegfried Line." Decca F.7265, 1939, 78 rpm 10-inch.

Fleischer, Robert, dir. *The Girl in the Red Velvet Swing*. Twentieth Century-Fox Film, 1955.

Forman, Miloš, dir. *Ragtime*. Ragtime Productions and Sunley Productions, 1981.

Hooper, Louis Stanley. *Lou Hooper, piano*. Radio Canada International RCI 380, 1973, 33⅓ rpm LP.

Jenkins, Sacha, dir. *Louis Armstrong's Black & Blues*. Imagine Documentaries, 2022.

Lam, Meilan, dir. *Show Girls*. National Film Board of Canada, 1998.

Loss, Joe, and His Band. "The Washing on the Siegfried Line" b/w "And That Started It." Regal Zonophone (EMI) MR 3139, 1940, 78 rpm 10-inch.

Micheaux, Oscar, dir. *Harlem After Midnite*. Micheaux Pictures, 1934.

Perry, Julia. *Stabat Mater*. Performed by Les Angles Mortes. *SuoniTV*, 1 April 2021, video file. https://suoniperilpopolo.org/en/program/tele-suoni-tv-s2-4-angles mortes-amahl.

Stone, Andrew L., dir. *Stormy Weather*. Twentieth Century-Fox Film, 1943.

Three Jolly Miners. "House Party Stomp" b/w "Grand Opera Blues." Vocalion 15164, 1926, 78 rpm 10-inch.

– *The Three Jolly Miners, 1925–1928*. Historical Records 5829-23, 1967, 33⅓ rpm LP.

Various. *Collectors' Items, 1922–1930*. Historical Records 5829-11, 1967, 33⅓ rpm LP.

– RARE and HOT! *Female Vocals with Accompaniment, 1923–1926*. Historical Records 5829-14, 1967, 33⅓ rpm LP.

– *The World at War*. Carl Davis Collection CDC006, 2010, CD.

Waters, Ethel. "Refrigeratin' Papa (Mama's Gonna Warm You Up)" b/w "Throw Dirt in Your Face." Columbia 14132-D, 1926, 78 rpm 10-inch.

Williams, George, and Bessie Brown. "Hit Me but Don't Quit Me" b/w "You Can't Proposition Me." Columbia 14135-D, 1926, 78 rpm 10-inch.

Wise, Robert, dir. *Desert Rats*. Twentieth Century-Fox Film, 1953.

Printed and Online Sources

Adjetey, Wendell Nii Laryea. *Cross-Border Cosmopolitans: The Making of a Pan-African North America*. Chapel Hill: University of North Carolina Press, 2023.

– "From the North Star to the Black Star: African North Americans and the Search for a Land of Promise, 1919–1984." PhD diss., Yale University, 2018.

"African-Americans Find Home in Macomb County from Detroit." BLAC *Detroit*, 2 September 2014. https://www.blac.media/news-features/african-americans-find-home-in-macomb-county-from-detroit/.

Allen, Robert. *Horrible Prettiness: Burlesque and American Culture*. Chapel Hill: University of North Carolina Press, 1991.

Anderson, Iain. *This Is Our Music: Free Jazz, The Sixties, and American Culture*. Philadelphia: University of Pennsylvania Press, 2007.

Antracoli, Alexis A., and Katy Rawdon. "What's in a Name? Archives for Black Lives in Philadelphia and the Impact of Names and Name Authorities in Archival Description." In *Ethical Questions in Name Authority Control*, ed. Jane Sandberg, 307–36. Sacramento: Library Juice Press, 2019.

Archives of Ontario. "Resources Relating to Black History at the Archives of Ontario." *Archives of Ontario*, n.d. http://www.archives.gov.on.ca/en/access/black_history.aspx.

Armentrout, Don S., and Robert Boak Slocum, eds. *An Episcopal Dictionary of the Church: A User-Friendly Reference for Episcopalians*. New York: Church Publishing, 2000.

Austin, David. *Fear of a Black Nation: Race, Sex, and Security in Sixties Montreal*. Toronto: Between the Lines, 2013.

Baade, Christina L. *Victory through Harmony: The BBC and Popular Music in World War II*. Oxford: Oxford University Press, 2012.

Bakriges, Christopher G. "Musical Transculturation: From African American Avant-Garde Jazz to European Creative Improvisation, 1962–1981." In *Jazz Planet*, ed. E. Taylor Atkins, 99–114. Jackson: University of Mississippi Press, 2003.

Balshaw, Maria. "Sugar Hill and Strivers' Row." In *Encyclopedia of the Harlem Renaissance: Volume 1 and Volume 2*, ed. Cary D. Wintz and Paul Finkelman, 478–9. New York: Routledge, 2004.

Bastian, Jeannette Allis. "Reading Colonial Records through an Archival Lens: The Provenance of Place, Space, and Creation." *Archival Science* 6, nos. 3–4 (August 2007): 267–84.

– "Taking Custody, Giving Access: A Postcustodial Role for a New Century." *Archivaria* 53 (2002): 76–93.

Bastin, Bruce. *The Melody Man: Joe Davis and the New York Music Scene, 1916–1978*. Jackson: University Press of Mississippi, 2012.

Batten, Jack. "Harlem Cakewalk: When Lou Hooper Played for Paul Robeson and Bessie Smith, It Was a 'Place of Decorum and Illustrious People.'" *Ottawa Citizen*, 23 July 1977, 8–10.

Beaulieu, Shawn. "Fred S. Stone – Ma Ragtime Baby (1893)." *Chatham Music Archive*, 3 June 2009. https://demokidblog.wordpress.com/2009/06/03/fred-s-stone-ma-ragtime-baby1893/.

Beissenhirtz, Alexander J. *Affirmation and Resistance: The Politics of Jazz Life in the Jazz Self-Narratives of Louis Armstrong, Art Pepper, and Oscar Peterson*. Kiel: Ludwig, 2012.

Bernard, Emily. *Carl Van Vechten and the Harlem Renaissance: A Portrait in Black and White*. New Haven: Yale University Press, 2012.

Berry, Dorothy. "When Black Celebrities Wore Blackface." *JSTOR Daily*, 12 August 2020. https://daily.jstor.org/when-black-celebrities-wore-blackface/.

Bethune, Brian. "A Gift Fit for the King." *Maclean's*, 18 July 2011, 48–9.

Björn, Lars. "From Hastings Street to the Blue Bird: The Blues and Jazz Traditions in Detroit." *Michigan Quarterly Review* 25, no. 2 (1986): 257–68.

Björn, Lars, and Jim Gallert. *Before Motown: A History of Jazz in Detroit, 1920–1960*. Ann Arbor: University of Michigan Press, 2001.

"Blackbirds Revue Outstanding Show." *The Gazette*, 18 May 1929, 16.

Blais-Tremblay, Vanessa. "Jazz, Gender, Historiography: A Case Study of the 'Golden Age' of Jazz in Montreal (1925–1955)." PhD diss., McGill University, 2018.

Boggs, John Williams. "Music Instruction in Detroit from 1874 to 1929." PhD diss., University of Michigan, 1970.

Bohlman, Philip V., and Goffredo Plastino, eds. *Jazz Worlds / World Jazz*. Chicago: University of Chicago Press, 2016.

Bradford, Perry. *Born with the Blues: Perry Bradford's Own Story. The True Story of* the Pioneering Blues Singers and Musicians in the Early Days of Jazz. New York: Oak Publications, 1965.

Breakell, Sue, and Victoria Worsley. "Collecting the Traces: An Archivist's Perspective." *Journal of Visual Art Practice* 6, no. 3 (2007): 175–89.

Brooks, Tim. *Lost Sounds: Blacks and the Birth of the Recording Industry, 1890–1919.* Chicago: University of Chicago Press, 2005.

Brophy, John, and Eric Partridge. *The Long Trail: What the British Soldier Sang and Said in the Great War of 1914–18.* London: Andre Deutsch, 1965.

Brothers, Thomas. *Louis Armstrong: Master of Modernism.* New York: W.W. Norton, 2014.

Brown, Elspeth H. *Work! A Queer History of Modeling.* Durham: Duke University Press, 2019.

Brown, Simone. *Dark Matters: On the Surveillance of Blackness.* Durham: Duke University Press, 2015.

Broyld, dann j. *Borderland Blacks: Two Cities in the Niagara Region during the Final Decades of Slavery.* Baton Rouge: Louisiana State University Press, 2022.

– "Harriet Tubman: Transnationalism and the Land of a Queen in the Late Antebellum." *Meridians: Feminism, Race, Transnationalism* 12, no. 2 (2014): 78–98.

– "'Justice Was Refused Me, I Resolved to Free Myself': John W. Lindsay. Finding Elements of American Freedoms in British Canada, 1805–1876." *Ontario History* 109, no. 1 (2017): 27–59.

Bryant, William R. *Ajax Records: A History and Discography.* Denver: Mainspring Press, 2013.

Campbell, Arlene. "Life Notations of Daisy Sweeney: Reflections of Othermothering, Musicianship, and Montreal." PhD diss., York University, 2012.

Campt, Tina. *Listening to Images.* Durham: Duke University Press, 2017.

Canada. "The Dieppe Raid: 19 August 1942." *Government of Canada, Veterans Affairs,* n.d. https://www.veterans.gc.ca/eng/remembrance/wars-and-conflicts/second-world-war/battle-of-dieppe.

Cantor, Eddie. *My Life Is in Your Hands & Take My Life: The Autobiographies of Eddie Cantor.* New York: Cooper Square Press, 2000.

Caron, Matthieu. "Dissipating Darkness: Governing Nighttime in Montreal, 1954–1986." PhD diss., University of Toronto, 2022.

Carr, James Revell. *Hawaiian Music in Motion: Maritimers, Missionaries, and Minstrels.* Chicago: University of Illinois Press, 2014.

Carter, Rodney G.S. "Of Things Said and Unsaid: Power, Archival Silences, and Power in Silence." *Archivaria* 61 (2006): 215–33.

Casey, Kathleen B. *The Prettiest Girl on Stage Is a Man: Race and Gender Benders in American Vaudeville*. Knoxville: University of Tennessee Press, 2015.

Caswell, Michelle, Alda Allina Migoni, Noah Geraci, and Marika Cifor. "'To Be Able to Imagine Otherwise': Community Archives and the Importance of Representation." *Archives and Records* 38, no. 1 (2017): 5–26.

Chauncey, George. *Gay New York: Gender, Urban Culture, and the Making of the Gay Male World, 1890–1940*. New York: Basic Books, 1995.

Chilton, John. *The Song of the Hawk: The Life and Recordings of Coleman Hawkins*. Ann Arbor: University of Michigan Press, 1990.

Cohan, George M. *Twenty Years on Broadway and the Years It Took to Get There: The True Story of a Trouper's Life from the Cradle to the "Closed Shop."* New York: Harper and Brothers, 1925.

Collier, Zakiya, and Tonia Sutherland. "Witnessing, Testimony, and Transformation as Genres of Black Archival Practice." *The Black Scholar* 52, no. 2 (2022): 7–15.

Conley, Darlene C. "Driven and Pursued: Black Migrant Detroit an Analysis of the Neighborhoods Black Bottom and Paradise Valley, 1916–1968." Master's thesis, Morgan State University, 2016.

Conyers, Claude. "Texas Tommy." In *Grove Music Online*. N.p.: Oxford University Press, 2011. https://doi-org.proxy.queensu.ca/10.1093/gmo/9781561592630. article.A2092757.

Cooper, Afua. "The Fluid Frontier: Blacks and the Detroit River Region: A Focus on Henry Bibb." *Canadian Review of American Studies / Revue canadienne d'études américaines* 30, no. 2 (2000): 129–50.

Cornelius, Steven H. *Music of the Civil War Era*. Westport, CT: Greenwood Press, 2004.

Crease, Robert P. "Jazz and Dance." In *The Cambridge Companion to Jazz*, ed. Mervyn Cooke and David Horn, 69–80. New York: Cambridge University Press, 2002.

Cuccioletta, Donald. "The Américanité of Quebec Urban Popular Culture as Seen through Burlesque Theater in Montreal (1919–1939)." PhD diss., Université du Québec à Montréal, 1997.

Cummings, Ronald, and Nalini Mohabir, eds. *The Fire That Time: Transnational Black Radicalism and the Sir George Williams Occupation*. Montreal: Black Rose Books, 2021.

Cuney-Hare, Maud. *Negro Musicians and Their Music*. New York: Da Capo Press, 1974.

Currie-Williams, Kelann. "Life after Demolition: The Absented Presence of Montreal's Negro Community Centre." *Urban History Review / Revue d'histoire urbaine* 48, no. 2 (2021): 56–75.

Curto, José C., and Arshad Desai. "The Early Demography of Moçamedes, 1839–1869, a Preliminary Analysis." *Revista Historiae* 10, no. 2 (2019): 11–32.

Dancocks, Daniel G. *The D-Day Dodgers: The Canadians in Italy, 1943–1945*. Toronto: McClelland & Stewart, 1991.

Davis, Angela Y. *Blues Legacies and Black Feminism: Gertrude "Ma" Rainey, Bessie Smith, and Billie Holiday*. New York: Pantheon Books, 1998.

Davis, John, and Gray Clarke. "Recordiana: John Davis and Gray Clarke Discuss Lizzie Miles." *Musical Express*, 27 February 1948, 2.

DeMichael, Don. "Oscar Peterson: On the Teaching of Jazz." *DownBeat*, 27 September 1962, 24–5, 44.

Denning, Michael. *Noise Uprising: The Audiopolitics of a World Musical Revolution*. New York: Verso, 2015.

"Dizzy Gillespie Due in Montreal Tuesday." *The Gazette*, 15 April 1948, 6.

Doctorow, E.L. *Ragtime*. New York: Random House, 1975.

Douglas, Jennifer, and Alexandra Alisauskas. "'It Feels Like a Life's Work': Record-keeping as an Act of Love." *Archivaria* 91 (2021): 6–37.

Downs, Kenya. "When Black Death Goes Viral, It Can Trigger PTSD-Like Trauma." *PBS NewsHour*, 22 July 2016. https://www.pbs.org/newshour/nation/black-pain-gone-viral-racism-graphic-videos-can-create-ptsd-like-trauma.

Drake, Jarrett M. "Diversity's Discontents: In Search of an Archive of the Oppressed." *Archives and Manuscripts* 47, no. 2 (2019): 270–9.

– "Liberatory Archives: Towards Belonging and Believing (Part I)." *Medium*, 22 October 2016. https://medium.com/on-archivy/liberatory-archives-towards-belonging-and-believing-part-1-d26aaeboedd1.

Drawbell, James W. "This Is London Calling." *Maclean's*, 15 February 1941, 9, 24.

Duberman, Martin B. *Paul Robeson: A Biography*. New York: Ballantine Books, 1989.

Du Bois, W.E.B. *The Souls of Black Folks*. New Haven: Yale University Press, 2015.

Duggan Murphy, Michael. "Detroit Blues Women." PhD diss., Wayne State University, 2011.

Dumas, Evelyn. *The Bitter Thirties in Québec*, translated by Arnold Bennett. Montreal: Black Rose Books, 1975.

Ensemble Obiora. "Concert Inaugural." *Ensemble Obiora*, 28 August 2021. https://ensembleobiora.com/concerts/concert-inaugural.

Fahrni, Magda. "The Second World War: Wartime Production and War Efforts." In *Montreal: The History of a North American City*, ed. Dany Fougères and Roderick MacLeod, 37–73. Montreal and Kingston: McGill-Queen's University Press, 2017.

Fearnley, Andrew Michael. "Eclectic Club." In *Encyclopedia of the Harlem Renaissance: Volume 1 and Volume 2*, ed. Cary D. Wintz and Paul Finkelman, 327–8. New York: Routledge, 2004.

Feld, Steven. *Jazz Cosmopolitanism in Accra: Five Musical Years in Ghana*. Durham: Duke University Press, 2012.

Fields, Armond. *Tony Pastor, Father of Vaudeville*. Jefferson, NC: McFarland, 2007.

Fillion, Eric. *JAZZ LIBRE et la révolution québécoise: Musique-action, 1967–1975*. Saint-Joseph-du-Lac: M Éditeur, 2019.

"Fire Destroys Resort Building." *The Gazette*, 16 July 1952, 3.

Flinn, Andrew. "Archival Activism: Independent and Community-Led Archives, Radical Public History, and the Heritage Professions." *InterAction: UCLA Journal of Education and Information Studies* 7, no. 2 (2011): 1–20.

Flinn, Andrew, Mary Stevens, and Elizabeth Shephard. "Whose Memories, Whose Archives? Independent Community Archives, Autonomy, and the Mainstream." *Archival Science* 9, nos. 1–2 (June 2009): 71–86.

Frith, Simon, Matt Brennan, Martin Cloonan, and Emma Webster. *The History of Live Music in Britain*, vol. 1: *1950–1967: From Dance Hall to the 100 Club*. London: Routledge, 2013.

Fuhrer, Urs. *Cultivating Minds: Identity as Meaning and Making Practice*. London: Routledge, 2004.

Garvey, Marcus, and Robert Abraham Hill. *The Marcus Garvey and Universal Negro Improvement Association Papers*, vol. 12: *The Caribbean Diaspora, 1920–1921*. Durham: Duke University Press, 2014.

Gaudet, Harold. "Town Talk." *Evening Patriot*, 8 July 1978, 3.

Gelatt, Roland. *The Fabulous Phonograph, 1877–1977*. New York: Macmillan, 1977.

Gervais, Raymond. "Black Music: un art absent ici qui dit pourtant aux Québécois la révolution qu'ils ont à faire." *Tilt* 1, no. 2 (1974): 34–42.

Ghaddar, Jamila J. "The Spectre in the Archive: Truth, Reconciliation, and Indigenous Archival Memory." *Archivaria* 82 (2016): 3–26.

Gilbert, David. *The Product of Our Souls: Ragtime, Race, and the Birth of the Manhattan Musical Marketplace*. Chapel Hill: University of North Carolina Press, 2015.

Gilmore, John. *Swinging in Paradise: The Story of Jazz in Montreal*, 2nd ed. Montreal: Ellipse Editions, 2011.

– *Who's Who of Jazz in Montreal: Ragtime to 1970*. Montreal: Véhicule Press, 1998.

Gingras, Claude. "Ella Fitzgerald et les autres." *La Presse*, 3 April 1967, 21.

Gioia, Ted. *The History of Jazz*. New York: Oxford University Press, 2021.

Godoy, Nancy Liliana. "Community-Driven Archives: Conocimiento, Healing, and Justice." *Journal of Critical Library and Information Studies* 3, no. 2 (2021). https://doi.org/10.24242/jclis.v3i2.136.

"Golden Jazz Age Pianist Dies." *The Gazette*, 20 September 1977, 42.

Greenberg, Cheryl Lynn. *Or Does It Explode? Black Harlem in the Great Depression*. New York: Oxford University Press, 1991.

Halladay, Laurel. "'It Made Them Forget about the War for a Minute': Canadian Army, Navy, and Air Force Entertainment Units during the Second World War." *Canadian Military History* 11, no. 4 (2002): 21–35.

– "'Ladies and Gentlemen, Soldiers and Artists': Canadian Military Entertainers, 1939–1945." Master's thesis, University of Calgary, 2000.

– "A Lovely War: Male to Female Cross-Dressing and Canadian Military Entertainment in World War II." *Journal of Homosexuality* 46, nos. 3–4 (2004): 19–34.

Hamilton, Carolyn, et al., eds. *Refiguring the Archive*. Dordrecht: Springer Netherlands, 2002.

Hartman, Saidiya V. *Scenes of Subjection: Terror, Slavery, and Self-Making in Nineteenth-Century America*. Oxford: Oxford University Press, 1997.

Hay, Samuel A. *African American Theatre: A Historical and Critical Analysis*. Cambridge: Cambridge University Press, 1994.

Hay, Sheridan. "Blacks in Canada: The Invisible Minority." *Canadian Dimension* 30, no. 6 (1996): 14–17.

Hébert, Chantal. *Le burlesque au Québec: Un divertissement populaire*. Montreal: Hurtubise, 1981.

Heble, Ajay. *Landing on the Wrong Note: Jazz, Dissonance, and Critical Practice*. New York: Routledge, 2000.

Heffley, Mike. *Northern Sun / Southern Moon: Europe's Reinvention of Jazz*. New Haven: Yale University Press, 2005.

Helton, Laura, Justin Leroy, Max A. Mishler, Samantha Seeley, and Shauna

Sweeney. "The Question of Recovery: An Introduction." *Social Text* 33, no. 4 (2015): 1–18.

Henry, Natasha. "Slavery Abolition Act, 1833." *The Canadian Encyclopedia*, 14 July 2014. https://www.thecanadianencyclopedia.ca/en/article/slavery-abolition-act-1833.

Hepburn, Sharon A. Roger. *Crossing the Border: A Free Black Community in Canada*. Chicago: University of Illinois Press, 2007.

Heppenheimer, T.A. "Elijah McCoy." In *Notable Black American Scientists*, ed. Kristine Krapp, 225–7. Detroit: Gale Research, 1999.

Hill, Errol G., and James V. Hatch. *A History of African American Theatre*. Cambridge: Cambridge University Press, 2003.

Hitchens, Bob. "The Choo Choo Jazzers and Similar Groups: A Musical and Discographical Reappraisal [Part I]." *Vintage Jazz Mart – The Original Jazz & Blues Record Trading Magazine* 175 (2016).

– "The Choo Choo Jazzers and Similar Groups: A Musical and Discographical Reappraisal [Part II]." *Vintage Jazz Mart – The Original Jazz & Blues Record Trading Magazine* 176 (2016). https://www.vjm.biz/176-choochoojazzers-print.pdf.

– "The Choo Choo Jazzers and Similar Groups: A Musical and Discographical Reappraisal [Part III]." *Vintage Jazz Mart – The Original Jazz & Blues Record Trading Magazine* 177 (2017). https://www.vjm.biz/177-choo-choo-jazzers.pdf. https://www.vjm.biz/175-choochoojazzers-web-low.pdf.

Hogg, Ian V. *The Complete Illustrated Encyclopedia of the World's Firearms*. New York: A&W Publishers, 1978.

Hudson, Peter James. "The Geographies of Blackness and Anti-Blackness: An Interview with Katherine McKittrick." *The CLR James Journal* 20, nos. 1–2 (2014): 233–40.

Hugues, Sakina Mariam. "Under One Big Tent: American Indians, African Americans, and the Circus World of Nineteenth-Century America." PhD diss., Michigan State University, 2012.

Imada, Adria L. *Aloha America: Hula Circuits through the U.S. Empire*. Durham: Duke University Press, 2012.

Jackson, Jeffrey H. *Making Jazz French: Music and Modern Life in Interwar Paris*. Durham: Duke University Press, 2003.

Jasen, David A. *Ragtime: An Encyclopedia, Discography, and Sheetography*. New York: Routledge, 2007.

- *Tin Pan Alley: An Encyclopedia of the Golden Age of American Song*. New York: Routledge, 2003.
"Johnny Canuck's Revue." *Radio Times*, 13 June 1943, 7.
Johnson, Robert E. *A Global Introduction to Baptist Churches*. New York: Cambridge University Press, 2010.
Joost, Mathias. "Racism and Enlistment: The Second World War Policies of the Royal Canadian Air Force." *Canadian Military History* 21, no. 1 (2015): 1–18.
Jost, Ekkehard. *Free Jazz*. New York: Da Capo Press, 1994.
Kallmann, Helmut. "Nathaniel Dett." *The Canadian Encyclopedia*, 4 January 2016. https://www.thecanadianencyclopedia.ca/en/article/robert-nathaniel-dett.
Katz, Mark. *Capturing Sound: How Technology Has Changed Music*. Berkeley: University of California Press, 2004.
Keillor, Elaine. *Music in Canada: Capturing Landscape and Diversity*. Montreal and Kingston: McGill-Queen's University Press, 2006.
Kelley, Robin D.G. *Africa Speaks, America Answers: Modern Jazz in Revolutionary Times*. Cambridge: Harvard University Press, 2012.
- *Thelonious Monk: The Life and Times of an American Original*. New York: Free Press, 2010.
Kenney, William Howland. *Chicago Jazz: A Cultural History, 1904–1930*. New York: Oxford University Press, 1993.
- "'Going to Meet the Man': Louis Armstrong's Autobiographies." *MELUS* 15, no. 2 (1988): 27–46.
Ketelaar, Eric. "Archives as Spaces of Memory." *Journal of the Society of Archivists* 29, no. 1 (2008): 9–27.
- "Cultivating Archives: Meanings and Identities." *Archival Science* 12, no. 1 (2012): 19–33.
Kidd, Jim. "Listening with Louis – Hooper, That Is." *Vintage Jazz Mart – The Original Jazz & Blues Record Trading Magazine* 175 (2016): 17.
- "Louis Hooper." *Record Research* 77 (1966): 2–5.
- "Louis Hooper Discography." *Record Research* 77 (1966): 6–9.
King, Shannon. *Whose Harlem Is This, Anyway? Community Politics and Grassroots Activism during the New Negro Era*. New York: New York University Press, 2015.
"Koppin Theatre, The." *The Chicago Defender*, 17 September 1927, 6.
"Landlords Taking Last Minute Gouge." *New York Times*, 16 September 1920, 11.
Lanken, Dane. "A Life-Time of Music on Stage." *The Gazette*, 23 May 1973, 18.

– "'Lou Hooper: As Full of Music as Ever,' Lively Arts." *The Gazette*, 7 August 1971, 35.

Lapointe, Mathieu. *Nettoyer Montréal. Les campagnes de moralité publique, 1940–1954*. Quebec City: Septentrion, 2014.

"L'école de musique de Pat Marrazza." *L'Illustration Nouvelle*, 21 October 1938, 8.

Lévesque, Andrée. "Les midinettes de 1937: culture ouvrière, culture de genre, culture ethnique." In *1937: un tournant culturel*, ed. Yvan Lamonde and Denis Saint-Jacques, 71–88. Quebec City: Presses de l'Université Laval, 2009.

Lewis, David. *Louis Hooper: The Harlem Years. A Bio-Discographical Dossier*. Montreal: Montreal Vintage Music Society, 1989.

Lewis, David Levering. *W.E.B. Du Bois: Biography of a Race, 1868–1919*. New York: Henry Holt, 1993.

– *W.E.B. Du Bois: The Fight for Equality and the American Century, 1919–1963*. New York: Henry Holt, 2000.

– *When Harlem Was in Vogue*. New York: Alfred A. Knopf, 1981.

Library and Archives Canada (LAC). "Black History in Canada." *Library and Archives Canada*, n.d. https://www.bac-lac.gc.ca/eng/discover/immigration/history-ethnic-cultural/Pages/blacks.aspx#a.

– "Lou Hooper Fonds [Textual Record, Graphic Material]." *Library and Archives Canada*, n.d. https://recherche-collection-search.bac-lac.gc.ca/eng/home/record?app=FonAndCol&IdNumber=616793.

Linteau, Paul-André, with René Durocher, Jean-Claude Robert, and François Ricard. *Quebec since 1930*. Translated by Robert Chodos and Ellen Garmaise. Toronto: James Lorimer, 1991.

Lobo, Rachel. "Archive as Prefigurative Space: Our Lives and Black Feminism in Canada." *Archivaria* 87 (2019): 68–86.

Lord, Tom. *Clarence Williams*. Essex: Storyville Publications, 1976.

Lott, Eric. *Love and Theft: Blackface Minstrelsy and the American Working Class*. New York: Oxford University Press, 1993.

Macaulay, Thomas Babington. *Lays of Ancient Rome*. London: T. Nelson & Sons, 1908.

Macdonald, Marilyn. "Louis Hooper's Musical Career Spans 70 Years." *The Journal-Pioneer*, 19 March 1976, 2.

Magee, Jeffrey. *The Uncrowned King of Swing: Fletcher Henderson and Big Band Jazz*. New York: Oxford University Press, 2005.

Mansbridge, Joanna. "In Search of a Different History: The Remains of Burlesque in Montreal." *Canadian Theatre Review* 158 (2014): 7–12.

Marrelli, Nancy. *Stepping Out: The Golden Age of Montreal Night Clubs*. Montreal: Véhicule Press, 2004.

Martin, Tony. "Garvey, Marcus." In *Encyclopedia of the Harlem Renaissance: Volume 1 and Volume 2*, ed. Cary D. Wintz and Paul Finkelman, 420–4. New York: Routledge, 2004.

Mathieu, Sarah-Jane. *North of the Color Line: Migration and Black Resistance in Canada, 1870–1955*. Chapel Hill: University of North Carolina Press, 2010.

McCracken, Krista, and Skylee-Storm Hogan. "'That's My Auntie': Community-Guided Residential School History." *KULA* 5, no. 1 (2021): 1–6.

McKay, Claude. *A Long Way from Home*. New York: Arno Press / New York Times, 1969.

McKemmish, Sue, Shannon Faulkhead, and Lynette Russell. "Distrust in the Archive: Reconciling Records." *Archival Science* 11, nos. 3–4 (2011): 211–39.

McKittrick, Katherine. *Dear Science and Other Stories*. Durham: Duke University Press, 2021.

McRae, Matthew. "'A Cauldron of Hell': The Story of Canada's Hong Kong Veterans." *Canadian Museum for Human Rights*. n.d. https://humanrights.ca/story/a-cauldron-of-hell-the-story-of-canadas-hong-kong-veterans.

McStay, "In Abraham's Bosom." *Variety*, 15 November 1932, 50.

McWhirter, Christian. "The Civil War: Music in the Armies." In *Music and War in the United States*, ed. Sarah Kraaz, 55–66. New York: Routledge, 2018.

Mensah, Joseph. *Black Canadians: History, Experiences, Social Conditions*. Halifax: Fernwood, 2002.

Metropolitan Opera. "*Fire Shut Up in My Bones*." The *MET* Opera, n.d. https://www.metopera.org/season/2021-22-season/fire-shut-up-in-my-bones/.

Milan, Jon. *Detroit: Ragtime and the Jazz Age*. Charleston, SC: Arcadia Publishing, 2009.

Miller, Mark. *The Miller Companion to Jazz in Canada and Canadians in Jazz*. Toronto: Mercury Press, 2001.

– *Such Melodious Racket: The Lost History of Jazz in Canada, 1914–1949*. Toronto: Mercury Press, 1997.

Mills, Alexandra, Désirée Rochat, and Steven High. "Telling Stories from Montreal's Negro Community Centre Fonds: The Archives as Community-Engaged Classroom." *Archivaria* 89, no. 1 (2020): 34–68.

Mills, Sean. "Democracy in Music: Louis Metcalf's International Band and Montreal Jazz History." *Canadian Historical Review* 100, no. 3 (2019): 351–73.

– *The Empire Within: Postcolonial Thought and Political Activism in Sixties Montreal*. Montreal and Kingston: McGill-Queen's University Press, 2010.

– *A Place in the Sun: Haiti, Haitians, and the Remaking of Quebec*. Montreal and Kingston: McGill-Queen's University Press, 2016.

Monson, Ingrid. *Freedom Sounds: Civil Rights Call Out to Jazz*. New York: Oxford University Press, 2010.

"Much Expected of Orchestra." *New York Amsterdam News*, 9 February 1927, 10.

Mukurtu. "The Mukurtu Community." *Mukurtu*, n.d. https://mukurtu.org/show case-2/.

Mull, Carol E. *The Underground Railroad in Michigan*. Jefferson: McFarland, 2010.

Murphy, Donna. "Music Man, Island Style." *Axiom Magazine*, n.d., 40–1.

Nelson, Charmaine A., ed. *Ebony Roots, Northern Soil: Perspectives on Blackness in Canada*. Newcastle upon Tyne: Cambridge Scholars Publishing, 2010.

Nesmith, Tom. "The Concept of Societal Provenance and Records of Nineteenth-Century Aboriginal-European Relations in Western Canada: Implications for Archival Theory and Practice." *Archival Science* 6, no. 3 (2006): 351–60.

– "Re-Exploring the Continuum, Rediscovering Archives." *Archives and Manuscripts* 36, no. 2 (2008): 34–53.

Ngô, Fiona. *Imperial Blues: Geographies of Race and Sex in Jazz Age New York*. Durham: Duke University Press, 2014.

Norris, John. "Jazz: Expect 100 Collectors at Toronto Convention." *Globe and Mail*, 17 July 1967, 12.

Orchestre Métropolitain. "Hélène Grimaud and Yannick Nézet-Séguin." OM, n.d. https://orchestremetropolitain.com/en/concerts/helene-grimaud-yannick-nezet-seguin/.

Palmer, Al. *Montreal Confidential*. Montreal: Véhicule Press, 2009.

– "Ourtown: Our Tune." *The Gazette*, 29 March 1967, 3.

Pelletier, Wilfrid. *Une symphonie inachevée*. Montreal: Leméac, 1972.

Perreten, Peter F. "Eco-Autobiography: Portrait of Place/Self-Portrait." *Auto/biography Studies* 18, no. 1 (2003): 1–22.

Pesotta, Rose. *Bread upon the Waters*. Edited by John Nicholas Beffel. New York: Dodd, Mead, 1944.

Peterson, Oscar. *Jazz Odyssey: The Life of Oscar Peterson*. New York: Continuum, 2004.

Préfontaine, Yves. "Musicojazz." *Liberté* 3, nos. 3–4 (1961): 672–4.

Prince, Shannon. "Elgin Settlement." *Canadian Encyclopedia*, 10 November 2021. https://www.thecanadianencyclopedia.ca/en/article/elgin-settlement.

"Professional Music Career Provides Exciting Highlights." *Evening Patriot*, 20 March 1976, n.p.

Putnam, Lara. *Radical Moves: Caribbean Migrants and the Politics of Race in the Jazz Age*. Chapel Hill: University of North Carolina Press, 2013.

Rachwal, Maria Noriega. *From Kitchen to Carnegie Hall: Ethel Stark and the Montreal Women's Symphony Orchestra*. Toronto: Second Story Press, 2015.

"Récital de jazz, ce soir, au Majesty's." *Le Canada*, 29 September 1947, 8.

Redmond, Shana L. *Everything Man: The Form and Function of Paul Robeson*. Durham: Duke University Press, 2020.

Roberts, Brian. *Blackface Nation: Race, Reform, and Identity in American Popular Music, 1812–1925*. Chicago: University of Chicago Press, 2017.

Robeson, Paul. *Here I Stand*. Boston: Beacon Press, 1998.

Robeson, Paul, Jr. *The Undiscovered Paul Robeson: An Artist's Journey, 1898–1939*. New York: John Wiley & Sons, 2001.

Ross, Alex. *The Rest Is Noise: Listening to the Twentieth Century*. New York: Picador, 2007.

Rust, Brian. *Jazz and Ragtime Records (1897–1942)*, vol. 2: *L–Z, Index*. Denver: Mainspring Press, 2002.

Sacks, Marcy S. *Before Harlem: The Black Experience in New York City before World War I*. Philadelphia: University of Pennsylvania Press, 2006.

Saito, Yoshiomi. *The Global Politics of Jazz in the Twentieth Century: Cultural Diplomacy and "American Music."* London: Routledge, 2020.

Savage, Jon. "Pop at the Pictures: Wartime London Dances to America's Tune." *The Guardian*, 26 October 2011. https://www.theguardian.com/music/musicblog/2011/oct/26/1940s-london-rainbow-corner-swing.

Schenbeck, Lawrence. *Racial Uplift and American Music, 1878–1943*. Jackson: University of Mississippi Press, 2012.

Schenker, Frederick J. "'A Circuit Tour of the Globe': 'Hiawatha' and the Double-Stake of Imperial Pop." *Journal of the Society for American Music* 13, no. 1 (2019): 1–26.

"Services Held for Veteran Jazz Pianist." *Calgary Herald*, 21 September 1977, 20.

Shilton, Katie, and Ramesh Srinivasan. "Participatory Appraisal and Arrangement for Multicultural Archival Collections." *Archivaria* 63, no. 1 (2007): 87–101.

Siegfried, Matt. "Emancipation Day." *What's Left, Ypsilanti* no. 2 (2019). https://whatsleftypsi.com/old/issue-2/emancipation-day/.

Siemerling, Winfried. "Jazz, Diaspora, and the History and Writing of Black Anglophone Montreal." In *Unsettling the Great White North: Black Canadian History*, ed. Funké Aladejebi and Michele A. Johnson, 199–213. Toronto: University of Toronto Press, 2022.

Slatin, Sonia, and Maria L. Noriega. "Montreal Women's Symphony Orchestra/Symphonie féminine de Montréal." *The Canadian Encyclopedia*, 15 December 2013. https://www.thecanadianencyclopedia.ca/en/article/montreal-womens-symphony-orchestrasymphonie-feminine-de-montreal-emc.

Smardz Frost, Karolyn, and Veta Smith Tucker, eds. *Fluid Frontier: Slavery, Resistance, and the Underground Railroad in the Detroit River Borderland*. Detroit: Wayne State University Press, 2016.

Smith, Sidonie, and Julia Watson. *Reading Autobiography: A Guide for Interpreting Life Narratives*. Minneapolis: University of Minnesota Press, 2010.

Snyder, Robert W. *The Voice of the City: Vaudeville and Popular Culture in New York*. Chicago: I.R. Dee, 2000.

South Adams Street @ 1900. "Home." *South Adams Street @ 1900: An Historic Ypsilanti African-American Neighborhood*, n.d. https://southadamstreet1900.wordpress.com.

South Asian American Digital Archive. "Browse the Archive." SAADA, n.d. https://www.saada.org/browse.

Stacey, C.P., and Barbara M. Wilson, *The Half-Million: The Canadians in Britain, 1939–1946*. Toronto: University of Toronto Press, 1987.

Stanger-Ross, Jordan, and Pamela Sugiman. *Witness to Loss: Race, Culpability, and Memory in the Dispossession of Japanese Canadians*. Montreal and Kingston: McGill-Queen's University Press, 2017.

Stanley, Ruth. *A Different Type of Bombshell: The Tin Hats' Journey through World War II*. Victoria: Tellwell Talent, 2021.

Stephens, W. Ray. *The Canadian Entertainers of World War II*. Oakville: Mosaic Press, 2013.

– *The Harps of War*. Oakville: Frederick Harris Music, 1985.

Stoler, Ann Laura. "Colonial Archives and the Arts of Governance: On the Content in the Form." In *Refiguring the Archive*, ed. Carolyn Hamilton, Verne Harris, Jane Taylor, Michèle Pickover, Graeme Reid, and Razia Saleh, 83–101. Dordrecht: Springer, 2002.

Straram, Patrick. "Les divertissements: jazz dans la vie quotidienne." *Parti pris* 1, no. 3 (1963): 55–7.

Stryker, Mark. *Jazz from Detroit*. Ann Arbor: University of Michigan Press, 2019.

Sugrue, Thomas. *The Origins of Urban Crisis: Race and Inequality in Postwar Detroit*. Princeton: Princeton University Press, 1996.

Sutherland, Tonia, and Alyssa Purcell. "A Weapon and a Tool: Decolonizing Description and Embracing Redescription as Liberatory Archival Praxis." *International Journal of Information, Diversity, & Inclusion* 5, no. 1 (2021): 60–78.

Tamboukou, Maria. "Archival Rhythms: Narrativity in the Archive." In *The Archive Project: Archival Research in the Social Sciences*, ed. Niamh Moore, Andrea Salter, Liz Stanley, and Maria Tamboukou, 71–95. London: Routledge, 2016.

– "Relational Narratives: Auto/biography and the Portrait." *Women Studies International Forum* 33, no. 3 (2010): 170–9.

Tansey, Eira. "Institutional Silences and the Digital Dark Age." *The Schedule*, 23 May 2016. https://saarmrt.wordpress.com/2016/05/23/institutional-silences-and-the-digital-dark-age/.

Thériault, Jacques. "Ella Fitzerald et chats 'jazzés.'" *Le Devoir*, 4 April 1967, 10.

Thompson, Cheryl. "Black Canada and Why the Archival Logic of Memory Needs Reforms." *Les Ateliers de l'Éthique* 14, no. 2 (2020): 76–106.

– "Searching for Black Voices in Canada's Archives: The Invisibility of a 'Visible' Minority." *public: Art/Culture/Ideas* 29, no. 57 (2018): 88–95.

Thompson, Debra. *The Long Road Home: On Blackness and Belonging*. New York: Simon & Schuster, 2022.

Todd, Malcolm. "Power, Identity Integrity, Authenticity, and the Archives: A Comparative Study of the Application of Archival Methodologies to Contemporary Privacy." *Archivaria* 61 (2006): 181–214.

"Trio Held as Police Block Harlem Riot." *New York Times*, 27 July 1926, 21.

Trouillot, Michel-Rolph. *Silencing the Past: Power and the Production of History*. Boston: Beacon Press, 1995.

Vance, Jonathan F. *A History of Canadian Culture*. Don Mills, ON: Oxford University Press, 2009.

Von Eschen, Penny M. *Satchmo Blows Up the World: Jazz Ambassadors Play the Cold War*. Cambridge: Harvard University Press, 2006.

Wade, Jill. "Wartime Housing Limited, 1941–1947: Canadian Housing Policy at the Crossroads." *Urban History Review/Revue d'Histoire Urbaine* 15, no. 1 (1986): 40–59.

Walcott, Rinaldo. "'Who Is She and What Is She to You?': Mary Ann Shadd Cary and the (Im)possibility of Black/Canadian Studies." *Atlantis: Critical Studies in Gender, Culture & Social Justice* 24, no. 2 (2000): 137–46.

Walden, Keith. *Becoming Modern in Toronto: The Industrial Exhibition and the Shaping of a Late Victorian Culture.* Toronto: University of Toronto Press, 1997.

Wallascheck, Richard. *Primitive Music: An Inquiry into the Origin and Development of Music, Songs, Instruments, Dances, and Pantomimes of Savage Races.* New York: Longmans, Green, 1893.

Walton, Genevieve Marie Julia. *History of St Luke's Parish.* Ypsilanti: n.p., 1916.

Whiting, Charles. *West Wall: The Battle for Hitler's Siegfried Line, September 1944 – March 1945.* Staplehurst: Spellmount, 1999.

Williams, Dorothy. *The Road to Now: A History of Blacks in Montreal.* Montreal: Véhicule Press, 1997.

– "Sankofa: Recovering Montreal's Heterogeneous Black Print Serials." PhD diss., McGill University, 2006.

Williams, Iain Cameron. *Underneath a Harlem Moon: The Harlem to Paris Years of Adelaide Hall.* New York: Continuum, 2002.

Williams, Jeremy. *Detroit: The Black Bottom Community.* Chicago: Arcadia Publishing, 2009.

Wilson, Jason. *King Alpha's Song in a Strange Land: The Roots and Routes of Canadian Reggae.* Vancouver: UBC Press, 2020.

– *Soldiers of Song: The Dumbells and Other Canadian Concert Parties of the First World War.* Waterloo: Wilfrid Laurier University Press, 2012.

"Wooden Acres [Ad]." *Canadian Jewish Review,* 15 July 1949, 5.

Wyndham, Tex. "Record Review: *Lou Hooper, piano.*" *The Ragtimer* (1975): 7.

Zarnowitz, Victor. *Business Cycles: Theory, History, Indicators, and Forecasting.* Chicago: University of Chicago Press, 1992.

Zuehlke, Mark, and Stuart C. Daniel. *The Canadian Military Atlas: The Nation's Battlefields from the French and Indian Wars to Kosovo.* Toronto: Stoddart, 2001.

Contributors

ARSHAD DESAI is a PhD student at the University of Toronto. He earned a BA and MA in history and the Black Canadian Studies Certificate from York University, and he holds the Canada Graduate Scholarships to Honour Nelson Mandela. His research focuses on Black Canadian activism in Southern African liberation movements.

ERIC FILLION is adjunct professor and Buchanan Postdoctoral Fellow in Canadian history at Queen's University. He is the author of *JAZZ LIBRE et la révolution québécoise: Musique-action, 1967–1975* and *Distant Stage: Quebec, Brazil, and the Making of Canada's Cultural Diplomacy.*

SEAN MILLS is Canada Research Chair in Canadian and Transnational History at the University of Toronto. He is the author of *The Empire Within: Postcolonial Thought and Political Activism in Sixties Montreal* (2010) and *A Place in the Sun: Haiti, Haitians, and the Remaking of Quebec* (2016).

SUNITA NIGAM holds a PhD in English from McGill University and completed a two-year SSHRC postdoctoral fellowship in theatre and performance studies at York University in 2021. Sunita has published on the racial, gender, and class dimensions of performance in Quebec and Mexico, including stand-up, blackface, burlesque, activist theatre, and urban design.

JULIE RICHARD is a classically trained composer and musician with expertise in various musical genres, including jazz, experimental, and African music. She has performed extensively across North America and internationally. Her commitment to preserving the legacy of forgotten Black composers has inspired her to form the Black Ark Orchestra and Les Angles Mortes.

DÉSIRÉE ROCHAT is a community educator and transdisciplinary scholar with a PhD in educational studies from the Department of Integrated Studies in Education from McGill University. Guided by an integrative approach connecting historical research, community archival preservation, and education, her work documents, preserves, theorizes, and transmits (hi)stories of Black communities' activism.

JASON WILSON is a bestselling Canadian historian, a two-time Juno Award nominee, and winner of the Ontario Historical Society's Joseph Brant Award. An adjunct professor at the University of Guelph, Dr Wilson has eight books to his name and lives in Stouffville, Ontario, with his wife Alana.

KRISTEN YOUNG is an information management professional whose work highlights and engages in community-led records-keeping practices. As a Jamaican immigrant to Canada, Kristen is interested in the intersection of archives, history, memory, and identity and how they interact in community environments.